Justice For All: Liberalism in its Finest Hour

Acknowledgements

During the two years it took to write this book I had the good fortune to receive both encouragement and helpful suggestions from a select number of sound minded people. It goes without saying that my editor Kathryn Gallien deserves considerable credit for the fine job of copyediting she did. Others that are included in this list are the individuals who took the time to read what I wrote and offer me advice. In this vain I think that the following people deserve special mention: my loving wife, Lisa Aronson; longtime friends, Max Sloan and Jack Wallace; good friends and fellow activists, Charley Brown and Cessie Alfonso; and good friends, Herbert Straus and B. K. Keramati.

Preface

About Myself

Before asking you to read this book about the struggle for justice in America, I need to tell you about myself and why this topic is so important to me. It begins with the issue of health care and what I observed during the many years I was employed by an agency that administers part of the Social Security Disability Program. Being in contact with individuals who were experiencing a broad range of medical difficulties would lead me to understand the importance of the ideal we call "justice." I found that the biggest obstacle faced by disability applicants wasn't poor health, but lack of adequate care due to inadequate insurance coverage. I witnessed firsthand how this cost people their lives.

What most struck me was the unfairness of the entire situation. We lived in one of the wealthiest countries in the world; yet for millions of Americans, lacking access to decent health care was still a life-threatening reality. We hold so many material things to be important. Madison Avenue has profited greatly by playing off this truism. Yet one of the most important human concerns—justice—is rarely the focus of their ads. The reason may be that it is not a commodity that can be assigned a monetary value. Nevertheless, the absence of a market price doesn't change the fact that a person can't hope to live in a civilized society if justice is not respected. My life experience has taught me that without a commitment to this concept, civilization becomes just another name for a jungle.

Since retiring I have chosen a path dedicated to achieving a fairer nation for everyone. In this pursuit I have had the good fortune of coming to know many courageous activists who have unselfishly given of themselves to make our world more humane. There is one event in particular that stands out. As you might have guessed, it's related to one of my foremost concerns, establishing health care as a right of all Americans. Immediately following the passage of the Affordable Care Act in 2010, I was asked to participate in a Health Care for America Now (HCAN) teleconference. Grassroots volunteers from all over the country were on the call. It opened with HCAN's national campaign manager Richard Kirsch saying that he would like to ask a few of us to tell our stories. He then proceeded to ask specific individuals to talk.

It seemed like every person was literally a real-life Norma Ray. One volunteer was a minister in his 80s. He had been an activist since the 1950s. During the civil rights struggle he marched with Martin Luther King Jr., putting up with the shouts and debris of hostile onlookers. I was particularly impressed by a single mom who was economically struggling. She could have been a clone of Fannie Lou Hamer. Those who tried to intimidate and silence her had no idea of the strength of this person's character—no idea until now. She said something that I

3

won't ever forget. After describing all the emotionally draining battles she had to fight along with all the time they consumed, she said that if she had been getting paid she would have quit long ago. This rang a bell with me since I felt the same way. You couldn't have paid me enough money to subject myself to so much aggravation.

Then, unexpectedly, Richard called upon me to tell my story. I was so taken aback by being included in this group, I was virtually speechless. As a result, what I said wasn't so interesting. Nevertheless, a year later Richard included me in his book *Fighting for Our Health* which highlighted the role of grassroots activists in the recent struggle for universal health care.

I can't fully express how inspired I was by these grassroots Americans who had spent the better portion of their lives making our world a more livable one. They weren't presidents, senators, governors or wealthy philanthropists. They weren't famous or academically accredited. Yet without their sacrifice and strength of character we all would be worse off today. They made the impossible possible. To paraphrase Howard Zinn, they were the people making history.

This experience would renew my interest in justice. I couldn't stop asking myself why people without any hope of personal gain or financial reward would give so much of themselves in a quest for a fairer world. Therefore, with this idea already in mind, it didn't take much of a catalyst to start me doing some in-depth historical research into the question. Such an undertaking was natural for me, since I have had a lifelong love affair with history. In the last forty years, I have read hundreds of books by leading historical scholars, with American history topping the list. Therefore, my activist experience and intellectual interests conveniently converged to create what would eventually become the final product you see now.

I would discover that these two sides of me would be a perfect fit for the book's message. Yet even before being fully aware of this, I quickly saw that if there ever was a need to highlight the crucial role played by America's great grassroots justice movements it was now. As an activist with firm convictions, I have had many interchanges with individuals of all political persuasions—from like-minded allies to Tea Party diehards. Of all of these people it was the activists dedicated to the struggle for justice in America who were the most instrumental in encouraging me to continue on with this endeavor. They succeeded in convincing me that a story written by a grassroots activist about our great grassroots justice movements has something unique to offer. The book would never have been written without their urging and steadfast support.

All our great justice movements were born of the same energy and commitment that the heroes on the HCAN teleconference had shown. Every one of them arose spontaneously from America's people. They all left us with a deeper appreciation of justice and, along with it, a more just America. Most important, my researching and writing would lead me to a deeper truth: their America is our America. This book strives to convey that message.

In doing so it's not neutral; I have a definite point of view. My compatriots have never let me forget that in the end the best that can be said about any work is the truth it tells; this will stand the test of time. If what's good about our country and its connection to advancing the cause of justice is of importance to you, I think you will find this book worth your while, not to mention an enjoyable read.

Addendum

Before beginning, you should be aware of three things.

First, as you will quickly see, I have placed the heroes of America's great justice movements front and center. I chose to use them as focal points for the larger movement because it's simply easier than talking about millions of people individually. The fact that these heroes never abandoned the grassroots base from which they came is what's important. All of them have earned the right to stand in for the millions who inspired them and who they in turn inspired. To place everything in context, I have also zeroed in on their primary adversaries to present contrasting opinions.

Second, I have tried to let history's leading actors speak, as much as possible, for themselves. This way the reader can better judge whether my take on things is accurate or not. I think that ordinary people like you and me are capable of making an informed opinion about what is being said when we are the ones being spoken to. Although it would be nice if you read every word of every quote, it's really not necessary. For the most part a general scan will give the reader a good idea of what the speaker wishes to convey. Grasping the message is what's important.

Third, all highlighted words contained in the book's quotations represent my emphasis alone and cannot be attributed to the original authors.

So if you are still with me, let's begin.

Chapter I

Overview

What is the origin of today's America? The nation's "official" story credits the Founding Fathers. For the most part, this fable has gone unchallenged. Of course, as with any good work of fiction it contains more than a grain of truth. Yet it is a woefully incomplete truth. Right from the beginning of the Republic, the nation has experienced successive grassroots movements that have advanced a "just" cause of one sort or another. I maintain that the accumulated successes of America's grassroots justice movements deserve as much credit as the Founding Fathers for creating the America that we currently live in. In fact, without their selfless efforts to moderate the Founding Fathers' ideals of liberty with that of justice, the country we know and love would be unrecognizable today. This is what the official story leaves out.

You are probably asking, where is your evidence? Before going there, it would be helpful to first explain how I came to be concerned with this question. In addition to my heightened awareness of the importance of justice, there was a specific catalyst that triggered my actions. Strangely, it was the Pledge of Allegiance. My original view of the pledge wasn't very inspiring. I grew up during the height of the Cold War and in the reflection of Joe McCarthy's anticommunist hysteria. The American right wing succeeded in its efforts to amend the Pledge of

Allegiance by including in it the words "one nation under God." Supposedly, their purpose was to draw a clear distinction between atheistic communism and "God-fearing" American democracy. Of course they also had a hidden purpose. By making the pledge more parochial (i.e., religious), they knew that more "eggheaded liberals" would follow their principals and scoff at reciting it. This situation delighted the right wing, since they could now ostracize a greater number of left-leaning nonconformists. As an added bonus, they would also be able to challenge the loyalty of people who they were able to associate with them. Therefore, for me and others of my generation, the Pledge of Allegiance was America's loyalty oath. The loyalty-oath-loving Right was the group pushing the pledge and the civil-liberties-loving Left was the group that was uncomfortable with any type of mandatory oath, official or unofficial.

Now we come to the anomaly that led me to examine our origins. Ron Paul's negative view of the Pledge of Allegiance surprised me since he is a leading (libertarian) conservative. Paul is so hostile to the pledge" that he even disses its author, accusing him of being a Socialist. He implies that the pledge's original words "one nation indivisible with liberty and justice for all" represent (misguided) liberal values. This made me stand up and take notice. Could it be that the pledge—which the Right of my generation tried to turn into a loyalty oath—was the work of a Socialist and speaks to the liberal values that they hate?

By now my curiosity had gotten the better of me. I was driven to acquaint myself with more of Paul's views. In doing so I discovered that he wasn't afraid to say what he really thought, no matter how startling. For example, he does what most mainline conservatives would be afraid to do: he concedes that Lincoln wasn't one of them. In fact, he openly blames Lincoln for destroying the Constitution and being responsible for virtually all the "bad" politics that has befallen the country in the last 150 years. For Paul, Lincoln is the anti-leader who subverted the Founding Fathers' intentions. Now my interest was intensified. What the hell was he talking about? At this point I felt that I had to do a little research on Paul's allegations. The more I got into it, the more interested I became, and "a little research" would inevitably turn out to be a little more and then again a little more, and so on. What I discovered in this process would eventually lay the groundwork for this book.

Since Paul placed a lot of credence on his interpretation of the Founding Fathers' intentions, I began my research with them. I, like most Americans, saw the Founding Founders as demigods who left us holy books that would always be there to guide us. In fact, much of our political debate has revolved around the question of who best speaks for them. If alive today, would founders like Jefferson or Madison be liberal or conservative? This has become an important question, because it is believed that these giants best symbolize America's great democratic traditions.

However, I found some glaring contradictions in this picture. Although I knew that both of these Founding Fathers were slaveholders, I was amazed to discover that neither of them was as opposed to slavery as "official" history has portrayed them to have been. In fact, they had no concept of the abolition of slavery occurring in their lifetimes or any time soon after their deaths. And both of them thought if abolition were to occur in the future it would have to involve some vague type of peaceful consensus that all regions of the country agreed to. In other words, slavery equated with current realty and abolition equated with some far-off visionary world that they would supposedly like to live in, but that wasn't feasible for the foreseeable future.

Yet it wasn't only this viewpoint that shocked me. When I read the letters of the elder Thomas Jefferson and James Madison I saw their unease over the rising antislavery movement that was beginning to take hold and challenge the prerogatives of slave masters like themselves. In fact, Jefferson was so upset by the Northern abolitionists that he even hypothesized that their reckless actions would one day lead to the dissolution of the Union. They appeared to be both offended and perplexed by the people who wanted to take immediate action against slavery instead of putting it off to some unspecified future time. After all, how could anyone think that slaveholders such as themselves weren't the proper group to be entrusted with the task of ending slavery (in their own good time of course)? It was clear that Jefferson and Madison didn't see the early antislavery movement as having views that were in sync with their own.

Therefore it was no accident that the classical liberal ideals of Jefferson and Madison failed to keep the torch of freedom burning during the dark days of slavery. Instead, it would be the abolitionists' condemnation of slavery's stark injustices that would be responsible for repeatedly rekindling that fire. Their appeal to a "higher justice" is what laid the groundwork for slavery's elimination. In contrast, the idea of liberty that these two esteemed Founding Fathers were enamored of didn't appear to make them overly sensitive to the injustices that they were responsible for maintaining. I came to understand that without a strong sense of justice their idea of liberty was considerably compromised.

The traditional concept of "liberty" tends to have an individual bent (i.e., individual liberty), while justice tends to encompass a broader range of societal formations (i.e., criminal justice, social justice, economic and distributive justice, etc.). To the extent that "justice" is equated with "fairness" it also covers relationships that exist between different groups of people. Justice is a far less individualistic concept than liberty. I think that both Jefferson and Madison were so centered on the individual that it blurred their views of the bigger picture. Their sharp focus on the "self" caused them to underestimate what the well-being of the "whole" contributes to the grand mosaic. This would explain their failure to see how tarnished their precious ideal of liberty was in the absence of justice. Blind spots like this were more noticeable the more I read their correspondence as well as our nation's original documents. The preamble of the Constitution aside, the words "liberty" and "freedom" seemed to appear far more often than the word "justice" or its opposite, "injustice."

Yet Jefferson and Madison were still strong advocates of democracy. That's why I was even more dumbfounded by their extreme level of visceral hostility towards the people actively battling against slavery. How could this be? What was it about the belief system of those in the antislavery movement that so turned off these two great Founding Fathers? Why did they think that these reformers were endangering the classical concept of liberty they embraced? The more I read the more obvious the answer became. It's contained in the antislavery movement's rhetoric and writings.

While movement activists expressed support for the concept of liberty found in the Declaration of Independence, they added another dimension of understanding to it. They were strongly moralistic, much more so than our Founding Fathers were. The central focus of their moral perspective was man's treatment of his fellow man. In leading off with their outrage over the terrible treatment that the enslaved were subjected to, they put their sense of fairness and justice on the front line in the battle against slavery. The strong emotive messages that they delivered were in sharp contrast to the classical eighteenth-century philosophical thinkers who were immersed in logical reasoning and thought that an appeal to popular emotions (i.e., passions) was dangerous. It was no wonder that these Founding Fathers were so taken back by the abolitionist persona, since they saw liberty as a reasoned concept rather than a moral or emotional imperative.

Nevertheless, it is important that we understand the sentiments that inspired our original justice movement, abolition. If they didn't spring from the classical eighteenth-century liberal ideals that fueled the Revolution, what was their source? Cognitive linguist George Lakoff has written that human empathy is at the core of liberal thinking. Interestingly, if there ever was a movement in American history that was literally dripping with empathy it was the abolitionist movement. Abolitionism was conceived in the depths of American civil society and it was driven by a rising concern for the plight of enslaved persons. That's why what comes across most decidedly in abolitionist works is an incredibly powerful sense of identification with the oppressed. You might say that their feeling for the plight of others was their most observable and distinguishing feature.

Yet how does this tie into the Pledge of Allegiance? The answer to this question is dependent on an even deeper one. Given the Founders' intense focus on individual liberty at the expense of most other concerns, how did it come to be that the pledge's last five words—"liberty and justice for all"—include justice in the same breath as liberty? This query can only be resolved by understanding America's true evolutionary development.

The Founding Fathers never foresaw the critical role that would be played by grassroots movements that were spurred on by empathic concern for other human beings.

Nevertheless, these justice movements and the causes that they fought for have been the primary players in shaping our country's destiny. The antislavery movement that emerged soon after the founding of the Republic was the first in a long line of grassroots movements to hold that justice and fairness were necessary ingredients to maintaining the vitality of liberty. One of the great untold truths is that the American concept of justice postdates both the Revolution and the Constitution. It didn't originate from above, with the Founders, but instead from the grass roots below. You might say that it was the firstborn child of the new nation.

The notion of justice that is embedded in the Pledge of Allegiance speaks to the maturation of that child. It turns out that Paul was correct about the pledge's origin and intended meaning. The author, Francis Bellamy, was a self-identified Christian Socialist. Although the pledge was written some three decades after the Civil War, the ideological divide that the war engendered was still fresh in the minds of the populace. The pledge's intended purpose was to codify the war's accomplishments as well as Lincoln's legacy. One nation "indivisible" spoke to a new vision of America. After the Civil War our country became a union where the whole was greater than the sum of its parts and no part had the right to withdraw without the consent of the whole.

The emergent truths given birth to in that era are even more important. "Liberty and justice for all" spoke to the higher purpose that was articulated in Lincoln's Gettysburg Address. When Lincoln uttered the words "a new birth of freedom," he was immediately attacked by opponents. Sounding like today's Tea Partiers, they angrily declared that he lacked authority to proclaim a "new birth of freedom." They insisted that Lincoln's appeal to a higher justice had no constitutional merit. For the first time in American history, justice was being placed on an equal footing with liberty. It's no accident that the pledge's final five words—"liberty and justice for all"—parallel the greatest achievement of the Civil War period. A concept of liberty that was almost totally centered on the individual was expanded to encompass the well-being of the whole of society.

Paul's hostility to the pledge is now understandable since it enunciates nothing that he or his brethren believe in. The flirtation that the libertarian Right has had with secessionism is but one example of their rejection of the concept of "one nation indivisible." More important, the American Right in general is contemptuous of the notion that justice is liberty's equal. Like Lincoln's detractors, they have always feared extending the protections inherent in this concept. The idea that liberty requires moderation by justice is and has always been anathema to American conservatism. Paul really hit the nail on the head when he dissed the pledge's original words "one nation indivisible with liberty and justice for all," because they do indeed represent the core values of the liberal ideal that he so abhors.

Unfortunately, Paul misses the bigger picture by focusing so much on the founder's eighteenth-century ideology. For whatever their contemporary shortcomings were, they decidedly understood that posterity would need to update and rethink the flaws in their ideas as changing times demanded. What abolitionists added to the political equation was in keeping with that tradition. In accommodating democracy's rising tide, it insured that history's arrow would continue moving in the same direction as the founders had set it. Yet at the same time, their profound transformation of our national consciousness is as much part of what America means as is the Founding Fathers' original thinking. The theme and basic tenets of abolition would be transferred to future justice movements. Women's, children's, workers', and civil rights movements are all the offspring of this great emancipationist crusade. They would take up where the abolitionists left off, and in their struggles they too would further advance the cause of justice.

Paul's hatred of Lincoln is now explained. The "Lincoln America" that was conceived in the long struggle to end slavery and reached fruition when the Union was undergoing its post-Civil War transformation was the first great success story of what would become modern-day American liberalism. In the years that would follow, it would be liberalism that would pick up the torch and carry on as the conduit for intertwining the concept of "justice" with the ideal of "liberty."

Of course the most important question is: Why is this insight so crucial? Why write a book about it? The answer is that unlike Paul, we liberals see the grassroots movements that fought to include justice alongside that of liberty as America's Co-Founders. Therefore any dialogue that solely centers on where the Founding Fathers would stand on this issue or that issue minimizes the accomplishments of our country and its people; and in doing so, it subverts America's true ideals.

To confirm this fact one only needs to lower his or her emotive blinders and take a hard look at our actual history. For the most part, the colonial America that revolted against British rule had freely elected legislatures and freedom of the press, speech, and religion. These basic English principles had begun to take hold in America—albeit somewhat loosely—prior to both the Revolution and the writing of the Constitution. While the Republic forged by the Founding Fathers was an improvement over what came before it, it was also a continuation of much of what preceded it. This is obvious if we look at the kind of political systems countries like the U.K., Canada, Australia, and New Zealand have today. Yet none of these countries had such of an ingrained system of slavery or long-standing practice of racial segregation as the United States had.

Given this situation, compare the differences between life in precolonial versus postcolonial America with the differences between life in a country that tolerates legalized slavery versus one that accepts the concept that everyone is equal in the eyes of the law. Or compare the differences between life in the U.S. versus Canada today with the differences between life in a country that has a system of legal apartheid within its borders versus one that establishes as a goal respecting the worth of all human beings. In both cases the magnitude of the divide is far greater when the comparison concerns the existence of slavery or racial apartheid. Ending slavery and segregation as well as opening up the political process to all, regardless of gender, race, or economic status, has had the most profound impact on the kind of nation we have become. And that's exactly why America's grassroots justice movements deserve the lion's share of the credit for creating the America we know. In downplaying their contributions we downplay America itself.

In the following chapters, I will take you on a journey through time to view how the real flesh-and-blood America—the America that we actually live in—came to be. Included in the sightseeing will be a view of the central role played by American liberalism in its struggle to include alongside of liberty a concept of justice. Please stay with me; I think you will find the voyage worth your while.

Chapter II

What is Justice?

Before beginning our journey through time, a little pretravel preparation is needed. In the coming chapters you will be seeing the word justice quite often. Therefore it's necessary to say a little something about the concept itself. Many great scholars have made attempts to define what "justice" is, and it has proven to be a massive undertaking. Because of the complexity and difficulties involved, at chapters end don't expect a definitive answer to the question "what is justice?" Yet, in pondering its meaning a good enough understanding of the ideal may be reached, so that we can at least recognize what it's most likely *not*. More important, we can go a long way in establishing that justice is more than just a dream residing solely in our inner thoughts—it's also a potent force affecting the world outside.

The best place to begin this endeavor is with the works of a man who has been called the greatest political philosopher of the twentieth century, John Rawls. His work has had immense influence in academia and other intellectual circles. Rawls is thought of as a liberal philosopher. Given my assertion that liberalism has a unique relationship to justice, I don't think that it's an accident that the central focus of Rawls's work was its definition. Rawls equated justice with fairness. To uncover the nature of fairness, Rawls used what is known as a thought experiment.

A thought experiment involves setting up an impossible situation that, if it were real, would tell you a deep truth. Physicists like Einstein have used thought experiments to try to get a deeper insight into the nature of a difficult problem. For example, Einstein thought about what he would see if he were able to ride on a beam of light. His theory of special relativity came from this seemingly improbable thought experiment. On *Discover* magazine's blog *Cosmic Variance*, leading contemporary physicist Joe Polchinski noted that:

> Thought experiments have played a large role in figuring out the laws of physics. Even for electromagnetism, where most of the laws were found experimentally, Maxwell needed a thought experiment to complete the equations. For the unification of quantum mechanics and gravity, where the phenomena take place in extreme regimes, they are even more crucial.[1]

What appears to be a ridiculous method of gaining knowledge is and has been successfully employed by the best physical scientists. Therefore, we shouldn't be surprised when a social scientist or philosopher uses the very same method to gain a deeper understanding of human beings.

To decide what is fairness Rawls relies on a thought experiment known as the "veil of ignorance." Imagine a community of people who are aware of each other, but are completely ignorant of their own as well as everyone else's position in society. No individual knows any community member's race, gender, age, social standing, job, income, abilities, defects, or other identifying features. This won't be revealed until the veil that covers their reality is lifted. The important point is that no one has the foggiest idea what theirs or anyone else's parochial self-interest is.

Rawls then asks if there are any basic precepts that all of them would agree to if (while still ignorant of the overall situation) they were asked to come together and formulate the ground rules that would exist when the veil is removed. Rawls hypothesizes that they probably wouldn't agree to a society that was rigidly equal. However, as a protection against not knowing what their own self-interest is, they would most likely agree to everyone possessing the essential "primary goods" required for a decent life. These primary goods would include sufficient income and wealth as well as political liberties—in other words, the tools necessary to protect a human being's general well-being. Rawls writes:

> Thus even though the parties are deprived of information about their particular ends, they have enough knowledge to rank the alternatives. They know that in general they must try to protect their liberties, widen their opportunities, and enlarge their means for promoting their aims whatever these are.[2]

By narrowing the distinction between what's good for me and what's good for everyone else, we shrink the barriers between ourselves and others. Therefore for Rawls fairness is what one would do to the "other" if one thought it possible that he or she would be that other. Rawls's hypothesis is actually supported by a good deal of social science research. However, we will take that up a little later.

You could say that the outcome of this experiment sounds a lot like the golden rule—do unto others as you would have them do unto you. This may explain why some of the greatest justice movements in history began in places of worship and were driven by spiritual values. This was true of abolitionist movements in both Britain and America as well as our 1950–1960s Civil Rights Movement. A more recent example would be the rise of liberation theology in Latin America. In all these cases, the spiritual bent was characterized by concern for the well-being of others along with a strong conviction that individuals have a moral responsibility to be proactive in redressing wrongs foisted upon innocent and powerless people.

Interestingly, these justice movements were not motivated by Rawls's perspective. While Rawls the philosopher was focused on rational self–interest, the great justice movements like abolition were primarily driven by strong emotion, namely empathic concern. Yet despite this fact, their practical view of things matches up quite nicely with a number of other aspects of this famous thought experiment. For both, things are usually as they seem to be. If you are ignorant of your status and parochial interests, what you would want to see when the veil comes off isn't complicated. Elaborate rationalization isn't required to know the possible scenarios that must be avoided at all cost. Rawls addresses this question by employing the concept of generality and universality. He writes:

> It is a commonplace of moral philosophy to require first principles to be general and universal. Principles are general when it is possible to state them without the use of proper names or rigged definite descriptions. They are universal when they can be applied without inconsistency or self-defeating incoherence to all moral agents, in our case all citizens of the society in question.[3]

Rawls is saying that justice must be general enough to apply to everyone in the same way. Since nonspecific and clear-cut principles will suffice, one needn't know details about particular groups to formulate a meaningful definition of it. It follows that intricate explanations that contain a lot of exceptions (i.e., "buts") will seriously compromise the elementary principle. Looking at our first great justice movement, we see that abolitionist sermons portrayed freedom as simply freedom, justice as simply justice, and slavery as simply slavery—in other words, as the concepts are usually understood without explanation.

Another common factor is seeing the welfare of human beings as central to justice. We suspect that individuals in Rawls's thought experiment would have been less worried about their fellows taking advantage of society's generosity than the possibility that an arbitrary society might take advantage of them. The need to secure everybody's well-being means that a just society must be humane. Rawls thinks that the best way to measure this is by looking at how its least advantaged are treated. Their status is especially important because he reasons that a just society requires all its members to have at least a firm enough standing to act autonomously without fearing any of the negative consequences that could result from one's civic or material vulnerabilities. This entails some degree of not only political leveling but economic as well. He notes:

> To say that *inequalities in income and wealth are to be arranged for the greatest benefit of the least advantaged* simply means that we are to compare schemes of cooperation by seeing how well off the least advantaged are under each scheme, and then to select the scheme under which the least advantaged are better off than they are under any other scheme (my italics).[4]

The bottom line here is that for justice to be real people must have enough "primary goods" to be able to access the liberties that they supposedly possess—as Rawls puts it:

> … so long as their powers and abilities suffice for them *to be normal cooperating members of society* (my italics).[5]

If we once again look at our first great justice movement, we see that abolition was also centered on the well-being of people and likewise this focus was expressed by a humanitarian concern for the welfare of the most vulnerable and oppressed. Abolitionists were more worried about unscrupulous persons rigging the system to deny the less powerful their humanity than they were about the victims of such villainy maneuvering to gain something that they supposedly weren't entitled to. As with Rawls, they understood that justice demanded in addition to political liberties economic redress—or, to state it another way, some degree of material redistribution. Hence, the idea emerged that the freed population should receive the additional benefit of being allotted "forty acres and a mule." For without some degree of social leveling, their newly gained liberties would be greatly devalued, and this would hinder them from becoming "normal cooperating members of society."

Along similar lines, there is an additional affinity in that both mindsets hold that the harm done *by* society is more egregious than the harm done *to* society. Each of them sees the concept of justice as being much broader than just retribution. And certainly this is in keeping with the classical liberalism of the Enlightenment enunciated so well by Voltaire's famous quote from *Zadig, or the Book of Fate* (*Zadig ou la Destinée*, 1747): "it is better to risk sparing a guilty person than to condemn an innocent one." You might say that there is no debate over the idea that the most basic rule of justice is to do no harm to human beings. Rawls lists protection from political, judicial, economic, mental, physical, and personal abuses as his "first principle of justice." This list not only includes but entails, according to Rawls scholar Thomas Pogge,

> *Freedom and integrity of the person*, which are incompatible with slavery and serfdom and which also include freedom from psychological oppression, physical injury, and abuse, as well as freedom of movement and the right to hold personal property ... [6]

For the most part, the great justice movements were driven by the fact that society's most vulnerable (enslaved persons, laborers, women, children, etc.) were denied this "freedom and integrity of the person." Equally important, this explains why proactive justice seekers, spiritual and secular, have been so concerned about the harm–benefit ratio. Since in most situations this calculation correlates with the scope and degree of the "freedom and integrity of the person" an individual is able to lay claim to, it is one of the best indicators for what Rawls would call the first principle of justice being at the root of any arrangement. The pre-Civil War era supplies us an excellent example of this. Slavemasters held that ending slavery would harm the enslaved population; they were just looking out for their well-being. In this case the harm–benefit ratio for each group is quite telling. Independent of anyone's abstract welfare, the slavemasters received all the tangible advantages while the enslaved got to make all the hard-core sacrifices. The free space of one group was expanded at the same time that the other's space was greatly reduced. This could not help but affect the consideration that the individual was afforded and along with this the amount of personal latitude required to protect against arbitrary mistreatment. If we look even deeper it becomes noticeable that only the slavemasters were free to express an opinion without fear of retaliation. This is crucial, because for "freedom and integrity of the person" to be legitimate, one cannot be motivated by dread and apprehension. In such a situation any perceived material rewards will lose their value. In more recent times we have seen how in totalitarian states the benefits of socioeconomic leveling were more than cancelled out by the terror that was generated. Therefore, this inherent fear of retaliation may be the most revealing factor in deciphering the validity of the slavemaster's claim of just treatment. For this type of situation, Rawls states the case quite clearly when he writes:

> Now this agreement, like any other, must be entered into under certain conditions if it is to be a valid agreement from the point of view of political justice. In particular, these conditions must situate free and equal persons fairly and must *not permit some to have unfair bargaining advantages over others*. Further, *threats of force and coercion*, deception and fraud, and so on must be ruled out (my italics).[7]

Obviously, threats of "force and coercion" against the enslaved population cannot be "ruled out." Needless to say this was one reason why abolitionists were not convinced by slaveholder claims that they were motivated by their concern for their captives. Abolitionist rhetoric frequently focused on the particularly vulnerable position of enslaved persons. And this was seen as being an especially ripe situation for the slavemaster to abuse his power. It was fully understood to be incompatible with any arrangement the purpose of which was to prevent harm to human beings.

While Rawls's and history's great justice movements have significantly different starting points, the pathway traveled is amazingly similar. They each understand justice to be fairness, and fairness to be an elegantly simple and human-centered force. Both see the presence of a naked self-interest—in treating others differently than you would wish to be treated yourself—as almost always a red flag for the absence of justice. Likewise, when the focus is primarily centered on the transgressions of the most vulnerable and coupled with a minimal concern for the abuses of the most powerful, neither give claims of holding justice in high esteem much creditability.

Going deeper into it and observing how these justice seekers differ is also enlightening. Let us first look at it from Rawls's perspective. There are those who would claim that Rawls's view of things supports the notion that in the end it's all about "what's in it for me?" After all, he does seem to think that rational self-interest, albeit in the absence of prejudicial knowledge, lays a foundation for a just society. Some have claimed that Rawls chose the veil of ignorance because it eliminated sympathy from the equation. Since people wouldn't know which fellow community members were destined to wind up with the short end of the stick, they wouldn't know whom to be sympathetic to. Although this interpretation has its opponents, and the role that emotion plays in Rawls's experiment is still a question for debate, it wouldn't be too far a reach to say that one of the most important things that he was searching for was at least some semblance of a rational explanation for the existence of justice. In this vein he didn't wish to see the concept expanded to include life's nonrational realms—the religious, philosophical, and moral. He states:

> Finally, I stress a point implicit in what we have said: namely, that justice as fairness *is not a comprehensive religious, philosophical, or moral doctrine*—one that applies to all subjects and covers all values (my italics).[8]

Rawls also says that narrowing the scope of justice to just the rational domain entails restricting the fields of knowledge that are in play. He elaborates:

> … we allow the parties the general beliefs and forms of reasoning found in common sense, and the methods and conclusions of science, when not controversial.… So we say the parties have that kind of general knowledge and they use those ways of reasoning. *This excludes comprehensive religious and philosophical doctrines* (the whole truth, as it were) from being specified as public reasons (my italics).[9]

Limiting the applicability of a whole range of information insures that our points of reference will not be too divergent. But most important, by removing as much of the subjective as possible there is less room for favoritism and partisanship. A society is guided towards a more rational view of justice that is not specific to any person or tribe. This is probably the reason why Rawls is more concerned with one's attachment to the larger group rather than to any specific individual members. He says that:

> In any case, the citizen body as a whole is not generally bound together by ties of fellow feeling between individuals, but by the acceptance of public principles of justice. While every citizen is a friend to some citizens, no citizen is a friend to all. But their common allegiance to justice provides a unified perspective from which they can adjudicate their differences.[10]

While this idea has merit, can one's personal attachments be so easily separated from the concept of justice? If there were other members of the group that you really cared about and you were as concerned with their fate as your own, wouldn't it impact your thinking as well as your actions? And if so, isn't identifying with the plight or possible plight of another a step beyond pure rational self-interest?

For Rawls the answer is no; the connections that one makes with others "in the presence of the veil" are not included in it. Under the veil you wouldn't know anything about your attachments. In this regard, Pogge writes of Rawls's theory:

> Because citizens' constitutive attachments develop within social structures whose nature is yet to be agreed upon in the original position, they

cannot be presupposed as already known by the parties in their deliberations.[11]

This is where our great justice movements can add to our understanding of justice. If we take a look at our country's first one, abolition, we see a mosaic consisting of society's most advantaged members as well as its most disadvantaged ones. All of them were fully aware of their position and interests in relation to the others. So if it wasn't the veil of ignorance, what was the link that connected them? We can easily see that the most disadvantaged group had a great deal to gain in joining the movement. However, wasn't the reverse true for the most advantaged one? From a purely quantitative standpoint, yes; but this is where it gets interesting. If we look at what these people had to say, we see individuals who were deeply affected (moved) by the terrible treatment the most disadvantaged were subjected to. You might say that they "felt their pain" and it wasn't a political gimmick.

An individual who sacrifices his or her own life to save another—parent for a child, spouse for a partner, or friend for a buddy—acts this way out of connectedness to that person, not to get something for herself. Dedicating a significant portion of your life to redressing the injustices committed against those different from yourself is traveling down the same road as the people who literally sacrifice their very existence to save persons with whom they have a close bond. In both cases one's behavior results from the individual making a meaningful connection with the distress of another. Any differences rest solely with the intensity of one's emotions and the depth of one's commitment. The abolitionists represented a phenomenon that was bigger than them. Their reaction wasn't solely isolated or individualistic; it rested on a broader species-specific capacity for identifying with the plight of their brethren. It went to the very definition of what it means to be human.

In assessing the bigger picture we learn that we possess a unique ability to identify with what our fellow human beings are experiencing, and this capacity expresses itself along a spectrum that encompasses everything from literally to metaphorically placing one's life on the line, not for any predictable reward but solely for the benefit of another or even the group as a whole. Yet most significant, we see that such selfless inclinations transcend pure rational self-interest and as such are integral to the quest for justice.

We have reached the point in our discussion where I cannot resist superimposing another thought experiment onto Rawls's original one. Since it involves a situation that exists in real time, human emotions cannot be factored out. Let us look at the reaction of soldiers in a war zone. No soldier knows who will survive the fighting and who won't (*the presence of the veil*). This uncertainty can generate a very strong group loyalty that affects all levels of human interaction. It is not uncommon for soldiers in this situation to develop a personal closeness and concern for the welfare of their comrades (*forming attachments while veiled*). The starkest example of this would be a soldier sacrificing his life for a fellow mate (*acting contrary to one's own self-interest*). Even after the war ends and the survivors know who made it home and who didn't (*the veil is lifted*), this personal closeness has been known to last a lifetime (*attachments continue in the absence of the veil*).What's ultimately important is greater than extent of the knowledge that we have about our particular self-interests, but also includes the level of connectedness we have to our fellow human beings. That's why the deepest expression of justice is recognizing that an injustice to one is an injustice to all.

Independent of everything that's been said, can we find an even more fundamental truth that sheds light on this topic? The answer is maybe. We know from physics that "quantum entanglement" is a proven characteristic of our natural world. Particles that are in contact with each other remain connected even if they become separated and find themselves at opposite ends of the universe. The fact that the limitation imposed by the speed of light doesn't affect their connectedness is just as telling. Of course it's not being claimed that the connectedness that I speak of emanates from any proven scientific findings. I am using this example in physics purely as a metaphor. However, as far as metaphors go it's a particularly good one, since it does establish that when we speak of "connectedness" we are referring to a phenomenon that, unlike fairy dust, actually exists. This may be reason enough not to automatically dismiss the potential insights inherent in what appears to be a purely subjective abstraction.

Despite a multitude of speculation that has been derived from a classic academic thought experiment—as well as history's great grassroots movements—we are still unable to formulate a final definition of justice; the question is too far-reaching. Nevertheless, I think we can take a stab at establishing some broad parameters that can be used to identify the likely absence of justice. So here they are:

- Unfairness or treating others differently than you would wish to be treated yourself (in spiritual terms, the absence of the golden rule)
- Intricate explanations with many exceptions and "buts"
- A lack of human centeredness which includes:
  o Lacking any desire to protect the most vulnerable from abuse by the most predatory
  o Lacking any concern for preventing or stopping harm to human beings
  o Lacking any acute sensitivity to who is harmed and who benefits
- Lacking any sense of connectedness or putting oneself in another's place and being concerned for their well-being (in psychological terms, a lack of empathy and empathic concern)

To some degree these parameters overlap, and of course the fourth one is contained in all the others. Although this is informative, it isn't any surprise that in our scientific age the quest doesn't end here, with just philosophy. In establishing a foundation for society, modern-day neuroscience recognizes the important role that is played by the human capacity to empathize (identify/connect) with others. Such an understanding is consistent with the striving for fairness that characterized the great justice movements as well as the outcome of Rawls's thought experiment. Therefore, it would be helpful to look at what the objective data has to tell us about how humans perceive fairness.

During the last sixty years, social scientists have developed all kinds of laboratory experiments to test how people react in situations where a person's idea of fairness could be an important factor in human decision making. The "ultimatum game" is an example of one of these experiments. It involves giving a participant a particular amount of money; we will call her the first participant. The first participant can then decide how much she will give to a second participant. If this second participant refuses to accept what the first participant is willing to share with him, neither of the two participants will end up with anything. If the second participant accepts what the first one decides to give him, both of them keep this agreed upon amount of money. Obviously, since the second participant begins the game with nothing, he has nothing to gain by rejecting the offer of the first participant, no matter what it is. He has to come away with more than he started with.

Yet, the unexpected happens. What one would think is rational self-interest appears to be negated if the second participant perceives the first one's offer as being too low. In this situation he will reject the offer and willingly lose everything. The bottom line here is that people have a concept of fairness, quickly recognize when it's in play, and consistently act upon it even if it's to their own detriment.[12]

There are many other games that are concerned with the idea of fairness and correspondingly involve cooperation between people. It has been discovered that when a game participant acts unselfishly for another participant's benefit, the area of the brain that is associated with rewards is activated, and the more the action benefits other participants, the greater the brain activation. Whether one holds that this is the whole story or just a piece of it, the fact that when acting unselfishly we automatically exhibit a pleasurable neurophysiological response indicates that at least on this level we are biologically inclined to react positively towards one another.[13]

Numerous findings like this have convinced a large number of scientists that the idea of fairness is part of our hardwiring. Yet, there are additional scientific studies, particularly those involving children, that are even more convincing. A recent investigation involving children was undertaken by researchers at Harvard's Laboratory for Developmental Studies, with the results appearing in the journal *Cognition*. Eight-year-olds participated in a version of the ultimatum game where, instead of money, candy was the reward, and this time both children were allotted a particular amount. As before, just one child got to decide if both of them kept their candy or together they ended up empty-handed.

The purpose of the study was to see if the "decider," when given less candy than the other participant, chose to accept it or opt for nothing. Of course no matter how little the decider was given it was still more advantageous for her to accept it rather than wind up with no candy at all. The result showed that it wasn't the "bottom line" that was important; the children were far more concerned about being treated fairly. One of the Harvard researchers, Peter Blake, stated:

> We were able to show that 8-year-olds have a general sense of fairness and are willing to make large sacrifices to enforce it with other children.[14]

Another Harvard researcher, Katherine McAuliffe, added that:

> Children younger than 8 are more self-interested, yet they're still willing to deny themselves rewards in order to prevent a transaction that's unfair to them.[15]

It gets even more interesting. The eight-year-olds in the study did what no one had expected: they turned down the candy even if the unequal allocation benefited them! McAuliffe reported:

> We weren't expecting to see 8-year-olds willing to sacrifice so much candy to prevent a peer from getting less than them. In some cases, children were giving up 24 candies in a given session. It shows that fairness or inequity aversion is an important factor in determining how these children behave. Relative rewards do matter.[16]

That was with eight-year-olds; but how about with children much younger? On September 13, 2012, the *Harvard Gazette* published an article entitled "Figuring out Fairness," revealing the results of a study on young children conducted by Harvard University researchers. Children were taught to play a game where they competed against a "puppet," using poles and hooks to lift containers filled with coins out of a bucket. At the end of the game the children were given six stickers and had to choose how many the puppet should get and how many they should keep. What was discovered was that when the children collected more coins they kept more stickers than they gave the puppet. However, when the puppet collected the most coins the children either distributed the stickers evenly or gave the puppet more.

Surprisingly, children as young as three years old showed that they not only possessed a sense of fairness but were also willing to act on it. One of the researchers, Professor Felix Warnekin, explained:

> What this finding demonstrates, I think, is that merit seems to be an essential part of the earliest forms of fairness that children display. That challenges the idea that young children only have a very egocentric notion that everything should go to them, and shows that from a very early age they are sensitive to the work contributions partners make.[17]

The staff writer for the *Gazette* noted that:

Importantly, the study shows that the notion of merit isn't simply an abstract concept that children endorse, but one that they actually put into practice, even at a cost.[18]

The fact that even 3-year-olds show a resistance to take more than they deserve and possess an ability to recognize what another is entitled to suggests that at our core we humans are a good deal more complicated than just being concerned about "what's in it for me." This insight leads us to ask whether or not the previous discussion about justice has any practical merits independent of our lofty visions. I think that the answer to the question is a resounding yes! A crude concept of fairness appears to develop at a very early age. We recognize the distinction between fairness and unfairness when we interact with others and we willingly make personal sacrifices to insure a fairer outcome. More important, there are good objective indicators that reveal the situation goes beyond just achieving fairness for ourselves. We also recognize that others are entitled to it as well.

So how does all this stack up with the broad parameters we laid down? An awareness of what constitutes fairness and an understanding that if it's right for me it's right for others is very much in line with the golden rule. If we see this ancient precept missing from human interaction it should be a red flag for the absence of real justice. Similarly, we should be exceedingly guarded when someone sees justice from a purely self-centered viewpoint. A good example would be an individual who believes he is being victimized by the likes of "welfare cheats" and other "losers." These "undeserving lowlifes" are supposedly taking something away from him. For people like this, justice is never about putting oneself in another person's place or seeing his good fortune in the context of "for the grace of God go I." A "me only" perspective combined with contempt for the well-being of others usually indicates hostility towards justice.

Of equal importance, a basic sense of fairness doesn't appear to require intricate explanation. In fact it's so simple that, without any prompting, even a 3-year-old child is beginning to develop an understanding of it. Therefore, it's appropriate to be suspicious when a convoluted rationale is necessary to justify an action or situation. Although concepts like human centeredness and connectedness are more abstract and difficult to quantify, empirical evidence obtained by neuroimaging suggests that most individuals are sensitive other people's pain.[19] It is not something they have to think about; it's simply a human response. The absence of this response should be a warning.

By narrowing down the opposite attributes, we have come to a better understanding of fairness and its identical twin, justice. Yet, we have also accomplished something even more important than just establishing broad parameters to test for their absence. We have uncovered evidence that fairness and justice are tangible and innately human characteristics that shape our actions and history. The historical proof for this is evidenced by the achievements of great liberal justice movements such as nineteenth-century abolitionism. A large number of abolitionists, without the need of a veil, went to battle on behalf of others they did not know personally who were of a different race, social position, region, and historical rooting. And they did so without any expectation of tangible gain for themselves. The force that engaged them might be seen as an anomaly if it weren't for the fact that similar phenomena have regularly occurred throughout history. I contend that the force in question is a deeply seated human propensity for justice. In fact, it is almost certain that as long as there are human beings, the striving for justice will go on. Using modern-day terminology, I call this striving liberalism.

Chapter III

The Founders

Since the best place to start is at the beginning, let our journey commence with the Founding Fathers. The most prominent among them were proud sons of the Enlightenment. Included in this lot are the men most responsible for the nation's two founding documents, Thomas Jefferson and James Madison. For Jefferson it was the Declaration of Independence and for Madison the Constitution. This is why I have chosen them to be representative of the intellectual spirit that the founders imprinted on the new nation. Both Jefferson and Madison were larger than life, and all of us today are in their debt.

Yet they were fallible human beings, not gods. The political issues that they faced must be seen in the context of their time. It was before the nineteenth-century's industrial and communication revolutions. It was a period when women played no role in the body politic. It was an era when slavery was not only a legal but also a respected institution. Many of Jefferson's and Madison's political opinions were a parochial reflection of this more barbarous period. Admitting these truths doesn't lessen the stature of these founders. Despite the shortcomings of the age, their most distinguishing feature was willingness to question and challenge accepted dogma. They would expect and demand nothing less of us.

Since much of their eighteenth-century thinking remains part of our present-day political discourse, it is necessary to separate out the ideas that have become antiquated. In addition, those who have done what these two Founding Fathers would have been most upset with—namely, placed them on a pedestal—need to be counteracted. Therefore, let us take a retrospective look at the environment in which these two founders found themselves.

In the early years of the Republic forces were brewing in the underbelly of civil society that would take the new nation in directions Jefferson and Madison never conceived of. While these two giants were great philosophers of democracy, their formative years were not spent in the type of democratic society they idealized. Yet in their later years both of them would witness firsthand what life in a living and growing democracy was like. The speed of democratization that they began would soon overwhelm them. Reading what contemporaries reported about their conversations with the elder Jefferson, one gets the feeling that he was very uneasy with the rapid democratization that was occurring.

He didn't like Andrew Jackson and what he represented. He was uncomfortable with his appeal to the common man.[1, 2] What Jefferson and his fellow generation was observing was a fast-paced changing landscape characterized by a broadening base of popular participation. They experienced what all future American generations would have to deal with, the uncertainty of change and the pains of growth in a free, dynamic, and ever-accelerating democracy. Their reactive response would be typical of how most future generations would behave.

It's this democratic dynamic that shows no "man" mercy, the Founding Fathers included, that has not only shaped America but has become America. The democratic spark that would catch fire and spread beyond anybody's control started with America's first justice movement, abolitionism. Therefore, the reaction of prominent Founders like Jefferson and Madison to the emerging abolitionist movement gives us a much better understanding of America's true story. For this reason we need to take a good look at their response.

In order to have an unfettered view of how they thought, we first have to clear away the historical dissonance that surrounds their identities. There are people who classify Thomas Jefferson as an abolitionist. If you go to the website of the Thomas Jefferson Foundation (they oversee Jefferson's home at Monticello), you find a glowing picture of both Jefferson's distaste for and actions against slavery.[3] Both Jefferson and his good friend James Madison claimed to loathe the institution of slavery, and in both their private and public pronouncements they advocated its eventual elimination.

Yet to call either Jefferson or Madison abolitionists inappropriately associates them with the real abolitionists who embraced this designation without regard to the consternation of others or the potential risks involved. It does a great disservice to everyone, including these two Founding Fathers. But most important, it's a distortion of

45

history. Therefore, to dispel all the noise and obtain the objective truth about these men, it's necessary to define what constituted a "real" abolitionist.

I think that there are three reasonable requirements that anyone with basic common sense can agree to. First, a real abolitionist didn't enslave other human beings. Second, a real abolitionist favored eliminating slavery *now*, not at some unspecified future time. And third, a real abolitionist viewed abolition as central—not peripheral—in importance. These three requirements are simple and to the point. Since they provide some clarity on definitions, I will now refer, when appropriate, to "real" abolitionists as simply abolitionists.

Obviously, people who are normally thought of as abolitionists—like John Rankin, William Lloyd Garrison, Frederick Douglass, Wendell Phillips, John Brown, etc.—all easily qualify. Since both Jefferson and Madison were lifelong slaveholders and their slaves weren't even freed in their respective wills, they are immediately disqualified. However, this isn't any great revelation, since everyone concedes the fact that they owned slaves. What isn't conceded is that they wouldn't have qualified as abolitionists even if they hadn't been slaveholders. Despite wishes to the contrary, their written correspondence addressing the 1820 Missouri Compromise reveals substantial evidence supporting this assertion.

However, before viewing this evidence, one needs to understand the Missouri Compromise. By 1820 the individual states were beginning to become cognizant of their status as a free or slave state. In this regard the states were becoming aware of their relationship to other states. The same mindset was developing in states where the institution was seriously being challenged (on the way out) versus the states where it was deeply embedded. These two different categories of states were already evolving into separate camps, with each possessing a unique group identity and loyalty.

Thanks to the Louisiana Purchase, the areas of our country ripe for settlement were vastly expanded. Therefore, everyone knew that in the coming years there would be many new territories applying for statehood. Which camp these new states would line up with was a major concern. Neither side wanted to be numerically weakened in relation to the other. Maintaining the balance between the free and slave states was becoming increasingly important for tranquility of the whole. In addition, Southern slaveholders had another concern. They wanted to know where in this new land they could go and be assured that their slave property would be secure.

In the North an even more important consideration was working its way to the forefront. A significant rise in hostility towards this outdated institution was unfolding within Northern civil society. As a result a geographical opposition to slavery was taking shape. This growing Northern antislavery movement confronted a fixed reality. Preventing slavery from spreading ubiquitously across the massive new region was the only feasible course of action that could immediately and practically impact such a dismal situation.

These unfolding events were making a potentially explosive showdown more and more likely. To prevent this from occurring, a compromise that would afford each camp something of what they wanted was desperately needed. Therefore, the most important feature of the Missouri Compromise was an agreed-upon line of demarcation. A horizontal line was drawn across the former Louisiana Territory differentiating the area where slavery would be prohibited from the area where it would be permitted. With a singular exception made for the new state of Missouri, the slavery-prohibited area would be to the north of the parallel 36° 30' while the slavery-permitted area would be to the south.[4]

The Missouri Compromise was significant because it marked the emergence of slavery as a major political issue. In doing so it establishes a crucial timeline. While not telling us when the cause of abolition was first conceived, it roughly tells us when it was first born (i.e., became a real factor). For the four decades following 1820, the nation's most intense disagreements would revolve around the question of slavery. And for the first three of these decades the Missouri Compromise would be the established model for coping with this contentious issue. Clearly, such groundbreaking legislation suggests that by 1820 there was a significant level of discontent with the status quo.

This was particularly true in the North where political leaders were for the first time demanding that Congress do something to curtail what had been for centuries a legal and accepted institution. They were obviously receiving some palpable pressure from their constituents. Yet it's highly unlikely that this growing distaste for slavery would have appeared in the Northern body politic overnight, out of nowhere. Therefore, it is a good assumption that the evolving impetus to confront slavery head on (in the present and at every available opportunity) most likely began taking shape at some point in the decade prior to 1820.

This emerging development provided Jefferson and Madison a peek at what was going to characterize American politics for the next forty years. And through their writings we get a peek at their respective thoughts on the issue destined to fundamentally reshape our country. We discover that both of them saw the line drawn by the Missouri Compromise as about the worst thing that could have happened to the new nation. They thought that such a line would ultimately divide the Union into two separate halves that would in time have little interest in the other's concerns and therefore less incentive to cooperate with one another.

Beginning with Jefferson's perspective, we see his opinion on this situation expressed in a letter written to John Holmes, dated April 22, 1820:

> A geographical line, coinciding with a marked principle, moral and political, once conceived and held up to the *angry passions of men*, will never be obliterated; and every new irritation will mark it deeper and deeper [my italics].[5]

Note that he fears what the "the angry passions of men" will produce. In the following three sentences Jefferson cuts to the chase and tells us that he knows what's underlying all of this passion:

> I can say, with conscious truth, that there is not a man on earth who would sacrifice more than I would to relieve us from this heavy reproach, *in any practicable way.* The cession of that kind of property, for so it is misnamed, is a bagatelle which would not cost me a second thought, if, in that way, a general emancipation and expatriation could be effected; and gradually, and with due sacrifices, I think might be. *But as it is, we have the wolf by the ears, and we can neither hold him, nor safely let him go. Justice is in one scale, and self-preservation in the other* [my italics].[6]

Jefferson is obviously taking for granted that the reader understands that it's the issue of slavery that one needs to be speaking about next. He reveals that he doesn't like slavery very much and wishes to get rid of it. Yet this is where the big "but" comes in: slavery can only be eliminated if it's done in a "practicable way." Of course this way has yet to be precisely formulated. His "wolf by the ears" comment strikes up an image of grave danger. Although he can't be held forever (the future) he can't be let go (the present). Obviously, it's slavery that can't be let go. Why can't it be let go? This can be answered with another question: What is the wolf expected to do? The question is of course rhetorical. The "self-preservation" he refers to indicates an assessment that a freed slave population poses a great danger to the non-enslaved population, i.e., retaliation. That's why he links "general emancipation" together with "expatriation." The bottom line is that he clearly saw that for the "present time" the continued existence of slavery was necessary for "self-preservation," albeit under disagreeable circumstances.

In the second paragraph of this same letter he belittles the passions that this situation is stirring up by referring to them as "unworthy passions." He also speaks of the possible consequences that may well result from them:

> I regret that I am now to die in the belief, that the useless sacrifice of themselves by the generation of 1776, to acquire self-government and happiness to their country, is to be thrown away by the *unwise and unworthy passions* of their sons, and that my only consolation is to be, that I live not to weep over it [my italics].[7]

Once again we see Jefferson blaming the passions of men for what he sees as the deplorable situation signified by the Missouri Compromise. He feels that these passions could very well be the death knell of the Union. In a letter to William Short dated April 13, 1820, Jefferson was even more specific about where this could lead. He even used the word "separation" and indicated that there may come a time when it would be "preferable":

> But the coincidence of a marked principle, moral & political with a geographical line, once conceived, I feared would never more be obliterated from the mind; that it would be

recurring on every occasion & renewing irritations until it would kindle such mutual & mortal hatred, as to *render separation preferable to eternal discord* [my italics].[8]

He then says in this letter that he thinks that this feared breakup of the Union will most likely take place.

I have been among the most sanguine in believing that our Union would be of long duration. *I now doubt it much* ... [my italics].[9]

Since Jefferson sees the Union most likely ending on account of the passions that issue of slavery is conjuring up, he is not at all pleased with the people responsible for them. In the April 22, 1820, letter to Holmes he pontificates on this very concern:

If they would but dispassionately weigh the blessings they will throw away, against an abstract principle more likely to be effected by union than scission, they would pause before they would perpetrate this *act of suicide on themselves* ... [my italics].[10]

If only they could put their dispassionate rational facilities in control of their passions they could avoid a pending disaster. But whose passions is Jefferson referring to? On this question Jefferson gives us a hint. In the Holmes letter of April 22, 1820, he comments:

Of one thing I am certain, that as the passage of slaves from one State to another, would not make a slave of a single human being who would not be so without it ...[11]

It certainly sounds like Jefferson is basically saying that there is too much fuss being made over taking of slaves into the new territories; such concern over this issue is misguided. Therefore it follows that the people responsible for all this ferment are those (passionately) arguing in favor of the geographical containment of slavery.

Interestingly, he proceeds to say:

> ... so their [enslaved persons] diffusion over a greater surface would make them individually happier, and proportionally facilitate the accomplishment of their emancipation, by dividing the burthen on a greater number of coadjutors.[12]

In other words, allowing masters to take their slaves into all parts of the country would actually be better for the slaves. And conversely you would have to presume that preventing this migration would be injurious to them. Unfortunately, this is somewhat reminiscent of the people who opposed sanctions against South African apartheid because they claimed that such measures would only hurt the victims of apartheid. In addition, Jefferson appears to believe that letting slavery become more spread out within the country is a good thing because it will facilitate its elimination. Therefore he thinks that people who really want to get rid of slavery should support expanding its reach. It's no wonder that these

Jeffersonian opinions do not appear on his national memorial in Washington, DC. In any case, preventing restrictive geographic boundaries, rather than preventing the immediate expansion of slavery, is what Jefferson sees as most important.

These written statements indicate that Jefferson wasn't on the side that was pushing for the geographical containment of slavery. He saw their impassioned demands as dangerous. It should be noted that in the real political world the only side that was pushing for something to be done "now" against slavery was the side that Jefferson thought was causing the problem.

Looking at the perspective of Jefferson's compatriot James Madison on this subject is even more enlightening. In a letter to President James Monroe dated February 10, 1820, Madison writes:

> I find the idea is *fast spreading that the zeal* wth. which the *extension, so called, of slavery is opposed*, has, with coalesced leaders, an object very different from the welfare of the slaves, or the check to their increase … [my italics].[13]

Madison sees the opposition to the extension of slavery spreading along with the "zeal" of its supporters. And he doesn't think that these people really care about "the welfare of the slaves" or the lessening of their numbers. In other words, he doesn't like or respect them or what they are doing. He views their increasing numbers and intensity as problematic.

Once again, at that time in our history those pushing back against the geographical expansion of slavery were the only people engaging in any meaningful antislavery activity. Yet Madison believes that he, a lifelong slaveholder, is a fit judge of both their intentions and actions. If we fast forward to the American South in the 1950–1960s or South Africa in the 1950–1980s, we see this same attitude embraced by leaders trying to hold back the tide of change. In both cases those who benefited from the current setup claimed to know what was best for its victims and denounced active reformers as insincere frauds.

In fairness to Madison, like his mentor Thomas Jefferson, he wrote eloquently against slavery "in principle." For example, the Marquis de Lafayette wrote him a letter expressing his desire to see slavery ended. In his written response to Lafayette, dated February 1, 1830, Madison comments on Lafayette's sentiments:

> Your anticipations with regard to the slavery among us, were the natural offspring of your just principles & laudable sympathies.[14]

Yet his thoughts on the practicality of getting rid of slavery are similar to Jefferson's. In the sentences immediately following he writes:

> But I am sorry to say that the occasion which led to them, proved to be little fitted for the slightest interposition on that subject. A sensibility, morbid in its degree, was never more awakened among those who have the largest stake in that interest,

and are *most violent* against any Governmental movement in relation to it. The excitability at the moment, happened also to be augmented by party questions between the South & the North, and the efforts used to make the circumstance common to the former, a sympathetic bond of co-operation. I scarcely express myself too strongly in saying, that an allusion in the Convention to the subject you have so much at heart, would have been a *spark to a mass of Gun Powder* [my italics].[15]

Madison is telling Lafayette that at the present time there is no way of getting rid of slavery without suffering the most severe consequences, i.e., separation and war. Implied in this opinion is that these consequences trump the evils of continuing on with the institution intact. Also implied is that this topic is so volatile that at the present time it is better to refrain from public discourse on the subject. One could add that this is another way of implying that even advocating half measures could be dangerous. Remember that those fighting to contain slavery, as a practical first step towards achieving full abolition, could be considered pushing for a half measure to at least keep some active resistance alive.

At end of the letter he reveals to Lafayette what his hopes are:

It is certain nevertheless, that Time "the great Innovator" is not idle in its salutary preparations. The Colonization Societies are becoming more and more one of its agents. Outlets for the freed blacks are alone wanted for a rapid erasure of that blot from our Republican character.[16]

In his lifetime, Madison was actively involved with the colonization effort. In fact, it was really the only solution he had to the question of slavery, after the abolition of the external slave trade in 1808. Madison parallels Jefferson on expatriation. Like his mentor he doesn't appear to think that the country can exist with a significant population of freed blacks living within its borders. Why did he think this? Here again we have a version of Jefferson's "wolf by the ears" analogy. In a letter to Robert J. Evans dated June 15, /1819, Madison supplies us with more detail on this topic:

> If the blacks, strongly marked as they are by Physical & lasting peculiarities, be retained amid the Whites, under the degrading privation of equal rights political or social, they must be always dissatisfied with their condition as a change only from one to another species of oppression; *always secretly confederated agst.* [against] *the ruling & privileged class*; and always uncon-troulled [sic] by some of the most cogent motives to moral and respectable conduct. The character of the free blacks, even where their legal condition is least affected by their colour, seems to put these truths beyond question [my italics].[17]

The racism in this passage was virtually ubiquitous among the white population during this time period. Yet putting this aside, we still have Madison's strongly held belief that a large free black population posed a significant danger to the white population. He then adds an even deeper explanation of his position:

> It is material also that the removal of the blacks be to a distance precluding the *jealousies & hostilities* to be apprehended from a neighboring people stimulated by the *contempt* known to be entertained for their peculiar features; to say nothing of their *vindictive recollections*, or predatory propensities which their State of Society might foster [my italics].[18]

Freed blacks need to be moved as far away as possible because of their "jealousies," "hostilities," "contempt," "vindictive recollections," and "predatory propensities." With this perception of the enslaved population, it's no wonder that Madison wished to take special care to be sure things were safe before entertaining any real attempt at general emancipation. After all, the "wolf" may harbor, among other nasty things, too many "vindictive recollections." The bottom line here is that like Jefferson, Madison feared retaliation from enslaved people if they were freed.

There is something else on which Madison agreed with Jefferson. Namely, he saw the people who wanted to stop slavery from moving into a particular geographical area as ignorant of the constitutionality of their positions. The "Father of the Constitution" was disturbed by what he saw as the improper reading of that document. Addressing the issue of the impending Missouri Compromise and the constitutional questions it brings to life, he writes in a letter to Robert Walsh dated November 27, 1819:

> But whatever may have been intended by the term "migration" or the term "persons," it is most certain, *that they referred exclusively to a migration or importation from other countries into the U. States; and not to a removal, voluntary or involuntary, of slaves or freemen, from one part to another of the U. States.* Nothing appears or is recollected that warrants this latter intention [my italics].[19]

Madison questions the federal government's authority to regulate the internal migration of enslaved persons. He is basically saying that Congress has no constitutional authority to create a "no-slavery zone" within U.S. borders. This means it can't constitutionally contain the spread of slavery. Like Jefferson, Madison's primary concern was protecting what he saw as the proper institutional arrangements rather than being overjoyed that before he passed from the scene a real antislavery movement was emerging in America.

In their respective lifetimes, both Jefferson and Madison opposed slavery and simultaneously opposed taking any substantive action against it. Remember, even upon their deaths, neither freed their own slaves. They both feared what a freed black population might do to the society that had enslaved them for so long. Accordingly, each of them saw expatriation as a necessary part of any future emancipation. This explains why it was so difficult for them to take immediate steps towards emancipation. It was much more practical to put it off until some unspecified future time.

The last chapter in all this would be set in their golden years, when both men would have a final opportunity to cleanse themselves of the stain of slavery. Yet despite the fact that they lived to see the birth of the movement that would take the fight against slavery to its successful conclusion, they chose to ignore the reality of the present and remain fixated on a future fantasy world of their own creation. In the end they rejected engaging in any immediate and concrete actions against slavery. They saw those who engaged in such actions as unreasonable hot heads.

If we apply our three common-sense requirements for defining an abolitionist, these Founding Fathers came up short on every one of them. Jefferson and Madison cannot honestly be thought of as abolitionists. They were on the other side of the divide, thinking that the real abolitionists—not the slaveholders—were the Union's greatest danger.

We learn two important things from this chapter in our history. The first is that our Founding Fathers, even the most enlightened ones, were not always on the right side of history, particularly about questions in which they had self-interest. The second and most important is that although our nation's founders are a significant part of America's story, they are not by any means the whole story. What America has become is greater than any particular group of celebrated individuals, including the most renowned among them. We see that early on in the history of the Republic, other actors would arise from the grass roots who would ultimately turn out to be an even more determinant force in shaping the America we know and love.

Chapter IV

Justice Rising

As noted in the last chapter, Jefferson and Madison thought that abolition could be achieved in a genteel manner. We now know that reality couldn't have been more opposite. On this issue they were blind to how messy and jagged a dynamic democracy was. History has repeatedly shown us that in a popularly rooted society great objectives are accomplished not by the few sitting down and reasoning together but by the many engaged in the chaos of (metaphorically) bloody battle.

In this vein nineteenth-century abolitionism was the noblest cause that generated the biggest mess. And in doing so it would forever alter the course of our history. However, before looking at the crucial role played by this great nineteenth-century movement, it would be helpful to first understand its relation to the antislavery efforts that preceded it. An abundance of antislavery sentiments and activities existed prior to the nineteenth century. Here is a summary of a few of them:

- 1676: The Quakers had one of the longest histories of battling slavery. In this year they established (in Southern New Jersey) the first documented settlement in the New World that prohibited slavery.

- 1688: The first documented antislavery protest in the New World was jointly initiated by Quakers and Mennonites in Philadelphia (then Germantown).
- 1693: The first antislavery publication in what is now the United States—"An Exhortation & Caution to Friends Concerning the Buying or Keeping of Negroes"—was written by a group of Philadelphia Quakers.
- 1700s: It should be noted that Quaker antislavery activity would not only continue but progressively escalate during the eighteenth and of course the nineteenth centuries.
- 1775: The Pennsylvania Society for Promoting the Abolition of Slavery was founded (by whom else but the Quakers). Soon afterwards Benjamin Franklin became its honorary president. At the same time Thomas Paine publically denounced slavery and along with Benjamin Rush, an esteemed signer of the Declaration of Independence, joined the abolitionist society.
- 1777: In this decade Vermont was not part of the U.S. Nevertheless it is credited with being the first independent state in the world to abolish slavery.
- 1780: Pennsylvania became the first state that was at the time part of the U.S. to initiate a gradual abolition of slavery. A few years later Pennsylvania also amended its laws to forbid the forcible removal of blacks from the state.
- 1787: Rhode Island outlawed the slave trade.

- 1794: The American Convention for Promoting the Abolition of Slavery held its first conference in Philadelphia. It consisted of several state and local antislavery societies that joined together to oppose slavery.

During the eighteenth century antislavery and self-help activity by people of African blood existed in both America and Europe. The following is a partial summary of their actions:

- 1785: A black person's side of the story, an autobiography entitled *A Narrative of the Lord's Wonderful Dealings with John Marrant, a Black Man,* was published in London.
- 1787: African Americans in Philadelphia established the first independent African American organization and mutual aid society.
- 1791: The first American edition of Olaudah Equiano's work, *The Interesting Narrative of the Life of Olaudah Equiano, or Gustavus Vassa, the African,* was published. It was an eyewitness account of the Middle Passage and the first autobiography by an enslaved African.
- 1797: The first black-initiated petition to Congress, protesting North Carolina's attempt to re-enslave freed blacks, was received. Three years later, blacks petitioned Congress again, to protest the slave trade and the 1793 Fugitive Slave Act.

- 1800: An enslaved African American named Gabriel raised the stakes by attempting to organize (unsuccessfully) a massive slave insurrection.

These actions represent significant antislavery activity that took place prior to the nineteenth century.[1]

Yet despite some lofty endeavors as well as successes, the pre-nineteenth-century American antislavery groups were, for the most part, relegated to the peripheral edges of everyday politics. Their profile explains why. The victims—those of African descent—were obviously outside the mainline, lacking substantial civil and material resources. The Quakers (Mennonites as well) were thought of by the more down-to-earth churches as the (religious) hippies and peaceniks of their day. Well educated intellectuals with far sighted perspectives (aka eggheads) were usually given about as much credibility as they are currently. Notable figures like Franklin and Paine were in a unique category. As with today's celebrities, Franklin's sexual escapades at the French court or Paine's religious nonconformity were somewhat expected and mostly tolerated peccadilloes. The same could be thought about their opposition to slavery.

In the United States, it wouldn't be until the second decade of the nineteenth century that an antislavery momentum emerged as an aggressive political force demanding everyone's attention. For at that time a "militant" abolitionist sentiment would take off and begin a nonstop penetration into mainline society. In the introduction to his book *The Transformation of American Abolitionism: Fighting Slavery in the Early Republic*, Richard Newman outlines how a good number of historians have viewed this occurrence. Although Newman himself retains reservations about the exact degree of change that took place, he notes that:

> In both the popular imagination and in many scholarly accounts, Garrison's [founder of the nation's premier abolitionist newsletter] debut [1831] remains the benchmark for abolitionism. Against the backdrop of religious revivals, a broader reform sensibility, and an emerging market system of free labor, a radical abolition movement appeared almost overnight. The early struggle against slavery (described variously as "gradualist" and "Quaker-oriented") had long since died out; a brand new age was born.[2]

A major overnight shift in abolitionist intensity has been commented on by many students of history. The exact time of its conception is up for debate. While it has been commonly seen to have started in the 1830s, Newman astutely points out:

> Indeed, despite the impressive growth in abolitionist literature over the previous two decades (described by one well-known scholar as

an "avalanche"), abolitionism as an organized movement is still understood in this post-1830 context.[3]

This astounding "avalanche" of antislavery literature that Newman refers to coincides perfectly with the decade leading up to the Missouri Compromise and what correspondingly must have been the first rumblings of this new abolitionist era. The very same Garrison Newman refers to claimed that he was significantly influenced by an earlier (great) abolitionist who began his antislavery activism in the 1810s. What we see is that from this earlier time on, the movement was progressively growing stronger and stronger, until it would—in what is historically a relatively short time span (about a half century)—succeed in its goal of abolishing slavery. Those involved in this endeavor are referred to today as "the abolitionists."

These abolitionists comprised our first grassroots "justice movement." The ascendency of their cause began primarily in America's (mostly Northern) churches and pulpits. In this regard, Bertram Wyatt-Brown, Professor Emeritus at the University of Florida, has noted that:

> The cause of immediate emancipation, as the abolitionists came to define it, had a different germ of inspiration from those Enlightenment ideals that Jefferson had articulated: the rise of a fervent religious reawakening just as the new

Republic was being created. That impulse sprang from two main sources: the theology and practice of Quakerism and the emergence of an aggressive, interdenominational evangelicalism.[4]

As shown in Chapter III, this new and radical abolitionism didn't come from the classical (or rational) concept of liberty that was present at the nation's founding but rather from a mass empathic crusade inspired by what could be called a connection to universal humankind. James Brewer Stewart, a distinguished historian who has written or edited eleven books and some fifty articles on slavery and emancipation in the Western Hemisphere, notes—albeit in the context of the commonly seen connection between "militant" abolitionism and the 1830s—that:

> Radical abolitionism was partly fueled by the religious fervor of the Second Great Awakening, which prompted many people to advocate for emancipation on religious grounds. Abolitionist ideas became increasingly prominent in Northern churches and politics beginning in the 1830s, which contributed to the regional animosity between North and South leading up to the Civil War.[5]

While this "religious fervor" provided the fuel, what's equally important is the effect it had on the character of the movement. Since churchgoing was the norm and therefore very widespread in the early nineteenth century, rising abolitionist sentiments were of a bottom-up and very plebian nature. If the cause had been first situated in the nation's elite universities, its character and prospects for expansion would have been totally different. It most likely would have been more academic and in permanent confinement, thereby assuring an early obituary.

Yet out in the grass roots one didn't attend church to study logic, philosophy, or history. Church sermons were centered on a moral—not a scholarly—message. Moral messages were perfectly designed for appealing to congregants' emotions, particularly their sense of outrage. For many of the day's religious followers the manner in which humans treated other humans was an unabashed moral concern and this included not just people who looked like them, but everyone. Speaking about the piety of the Quakers, Dr. Brown says that they:

> ... asserted the love of God for every human being, regardless of color, sex, or station in life.[6]

It wouldn't be a stretch to say that some of this Quaker zeal for greater humanity rubbed off on their "aggressive, interdenominational" evangelist compatriots. Once again Dr. Brown presents it quite nicely:

> Growing out of the Great Awakening, these Protestants, largely in New England, were

inspired less by earlier Calvinistic doom and gloom theology than by concepts of human betterment under God's grace and His gift of free will. Out of this fresh religious doctrine, called Arminianism, grew a movement that included the plea for the freedom of all of God's human creatures, especially the Southern slaves.[7]

While it's not uncommon today to associate strong religious faith and practice with a judgmentally conservative "fire and brimstone" mentality, 200 years ago a Sermon-on-the-Mount brand of religious morality was equally noticeable and prevalent. The abolitionist movement is both result and proof of this truth. As mentioned in Chapter II, the closest example in recent times would be the black (Southern) churches that gave birth to the civil rights movement of the 1950–1960s. The fact that prominent historians see this nineteenth-century religious awakening as being responsible for fueling later reforming "crusades such as temperance, pacifism, and women's rights" speaks to the abolitionist's depth of commitment as well as sincerity.[8] Unlike the American Revolution, which was driven in large part by self-interested shopkeepers concerned about taxes and mercantile practices, abolitionism was driven by grassroots people (many of them shopkeepers) genuinely concerned about the welfare of other human beings.

That's why the most distinguishing feature of American abolitionism was its willingness to show outrage, condemn injustice, and call for—in the strongest of terms—a righting of wrongs. This fresh and combative spirit can be seen right from the time that the movement first began its ascendancy. We can easily observe this by looking at some its most prominent nineteenth-century leaders.

There is no one better to start with than John Rankin. His antislavery activity began in the second decade of that century and thus paralleled the movement's rise. Rankin delivered his first antislavery sermon soon after his graduation from divinity school in 1814. A short time later he became one of the first "conductors" on the Underground Railroad, a clandestine operation that helped enslaved persons escape bondage. His antislavery writings inspired a future generation of abolitionist leaders and many of them openly credited him with their involvement in the movement. In fact, *Uncle Tom's Cabin* author Harriet Beecher Stowe even attributed the responsibility for ending slavery to Rankin (and his sons).[9] As previously alluded to, the editor of the historic abolitionist newsletter *The Liberator*, William Lloyd Garrison, acknowledged that he was his "anti-slavery disciple.[10]

Rankin's famous work *Letters on American Slavery* was first published in 1823. It would have successive editions with updated material. Now look at the intensity of his writings, taken from the 5th edition of his book:

Hence many poor slaves are *stript naked*, stretched and tied across barrels, or large logs, and *tortured* with the keenest lashes during hours and even whole days, until their flesh is mangled to the very bones. Others are stript and hung up by their arms, their feet are tied together, and a heavy piece of timber is put between their legs in order to stretch their bodies [like the medieval rack], and so prepare them for the torturing lash—and in this situation they are often whipt until their bodies are *covered with blood and mangled flesh*, and in order to add the greatest keenness to their sufferings, their wounds are *washed with liquid salt!* And some of the miserable creatures are permitted to hang in that position *until they actually expire* ... [my italics].[11]

It's quite obvious why even slaveholders like Jefferson and Madison, who symbolized earlier more genteel antislavery sentiments, would likely be offended by such in your face language. Rankin's prose generates vivid imagery to expose all the gruesome evils of what he is opposing. He has no hesitancy in appealing to human passions. In fact, Rankin's rhetoric shows that right from the early days of the nineteenth century abolitionist movement the evils of slavery were not glossed over by any highbrow politeness or philosophical language. In speaking about slaveholders, Rankin doesn't equivocate in outing the force that is driving them to commit such atrocity:

72

... what can break loose the ice-bound heart of the man who urged by the impetuous torrent of *avaricious* feeling to bind with the chains of mancipation a number of his fellow creatures, and cause them, hungry and naked, to toil throughout life in heaping up treasure to satisfy his covetous inordinate and rapidly increasing extortionate *thirst for gain* ... [my italics].[12]

There is no attempt to be gentlemanly about the culprit. It is clearly avariciousness and thirst for gain that is the motive behind the slaveholders' desire to preserve the institution. If you remember that about half of the delegates attending the Constitutional Convention of 1787 were slaveholders, you have to be amazed by how quickly in the nation's history sentiments against this group materialized. What was beginning to take hold was the idea that the slaveholders were not just wrong in their opinions but flawed in their moral values.

Rankin not only had the courage to call it like it was; he even did it before the last of the slaveholding Founding Fathers had passed from the scene. And he did it by appealing to people's sense of empathic concern and outrage against the injustices that powerless others were unfairly subjected to. Deep-seated human emotions were activated to communicate a message with a moral. Injustice perpetrated against other human beings is in itself wrong as is what it derives from, greed and selfishness. And what force does Rankin think will drive things in an exactly opposite direction and thereby rectify these wrongs?

> To this nothing can induce him while the covetous *love of gain* is the predominating principle, and such, doubtless, will be the case while slavery exists in the world; for the very moment the *principle of justice gains the ascendancy over that of avarice, must slavery cease to exist* [my italics].[13]

Only the ascendancy of the principle of justice over avarice will make the world right. It's not that classical concepts of liberty are being rejected, but it's now clearly being stated that a concept of justice is equally important. In a following sentence he contrasts what he sees to be two dialectically opposed states of mind and action. From the same letter:

> Avarice tends to enslave, but justice requires emancipation.[14]

You could easily reverse this without changing its meaning. Slavery promotes avarice (i.e., greed) and emancipation (i.e., freedom) requires justice. When speaking of justice he isn't talking about complicated intellectualizations, but about simple fairness and a moral obligation to treat "the other" as you would wish to be treated yourself. What's important is that we see the beginnings of what would become a loud and clear call for a more just American society.

Following Rankin's lead a new generation of abolitionists would escalate the focus on the injustices that enslaved persons were subjected to. Invoking empathic concern in their audiences would be the abolitionist's modus operandi. The more powerful emotion they triggered the stronger was the common people's revulsion against the inhumanity that the abolitionists were exposing. This in turn would serve to validate the importance of including human empathy in the political dialogue.

One of the best known of this new generation of abolitionists was Frederick Douglass. His efforts supply us with a good example of this approach. But first, a few words need to be said about him. Unlike Rankin, Douglass was born enslaved. In fact, he spent his first seventeen years of life in this dreadful institution. After escaping slavery in 1835 he found his way to the abolitionist movement. In the years that followed he would become one of its most esteemed spokesmen. In contrast to most of the other prominent leaders, Douglass was self-educated. Yet he was every bit as poignant a writer and speaker as any of them. His lifetime works fill many volumes.

Douglass first burst on to the national scene in 1845 with the publication of what was then his life story, the *Narrative of the life of Frederick Douglass, an American*

Slave, Written by Himself. In the *Narrative* we once again see an appeal to one's sense of moral outrage over unspeakable injustice. And of course coming from someone who experienced this himself it was all the more effective.

A review written by Lynn Pioneer of Douglass's book appeared in the antislavery newsletter *The Liberator* on May 30, 1845. Pioneer speaks to the horror he experienced as well as the elegance of his writing:

> The picture it presents of *slavery is too horrible to look upon*, and yet it is but a faint picture of what to millions is a vivid life. It is evidently drawn with a nice eye, and the coloring is chaste and subdued, rather than extravagant or overwrought … *Its eloquence is the eloquence of truth*, and so is as simple and touching as the impulses of childhood [my italics].[15]

By the time of Douglass's *Narrative* the abolitionist movement was into its third decade as a discernible force in American politics. And it was unapologetically upholding its tradition of interjecting vital moral and humanistic concerns into the political discussion. This story of slavery in an enslaved person's own words was fully in the spirit of this abolitionist tradition and would have a powerful impact on people. The following excerpt from the *Narrative* is an example of what Pioneer is talking about:

Before he commenced *whipping* Aunt Hester, he took her into the kitchen, and stripped her from neck to waist, leaving her *neck, shoulders, and back, entirely naked* ... He made her get upon the stool, and *tied her hands* to the hook ... Her arms were stretched up at their full length, so that she stood upon the ends of her toes. He then said to her, "Now, you d—d b—h, I'll learn you how to disobey my orders!" ... *he commenced to lay on the heavy cowskin, and soon the warm, red blood (amid heart-rending shrieks from her, and horrid oaths from him) came dripping to the floor. I was so terrified and horror-stricken* ... [my italics].[16]

Yet it wasn't only acts of direct physical cruelty and arbitrary violence that Douglass highlighted, but also material deprivation and horrid living conditions. This too was in keeping with central tenants of abolitionism. Their outrage over injustice included, in addition to civil violations, social wrongs as well (more to come on this). Genuine human concern is not bounded by artificial distinctions. Once again, from the *Narrative*:

> *There were no beds given the slaves, unless one coarse blanket be considered such, and none but the men and women had these....* This, however, is not considered a very great privation.... Their yearly clothing consisted of two coarse linen shirts, one pair of linen trousers, like the shirts, one jacket, one pair of trousers for winter, made

of coarse negro cloth, one pair of stockings, and one pair of shoes.... When these failed them, they went naked until the next allowance-day. Children from seven to ten years old, of both sexes, *almost naked, might be seen at all seasons of the year* [my italics].[17]

On September 11, 1846, in Sheffield, England, one year after publication of his autobiography, Douglass opened his speech with the following words:

> I am here to-night to let you know the *wrongs*, the *miseries*, and the stripes of three millions of human beings for whom the Saviour died and though time would fail me to give all the details of the *horrid system* by which they are held, *I yet hope to place before you sufficient acts to enlist your sympathies in their behalf* [my italics].[18]

We see again that Douglass's self- proclaimed intention is to illicit from his audience an empathetic response by presenting them vivid outrages against innocent victims. This method of persuasion was in sharp contrast to the legal and philosophical approach of an earlier era. Passions were now a good thing if they awoke in people their natural tendency towards fairness and assisting others. In this regard Douglass was a master at the art of awaking people.

Wendell Phillips was a comrade of Douglass's and another master of this art. He ranks right next to him as one of the greatest abolitionist leaders. Phillips' dissimilarity to Douglass underlined the broad base of the movement. Unlike Douglass, he was born into a family with high social standing. And also unlike him he was educated at the best schools of the day. Phillips was a Harvard graduate. Yet it's the similarities of these two men that embodied the abolitionist character. Like Douglass, Phillips was a prolific activist, writer, and lecturer who dedicated the better part of his life to fighting against the injustice of slavery as well as all varieties of racial and sexual discrimination. And also like him, he was considered one of the most effective orators of his age. Speaking before a gathering of the Massachusetts antislavery society on January 27, 1858, Phillips introduced the following resolution:

> Resolved, That the object of this society is now, as it has always been, to convince our countrymen, *by arguments addressed to their hearts and consciences*, that slave-holding is a *heinous crime*, and that the duty, safety, and interest of all concerned demand its immediate abolition, without expatriation [my italics].[19]

Arguments that are addressed to the "hearts and consciences" of people are what one would employ against a moral outrage. "Heinous crime" would be the legitimate underpinning of such an outrage. That's why there isn't anything mentioned about a compensated emancipation. One doesn't compensate people for immoral and criminal acts. This type of morality can't be separated from politics. Long gone are the days when liberal-thinking gentlemen sat around the table and discussed a rational ending of slavery where slaveholders are duly compensated, tranquility is maintained, and no feathers are ruffled.

We know that this was what some of the slaveholding Founding Fathers had naively envisioned. And of course "immediate abolition, without expatriation" was never envisioned. In respect to the issue of slavery the nation was moving beyond the world of these founders. Speaking at the same gathering, Phillips presents us with a good example of this when he outlines the charges that are levied against abolitionists:

> *The charges to which I refer are these: that, in dealing with slaveholders and their apologists,* we indulge in fierce denunciations, ... if we would have submitted to argue this question with a manly patience; but, instead of this, we have *outraged* the feelings of the community by *attacks,* unjust and unnecessarily severe, ... but hurried on in childish, reckless, blind, and *hot-headed zeal,—bigots* in the *narrowness* of our views, and *fanatics* in our blind fury ... [my italics].[20]

It's clear from Phillips well delivered words that the abolitionists are accused of appealing to raw emotions rather than carefully grafted intellect. They also are accused of childishly demanding their way without compromise. For the people living during that time period these were the most frequent complaints that they heard leveled against abolitionists. For better or worse most onlookers believed that these "hell-raisers" were being driven by their passions. Phillips then proceeds to answer those who see this as a problem.

> If a man ... speaks *for the down-trodden and oppressed*, he must be content to put a curb upon the tongue of holiest passion, and speak only as harshly as is compatible with the amelioration of the evil he proposes to redress.... But distant Europe honors William Lloyd Garrison because it credits him with seeking for the slave simply redress. We say, therefore, that "uncompromising" policy is not to be measured by absolute justice, but by practical amelioration of the slave's condition. *Amelioration as fast as you can get it,—absolute justice as soon as you can reach it* [my italics].[21]

Phillips doesn't retreat from the abolitionist's strongly held axiom: that given the scope of the wrongs that need to be redressed their outrage is fully justifiable. In seeking to ultimately redress all the wrongs perpetrated against the enslaved population, abolitionists recognize the necessity of tying this goal to whatever (moral) actions are necessary to move the arrow in that direction. There is absolutely no concept of planned gradualism or purposely taking it slowly. The well-being of the larger society is totally intertwined with the elimination of slavery. Therefore the faster it proceeds and the greater the extent the better for everyone.

Yet the abolitionist cause is not unbounded. In striving for "redress" over revenge it's fully committed to pursuing the moral high ground. For most situations this meant a commitment to nonviolence. A similar path would be taken by the twentieth-century civil rights movement. Like their future offspring the overwhelming majority of abolitionists refused to sanction violent acts. John Brown's raid at Harper's Ferry was almost universally condemned by prominent leaders of the movement.

Interestingly, one of the few well-known abolitionists who supported Brown's actions was Lysander Spooner (more about him in Chapter VI). Spooner would eventually become a Confederate sympathizer and is today an icon in some right-wing circles. Yet history joins most of the other abolitionists together with Martin Luther King Jr., for all of them understood the crucial connection between one's means and one's ends.

In Phillips' reply to the naysayers he speaks of the aforementioned newsletter founder, William Lloyd

Garrison. He says that he is honored in "distant Europe." What Phillips does is tacitly acknowledge that Garrison is understood to be the de facto leader of the movement. In fact it's fair to say that if people of the period heard the word abolition the first name that would most likely come to their minds would be Garrison's, and the second would be his famous newsletter *The Liberator*.

Between the founding of *The Liberator* in 1831 and the constitutional abolition of slavery in 1865, Garrison and his abolitionist publication occupied the most forefront position in the struggle against this dreaded institution. When you talk about abolitionist outrage and appeal to justice, no clearer examples can be found than in his speeches and writings. Garrison's original declaration in *The Liberator* was as follows:

> I am aware that many object to the severity of my language; but is there not cause for severity? I will be as harsh as truth, and as uncompromising as justice. I am in earnest,—I will not equivocate,—I will not excuse,—I will not retreat a single inch,—*and I will be heard* [my italics].[22]

And indeed, for the next thirty-four years Mr. Garrison was heard loud and clear. His outrage over injustice even spanned national boundaries. In 1867, during a testimonial dinner held on his behalf in London, he was hailed as the "preeminent agitator of the century" by both John Stuart Mill and John Bright. In his definitive biography of Garrison, Henry Mayer reports that at this dinner Garrison was credited with raising the consciousness of his countrymen. It was said that "he emancipated not only slaves, but the American mind."[23]

An agitator for justice is a good description of what Garrison saw as *The Liberator*'s mission, and this was reflected in its articles. Look at these examples:

The Liberator, January 4, 1834:

> It is not three years since I lifted up the banner of emancipation in this city, for the rescue of perishing millions, whose hire is kept back by fraud, *whose servitude is that of brutes*, whose wrongs disquiet the earth, and are as the sands upon the seashore innumerable, and whose cries have entered into the ears of the Lord Sabaoth.... What is able to overthrow the present system of slavery? An enlightened, consolidated, and wisely directed PUBLIC OPINION. How shall this be secured? By disseminating light, by preaching the truth. For this purpose we established The Liberator [my italics].[24]

Again, *The Liberator*, January 7, 1832:

> When we hear of the cruel conduct of the slaveholders, we often kindle into a flame, and

our judgments tell us that they are without excuse. We can hardly believe that such beings exist in our land. *This is a righteous indignation*; these feelings of abhorrence are creditable to our humanity. But what if it should appear, on a candid examination, that we are as guilty as the slave owners? that *we uphold a system which is full of cruelty and blood*? that the chains which bind the limbs of the slaves have been riveted by us? [my italics].[25]

And again, *The Liberator*, July 28, 1832:

The whole system of slavery is essentially and radically bad—*injustice and oppression are its fundamental principles*; whatever lenity may be requisite in speaking of the agent, none should be shewn, none should be expressed for the act. *Of his actions we should speak in the language of reprobation, disgust, and abhorrence* [my italics].[26]

These three passages are demonstrative of the phraseology and type of appeal that characterized Garrison's newsletter. The reaction of more conservative people to *The Liberator* was one of shock and disgust. And Garrison prided himself on this very fact. Notices like the following were published in his paper:

The Liberator, March 12, 1836:

From the Milledgeville, GA *Federal Union*

$10,000 REWARD
For A. A. Phelps
A Noted Abolitionist
February 1, 1836[27]

Or how about this one, from *The Liberator* of August 3, 1833:

A Bid for a Freeman of Massachusetts

Copy of a resolution in Georgia, adopted by its House & Senate, Nov 30, 1831

"Resolved that the sum of five thousand dollars is hereby appropriated, to be paid to any person or persons who shall arrest bring to trial and prosecute to conviction under the laws of this state; the editor or publisher of a certain paper called the Liberator, published in the town of Boston of the state of Massachusetts ... (or any persons who shall circulate said paper within the limits of this state)."[28]

In addition to publishing *The Liberator* Garrison made frequent speaking engagements to get the abolitionist message out. The injustice of the institution of slavery was his most common theme. To make his case he often focused the listener's attention on the hardships of slavery's victims. This can be seen in a speech he delivered in Boston on July 4, 1838:

> Tell him who wears *an iron collar upon his neck*, and a chain upon his heels, that his limbs are fettered, as if he knew it not! … In spite of all their *whippings, and deprivations, and forcible separations,* — it seems that the slaves must have realized a heaven of blissful ignorance, until their halcyon dreams were disturbed by the pictorial representations and exciting descriptions of the abolitionists! What! *Have not the slaves eyes? have they not hands, organs, dimensions, senses, affections, passions? Are they not fed with the same food, hurt with the same weapons, subject to the same diseases* … [my italics].[29]

In the same address he tells his audience that he makes no apology for his rhetoric or the strong emotions he conjurers up:

> I use strong language, and will make *no apology* for it, on this occasion. In contemplating this subject, *no man, who is true to his nature, can speak but in the language of hot displeasure*, and

caustic irony, and righteous denunciation. *Every word will burn like molten lead, and every sentence glow like flaming fire* ... [my italics].[30]

Remember, as of this July 4, two of the most prominent slaveholding Founding Fathers, Jefferson and Madison, had only recently passed from the scene. In fact, for Madison it had been just two years. Yet for Garrison, since right was right and truth was truth, we mortals had an obligation to respect both of these values no matter whose sacred toes were stepped on, or how much hostility it engendered. That's why it's no surprise that in pulling no punches in his attack on slaveholders he faced frequent charges of sedition. Responding to the people levying these charges, he said:

Is this preaching sedition? *Sedition against what?* Not the lives of southern oppressors—for I renew the solemn injunction. 'Shed no blood!'—but against unlawful authority, and barbarous usage, and unrequited toil. If slaveholders are still obstinately bent upon *plundering and starving their long-suffering victims,* why, let them *look well to the consequences* [my italics].[31]

Garrison fully understood that abolishing slavery was going to be quite messy. It couldn't be accomplished without really shaking things up and thereby upsetting lots of people. Without making enemies nothing would ever get done. Yet the discomfort of these people paled in comparison to the terrible injustices that enslaved persons had to endure. And this really mattered for Garrison since he acknowledged no hierarchy in regards to a human being's worth. A greater harm to one trumped a lesser discomfort to another, period—no racial, social, or gender exceptions. For Garrison, the odiousness of slavery overrode all other considerations. Therefore, no matter how esteemed some slaveholders had once been, no excuse was acceptable and no leniency was going to be offered. The escalating bitterness over the issue of slavery—which Jefferson had so feared—was no longer in the distant future but unfolding before people's eyes in the here and now.

Those who would be victimized one hundred years hence by the rantings of Joe McCarthy could have learned a lot from how Garrison answered his accusers on that July 4. He wasn't afraid to unapologetically stand his ground and expose what the naysayers really stood for. The enemies of freedom and justice weren't going to intimidate him into allowing them to frame the issue or set the debate's agenda. Equally important, Garrison never wavered in asserting that justice was the only true remedy to the hideous status quo. He always gave this concept prominent billing. In addressing the American Anti-Slavery Society in 1854, Garrison opened his speech with the following statement:

> To drop what is figurative for the actual. I have
> expressed the belief that, so lost to all self-respect

and all ideas of *justice* have we become by the corrupting presence of Slavery, in no European nation is *personal liberty* held at such discount, as a matter of principle, as in our own [my italics].[32]

The importance of justice is acknowledged in the same sentence as liberty. For Garrison, as with Rankin and most other abolitionists the obtaining of justice was indistinguishable from that of liberty. In fact it's fair to say that there could be no liberty without it. Garrison's language never failed to project an imagery that would clearly demonstrate this fact. In his fiery speeches one could feel the pain of the victims along with the outrage of the speaker. Garrison's words generated a powerful logic all their own.

The existence of the institution of slavery was certainly the most striking injustice in Garrison's time. Therefore it's no wonder that he was so focused on its abolition. Yet Garrison was sensitive to all transgressions against human dignity. And during his life he was a fighter for all the victims of unfair treatment. In 1840 Garrison attended an international convention in London sponsored by the British and Foreign Anti-Slavery Society. When women were excluded from the proceedings he refused to participate. This caused quite a stir at the time and publically raised the issue of sexism eight years prior to the first Women's Rights Convention in Seneca Falls and 125 years before the start of the modern women's liberation movement. The significance of this moment in history cannot be overstated. Henry Mayer notes that:

> The seed planted during Garrison's London protest at the world's convention in 1840 had germinated slowly as women took on influential roles in abolition.... When Lucretia Mott and Elizabeth Cady Stanton reencountered each other [after meeting at the convention] ... their passionate and searching conversations led to an impromptu women's rights convention in Seneca Falls ... that laid the foundation for the modern feminist movement.[33]

Years later Garrison responded to the ongoing furor over his action, by saying:

> I have been derisively called a *"Woman's Rights Man."* I know no such distinction. I claim to be a HUMAN RIGHTS MAN; and wherever there is a human being, I see God-given rights inherent in that being, whatever may be the sex or complexion.[34]

Fighting against injustices foisted upon African Americans and women were but two (although quite important) causes out of a slew of others that Garrison was concerned about. During the thirty-four years of *The Liberator*'s existence articles addressing all kinds of ill treatment would appear in it. Many would be in the form of letters that readers sent in to the paper. Here is one that speaks to the "slavery of wages":

The Liberator, March 26, 1847:

> From Thomas Ingersoll, Westfield, Chaut. Co. N .Y.: "I have seen the slavery of the South, and the *slavery of the North*; and, sir, I find little to choose between the *slavery of wages* and that of no wages; though the *slavery of wages* supposes, and indeed is proof, of the mental advance of this order of slaves, over him who is yet but a chattel. Yet, sir, the *system of wages*, as now established, is a biting, galling *enslavement* ... The laborer does not any where *enjoy the full fruits of his labor*. He is under the necessity of sharing with another, who does not labor. *By what order of morals is the product of labor thus divided*? Must it be said, that capital must draw its share? *But why shall capital draw the lion's share?"* [my italics].[35]

Here is a summary of another article (extracted by historical researcher Horace Seldon) that tells us of an event that is described as a "working men's revolution meeting":

The Liberator, May 26, 1848:

An article telling of a meeting at Faneuil Hall, largely attended, "to sympathize with the European Revolution and express the sentiments of the laboring class in regard to its application in this country." Resolutions are passed praising what has been done in France, and to "call upon the Working Men of New England to oppose a manly resistance to the insulting pretensions of a 'shabby genteel' aristocracy, who already assume to control the elections and direct the legislation of the State," and calls for measures to improve the status of the Working Men.[36]

Look at this excerpt from an October 26, 1849, *Liberator* article (originally from the New York correspondent of the *Washington Union*):

Capital and Labor

The article, with the above title, is from "The New York correspondent of the *Washington Union*." Without including the statistics used to advance the author's argument, here is the gist of what the article says: "The attention of the thinking men of the age has been attracted to the fact that the constant tendency of capital is to accumulate in magnitude at the expense of labor. Its efforts to enhance the rent which it annually exacts from industry are constantly strengthened by its success, and on every hand manifold evidences manifest themselves that poverty is increasing with fearful rapidity among the masses of the people, while individual fortunes are constantly swelling in magnitude … "[37]

In the 1840s *The Liberator* was actually publishing letters and articles questioning the profits of capitalists, using terms like "slavery of wages," reporting on international workers' struggles, and addressing issues of poverty while noting that "individual fortunes are constantly swelling in magnitude." Some of it was even before the publication of the Communist Manifesto and prior to the popularization of the term "wage slavery."

Let's turn to Horace Seldon's great website The Liberator Files, which much of this material has been taken from. Examining the headings of *The Liberator*'s articles, Seldon lists the wide range of human concerns that appeared in the newsletter. He notes that his list "is only a bare beginning list." He also notes that there is one nonhuman concern that is included—the humane treatment of animals. Looking at Seldon's list of concerns we see the true Garrison:

- Abolish capital punishment
- Support an Employment Office
- Capitalism profits/labor suffers
- Colored Support of Orphanage
- Equal School Rights for Colored Children
- Support woman suffrage

- Vassar Female College incorporation
- Article About Cooperative Living
- Interracial Marriage supported
- Interracial military supported
- Training for midwifery
- Lawrence tragedy kills 700 workers
- Racist Treatment of Indians
- Public Safety and Police
- Poor treatment of domestic servants
- Poor Conditions for Animals
- Warns of prejudice toward Irish
- Assistance for "street girls"
- Lectures by Mechanics
- Alcoholism/Smoking both to be avoided[38]

"Official" textbook history has done to Garrison what it's now attempting to do to Martin Luther King Jr. As with King, who is being relegated to just a fighter against racial discrimination, Garrison has been relegated to just a fighter against slavery. Yet in both cases the real truth is being distorted by a purposefully intended tunnel vision. King was a liberal in a broader sense, i.e., he opposed war and economic inequality while supporting unions and social programs. Likewise, Garrison was the premier liberal of his day, exposing among other injustices those based on race, ethnicity, gender and, yes, class.

One only has to look at Seldon's incomplete list for proof. Just a few of the classic progressive concerns that make the list are:

- Support for "equal school rights for colored children" as well as opposition to the "racist treatment of Indians" *[racial justice]*
- "Support [for] women's suffrage" as well as "Vassar Female College incorporation" i.e.: women's participation and access to higher education *[gender justice]*
- An active awareness that "capitalism profits" while "labor suffers" and "support [for] an employment office," i.e., opposition to the exploitation of labor and concern for the well-being of the lowest social strata *[social and economic justice]*[39]
- Assistance for "street girls" and "Lawrence tragedy kills 700 workers," i.e., active concern for those most "demonized" or subject to be taken advantage of *[gender, social, economic and industrial justice]*
- "Article About Cooperative Living" and "Poor Conditions for Animals," i.e., mutual respect, sharing, humane treatment, and aversion to cruelty *[a just society in the broadest sense]*

A word needs to be said about the last one. Henry Mayer tells us that Garrison's brother George, along with some friends, acquired assets in a silk manufacturing enterprise in Northampton Mass., where in 1842 they established a cooperative society "as an alternative to the harsh inequalities of modern life." As a consequence Garrison decided to give up his Cambridgeport home and live in Northampton for the summer. The lodgings there were so small that his three older boys had to sleep crossways in one bed. They took their meals in the community's "hospitable dining hall." Residents included fugitive slaves, one of whom was Sojourner Truth. During a lecture tour Frederick Douglass would visit the community and report that "The place and people struck me as the most democratic I had ever met."[40] The bottom line here is that as with King (more about King in Chapter VIII) the good that Garrison fought for was part and parcel of a larger theme—namely, justice in all its incarnations.

In the face of vile right-wing opposition, Garrison along with America's other great "justice fighters" were prime catalysts in changing our world for the better. And due to their efforts the face of America was forever altered. One cannot find any better example than the abolitionists to support my claim that our nation's grassroots activists are as responsible for today's America as are the Founding Fathers. The changes they helped to bring about were so enormous that even conservatives are forced to acknowledge them, albeit using tunnel vision to thin out their full identity.

After Civil War issues receded, attention would be turned elsewhere. For America's "justice seekers" women's suffrage, exploitation of industrial workers, and big business's abuse of farmers became the next most important struggles. For Garrison, the world's leading abolitionist and the nation's foremost liberal, this would have been a natural progression.

The principle of justice that the abolitionists would pass on to future generations didn't emanate from any long intellectual discourse but instead from a strong identification with the plight of others. Abolitionists purposely focused on the ordinary person's "instinctive" sense of fairness. In doing so, they spoke to the plebeian essence of the movement. Their arguments weren't normally thought of as academic treatises. Of course it's not that they couldn't have made a step by step logically reasoned case against the institution of slavery. In fact, all of these men did exactly that in other writings.

Abolitionists didn't reject reasoned argument, but at the same time they refused to put aside their righteous indignation over the terrible unfairness of slavery. And when they discovered that many others could identify with their outrage, they didn't hesitate to double down on it. They offered no apologies for their strong affinity for treating others as one would wish to be treated themselves. As such they made a statement to the larger society (as well to posterity) that when one embraces the "better angels of our nature" no apology is required.

It's clear from abolitionist speeches and writings that they struggled feverishly to move the concept of justice to a higher ground within the popular mind. They couldn't envision liberty without it, since they saw the two concepts as irrevocably joined together. By the end of the formal abolitionist period this vision was firmly implanted in the nation's psyche. It is no accident that that the last five words of the Pledge of Allegiance give "liberty" and "justice" equal standing (something they were not originally afforded). But most important, it's also no accident that the reform movements that followed would also be centered on the cause of justice.

While the Founding Fathers feared the potential destructiveness of human passion, the abolitionists saw within its bosom a common affinity for fairness. Their steadfast commitment, incredible linguistic imagery, and lofty purpose displayed the majesty of a newly emerging democratic society—one that's core value rested on trust in the common people. They would pass on to posterity a much enriched concept of freedom.

Before this chapter comes to an end I feel compelled to add some of my other deeply held feelings about the abolitionists. I see them as America's real heroes. They shaped our country more than any other group of people, our Founders notwithstanding. They never lost site of the bigger picture and the validity of the simple truth expressed so elegantly by the golden rule. They thought that all human beings should count equally and that morality is how we treat one another. And most important, they held that a just and moral person has an obligation to be proactive against the injustices that he or she observes.

Yet embracing these ideals was no easy matter. It required that they see through the accepted philosophy of many of their day's most esteemed and respected thinkers, some of whom were giants like the Founding Fathers who were still alive at the time. But even then, they still had to face some of the worst abuse and social ostracizing that any free American has ever had to confront. At times and in some places their lives were in grave danger. The vitriol against them was so intense that for one hundred years following their dissolution most "official" history books even in the North portrayed them in a bad light. They single-handedly took on the worst injustice in our history, and despite their success, the "establishment" chose to denigrate rather than honor them—while of course shamelessly claiming credit for their accomplishments.

Even today there are libertarian conservatives who deny that the unrest that abolitionists stirred up was necessary for the abolition of slavery. This ignorant perspective is akin to Holocaust denial. Yet in a strange way it's a quite fitting comparison, since the abolitionists are the closet people America has ever had to the "righteous gentiles," a group that risked everything during the Nazi era to save other people. Our nation will forever be indebted to them because despite overwhelming odds and incredible hostility they not only succeeded in redressing America's greatest wrong but, in the process, created the blueprint for all future grassroots "justice movements." From on high, the Founding Fathers gave us the institutional design; from America's grass roots, the people gave us justice.

Chapter V

Justice's Enemies

Since slavery's supporters set the standard for deception, we can better understand justice's enemies by first looking at the most common responses to the abolitionist scare. What we observe is a multitude of propositions that were exceedingly effective in convincing people that the obvious wasn't true. The logical structures that underlined them are not necessarily specific to any particular time period. It doesn't really matter if the injustice is slavery or something else; if you wish to oppose fundamental fairness, these are the most persuasive arguments to use. In fact many of them are still relied on today to defend contemporary injustices.

So let's begin with how the proslavers tried to counter abolitionist appeals to one's basic humanity. To defend their position they would frequently fall back on all kinds of highly intellectualized rationalizations. The fact that slavery had historically been the norm in America as well as the classical world—with many esteemed individuals owning slaves—made it easier for them to win people to their cause than one would think. In fact, I was surprised by the level of discourse on the part of some of the proslavery intelligentsia. Reading what both sides had to say—without any knowledge of what would transpire and absent any present-day perspective—one could easily think that the leading proslavery supporters were more deeply rooted in culture and history than their antislavery counter parts.

Many of the day's leading Southern writers expressed the South's contemporary thinking in the popular monthly publication *DeBow's Review*. In the *Review*'s July 1, 1857 edition, one of these writers, George Fitzhugh, contributed an article entitled "Black Republicanism in Athens," in which he defends slavery and attacks its opponents in exactly the highbrow manner that I refer to. Fitzhugh demonstrates knowledge of many past civilizations, including ancient Athens, Judea, Phoenicia, and Carthage. In explaining his position he refers to such works as Plato's *Republic*, Aristotle's *Politics*, Sir Thomas Moore's *Utopia*, and even Aristophanes' classical Greek play *Ecclesiazusae*. In discussing *Ecclesiazusae* he presents and comments on specific dialogue in the play. More contemporary notables, including Fourier, Blanc, and Hume, are spoken about as well.[1] I was amazed by how much Fitzhugh's highly intellectualized presentation was reminiscent of the Right's leading twentieth-century wit, William F. Buckley, Jr.

In the same vein, look at these excerpts from the work of another one of the South's distinguished writers, then former Chancellor of the University of South Carolina William Harper, published in 1852:

> The institution of domestic slavery exists over far the greater portion of the inhabited earth. Until within a very few centuries, it may be said to have existed over the whole earth —at least in all those

portions of it which had made any advances towards civilization. We might safely conclude then that it is deeply founded in the nature of man and the exigencies of human society.[2]

But this I will say, and not without confidence, that it is in the power of no human intellect to establish the contrary proposition—that it is better it should not exist. This is probably known but to one being, and concealed from human sagacity. There have existed in various ages, and we now see existing in the world, people in every stage of civilization, from the most barbarous to the most refined.[3]

Yet once it was not so, when Italy was possessed by the masters of slaves; when Rome contained her millions, and Italy was a garden; when their iron energies of body corresponded with the energies of mind, which made them conquerors in every climate and on every soil; rolled the tide of conquest, not as in later times, from the south to the north; extended their laws and their civilization, and created them lords of the earth.[4]

We see the chancellor presenting a broad historical perspective, including the history and glory of past slave civilizations, like ancient Rome. The practice of presenting a wealth of classical knowledge and relying on the authority of history's great (secular) thinkers was in sharp contrast to the abolitionists, whose modus operandi was characterized by outrage over injustice and empathic concern for the victims.

It was to be expected that the proslavers would present themselves as objectively dispassionate. If you accept that humans have a natural inclination to be fair and that real justice is elegant, simple, as well as humane, the proslavery side faced a significant problem. Once sprung, they had to push back into the box a formidable genie, namely concern for one's fellow man. Resorting to higher intellect allowed them to bypass emotive considerations thereby making empathy appear out of place. However, this elitist response was not without limitations. Since there was a need for a broader appeal, proslavery advocates were forced to devise a multitude of more commonplace arguments that, when stripped of the veneer of scholarship, exposed an ugly underbelly. Amazingly they were still able to camouflage enough of this unsightliness to continue defending the indefensible while simultaneously convincing large numbers of people that they were just being objective observers. What would emerge from all the schematics was a concept of freedom so devoid of justice that it would have shocked even the slaveholding Founding Fathers.

It is important that we examine the essential components of their convoluted reasoning. Since most defenders of the status quo knew that it would be disadvantageous to their position if the battlefield was the higher moral plane, they had to prevent the discussion from being taken there. This required placing the debate in a more favorable context, one that would be more aligned with their chosen destination. Of course the debate had to be altered without appearing to be avoiding the subject. What I call "confusing the issue" would turn out to be the best approach to accomplishing this feat. The most effective way of creating such confusion was to make things either as logically irrelevant or intricately complicated as possible. From a practical standpoint a myriad of techniques were employed. They included narrowing the focus, subtly changing definitions, adding erroneous qualifiers, and dissecting arguments so they could be either selectively analyzed or cleverly reconfigured. These techniques were not mutually exclusive; they frequently were combined and overlapped.

Let's take a closer look at how the proslavery side tried to avoid the higher moral plane. In his book *When Slavery Was called Freedom: Evangelicalism, Proslavery, and the Causes of the Civil War*, John Patrick Daly investigates the philosophical underpinnings of slavery's defenders. Daly sets the stage by writing:

> History textbooks often repeat the facile and inaccurate argument that the South defended slavery as a "necessary evil" before 1831 [the beginning of Garrison's famous abolitionist newsletter, *The Liberator*] and then became defensive, after abolitionist assaults, and argued after 1831 that slavery was a "positive good."[5]

Daly goes on to report that his research "found little support for the above argument."[6] He points out that Southerners "rarely argued that slavery would last forever or that it was a feature of an ideal society."[7] Then how did Daly portray the proslaver's point of view? He found that they frequently engaged in practical and technically oriented discussions. Daly implies that this served to obfuscate the larger issue. Therefore what one would normally think of as contradictory wasn't seen that way by proslavery advocates. He uses the word evangelical "to denote a sweeping cultural movement that celebrated individualism and moral self-discipline."[8]

Daly writes:

> Naturally, antebellum southerners applied evangelical moral concepts and *free market economic science* to the *question of slavery* … Southern evangelicals argued that free labor theory did not threaten the South, not because slavery was a superior economic system to a free economy but because the *South had a free economy* and because *slavery constituted* a form of *free labor* [my italics].[9]

Zeroing in on "free market economic science" can narrow the focus and thereby redirect the entire conversation. One is still able to talk about freedom (albeit in a quite limited way). The discussion of a "free economy" avoids the question of a free people. By assuming that your economic system is free it then follows that its constituent parts, like the labor force, must in some way contribute to and benefit from the overall structure. In a similar fashion, focusing on the practical aspects sidesteps any moral concerns. Since morality is not a category of what's being discussed, it's subliminally understood to be irrelevant to the point at hand. This is a quite convoluted way of ignoring the bigger picture while at the same time turning slave labor into some weird variant of free labor. Such logical irrelevance was how the bigger picture was often painted over and the real substance of a concept like freedom was bypassed. Once you get someone to accept a false starting point you can methodically apply standard logic to carry the idea to absurdity.

Such absurdity was carried even further by one of the South's foremost proslavery advocates, Thomas R. Dew. In discussing how slavery and the laws of a free marketplace are in perfect harmony, Dew writes:

> Adam Smith has well observed, that there is a strong propensity in man "to truck, barter and exchange, one thing for another," and both the parties generally intend to derive an advantage from the exchange. This disposition seems to extend to every thing susceptible of being impressed with the character of property or exchangeable value, or from which any great or signal advantage may be derived—it has been made to extend, at times, to life and liberty. Generals, in time of war, have pledged their lives for the performance of their contracts. At the conclusion of peace, semi-barbarous nations have been in the habit of interchanging hostages— generally the sons of princes and noblemen—for the mutual observance of treaties, whose lives were forfeited by a violation of the plighted faith; and in all ages, where the practice has not been interdicted by law, individuals have occasionally sold their own liberty, or that of others dependent

on them.… Throughout the whole ancient world, the sale of one's own liberty, and even that of his children, was common.[10]

The slave market is just another free market that should be left alone. Like the broad category of economic activity that it comprises, it has existed since the dawn of time and is as natural as the light of day. Daly notes that Dew didn't see any contradiction between the use of slave labor and a free economy. He remarks that for Dew:

> Southern *slavery* was *in harmony* with the development of *freedom* and a *freely operating economy* [my italics].[11]

Dew and other Southern spokespersons were geniuses at using the idea of freedom to justify slavery. In this pursuit they frequently relied on what might be called a double narrowing. First, they shrunk the range of the idea so much that economic prosperity along with the total absence of mercantile restraints became its most prominent feature. Therefore an unfettered and thriving slave market not only benefited society but was characteristic of a true land of liberty. Second, they reduced the significance of its labor force to such a degree that the economy's reliance on slavery was at best an afterthought. Bustling commercial activity not only trumped everything else but was also the one reality most synonymous with freedom itself.

Of course it was understood that for many people there would still be a lot of unanswered questions. To avoid having to deal with broader concerns, they appeared to be acting like scientists dissecting the whole and detailing the parts. The premise began with the dissected piece of their choosing, while they ignored the remaining ones. The natural and successful functioning of the economic system was the specimen to be studied, while the well-being of the labor force was the specimen to be conveniently shelved (although Dew and others claimed otherwise). Yet the enslaved population was still a dissected piece that could be observed. How might those defending the institution of slavery explain how enslaved people saw things? A good answer to this question is contained in the 1857 book *The Universal Law of Slavery* written by our "good friend" George Fitzhugh. He writes:

> The negro *slaves of the South* are the happiest, and, in some sense, *the freest people in the world.* The children and the aged and infirm work not at all, and yet have all the comforts and necessaries of life provided for them. *They enjoy liberty,* because they are oppressed neither by care nor labor. The women do little hard work, and are protected from the despotism of their husbands by their masters. The negro men and stout boys work, on the average, in good weather, not more than nine hours a day. The balance of their *time is spent in perfect abandon* [my italics].[12]

Fitzhugh was such a good writer that he could make a free person jealous that he wasn't born a slave; they seemed to have all the fun! The so-called objective observer sees that if one takes a close look at enslaved people while they were relaxing one would discover that

110

at least they appeared to be the most free of anyone. This theme was played nonstop in Southern newspapers and journals during the antebellum period. Here is a common example from the *Staunton Spectator*, January 17, 1860:

> The negroes alluded to, says the [Norfolk] Herald, like millions in the Southern States, are not only plentifully provided for in every way, but they are saving money to use as they may find best in coming years—and withal they seem as happy as lords. They work well and cheerfully in the day, and at night, during the holidays they sing, dance and smoke, eat sweet potatoes, drink hard cider, sit around big kitchen fires, "laugh and grow fat," regardless of all the "tomfoolery" and *nonsense about the "poor oppressed slaves"* [my italics].[13]

A less oppressed people (i.e., enslaved population) one could never see! This was another roundabout way of saying that slavery was freedom. Obviously this didn't speak to the totality of the experience but only covered one dissected segment. Yet that segment was the closet specimen to the enslaved population "being themselves." If you can break up reality into individual frames, the partisan eye saw the one closest to the slave as containing the most joy.

You could also confuse the issue by erroneously employing some type of qualifying language that would subtly change the definition or would once again narrow the focus. For example, you could either literally or metaphorically hyphenate the core concept. My favorite example of this was proslavery advocate Rev. James

Thornwell referring to "regulated freedom" when addressing the situation as he perceived it to be in 1860:

> The parties in this conflict are not merely Abolitionists and slaveholders, they are Atheists, Socialists, Communists, Red Republicans, Jacobins on the one side and the friends of *order and regulated freedom* on the other [my italics].[14]

Order and regulation (i.e., control] are now seen as synonymous with freedom. Therefore the many areas of this concept that cannot be reconciled with these traits (which is most of it) are no longer included in it. What's so interesting about what Thornwell said is that it could have very well been said by many on the Right today, without even the slightest hint that it was first expressed 150 years ago.

Another way to confuse the issue and thereby remove the idea of justice from any understanding of freedom was to disassemble the entire notion and rearrange it in such a fashion that its most fundamental characteristics were virtually nonexistent. This method was particularly effective if one was hard pressed to deny the greater truth—that in the usual sense slaves were not free. Look at this excerpt from the *Staunton Spectator*, December 6, 1859:

> There is a vast deal of foolish talk about the delights of freedom and the hardships of slavery. In one sense *no one, white or black, is free in this world*. The master orders his slave to work in a certain field, when he perhaps would prefer to go

elsewhere—this is slavery. But is the master free to do as he pleases! Not so.—He is driven by as stern a necessity to labor with his hands or confine himself to business, as the slave ever feels. *We are all therefore slaves* [my italics].[15]

Of course if one is to say that no one is free it is just another way of saying everyone is free. No one is free in the sense that we all have some restrictions placed on us, even if it's only the laws of physics and mortality. This has practically nothing to do with the concept of freedom as normally understood. Yet once you are suckered into accepting this false definition, it then follows that when it comes to what's important in life everyone is in the same position and therefore equally nonfree (or of course free).

Additional ways of rearranging the conceptual structure were also employed. For example the reconfigurations often retained classical liberal rhetoric while simultaneously being devoid of any substance. This gimmick was frequently used by those who dared to argue that the institution was an innate and positive good. Yet one's willingness to openly embrace the ceaseless wonders of slavery didn't dampen the desire to be seen as supporting (some vague notation of) freedom. One of these individuals was the South's preeminent pre-Civil War political leader, John C. Calhoun. His rhetoric never failed to refer to derivatives of the ideal. In a famous proslavery speech delivered before the U.S. Senate on February 6, 1837, Calhoun didn't neglect to allude to an abstract version of it:

... here I fearlessly assert that the existing relation between the two races in the South, against which these blind fanatics [abolitionists] are waging war, forms the most solid and durable foundation on which to rear *free* and stable political *institutions* [my italics].[16]

Note that Calhoun cleverly refers to free (and stable) institutions instead of free people. The concept of freedom is being broken down and reconstructed in all sorts of odd ways. But most essential, it's going from an ideal that implies a universalism to one that implies a parochialism—as in my group's freedom depends on your group's slavery. In the same speech Calhoun just about says as much:

I hold then, that there never has yet existed a wealthy and civilized society in which one part of the community did not, in point of fact, live on the labor of the other.[17]

Another leading Southern political leader who held that slavery was a positive good was Senator James Henry Hammond. In a speech before the U.S. Senate on March 4, 1858, he expressed similar sentiments to Calhoun by putting forth his [in]famous "mudsill theory" of history:

In all social systems there must be a class to do the menial duties, to perform the drudgery of life. That is, a class requiring but a low order of intellect and but little skill. Its requisites are vigor, docility, fidelity. Such a class you must have, or you would not have that other class which leads progress, civilization, and refinement. It constitutes the very mud-sill of society and of political government; and you might as well attempt to build a house in the air, as to build either the one or the other, except on this mud-sill.[18]

How does freedom fit into the "mudsill theory?" In this case, Senator Hammond doesn't mention the word at all. However he substitutes the idea that all social systems (universalism reconfigured) are the same (equality reconfigured). The definition of freedom is being subtly reformulated without even mentioning it. Hammond has more to say on the topic:

The Senator from New York said yesterday that the whole world had abolished slavery. Aye, the name, but not the thing; all the powers of the earth cannot abolish that. God only can do it when he repeals the fiat, "the poor ye always have with you;" for the man who lives by daily labor, and scarcely lives at that, and who has to put out his labor in the market, and take the best he can get for it; in short, your whole hireling class of manual laborers and "operatives," as you call them, are essentially slaves.[19]

Hammond sees no real enslavement existing in the South that isn't in existence everywhere else. Therefore what is called slavery is just the ordinary arrangement of any society. How could Southern social organization impinge on someone's liberty? You might say that there is an implied de facto freedom here—everyone is as free as the real world allows them to be. In the same speech the Senator repeats that the Southern social system is "everywhere," but he isn't done explaining his view of individual limits:

> We found them slaves by the common "consent of mankind," which, according to Cicero, *"lex naturae est."* The highest proof of what is Nature's law. We are old-fashioned at the South yet; slave is a word discarded now by "ears polite;" I will not characterize that class at the North by that term; but you have it; it is there; it is everywhere; it is eternal.[20]

This system of slavery that is everywhere is so because the laws of nature demand it. In fact, it's so much part of the natural world it's eternal. Without even referring to it by name, freedom's possibilities are being shredded and then put back together so elusively that just about any society can claim to be free (and thus there is no real slavery).

However, all these strategies paled in comparison to what would prove to be a method of confusing the issue that was so successful it still remains the most widely used one today. Many of the techniques are combined to achieve the intended goal. One of the most crucial elements involves narrowing the focus in a manner that places the individual at the center of the discussion. Only this time it's not that a select group of individuals, such as enslaved people, are free of life's burdens, but that freedom as a concept pertains solely to individual

116

character and is without external considerations. On this question, Daly has a good deal to say. He tells us:

> Evangelical moralists battled over the practical implications of *individual restraint*, but they agreed that it was the cardinal element of *freedom*. They believed that anyone capable of practicing *moral self-control* had obtained *true freedom* and therefore could enjoy the good life *regardless of material conditions....*William A. Smith, a leading proslavery philosopher, regularly told southerners that "*self-control is the abstract principle of freedom.*" ... Southern Presbyterian James Henley Thornwell said that "*true Freedom*" was "*discipline*" and that as such it was universally available [my italics].[21]

While the abolitionists saw morality in the context of man's treatment of his fellow man, slavery's defenders viewed it as an individual's inner struggle to be free of ungodly desires. The extent that the individual succeeds in this effort corresponds to the extent that he or she is free. We see other good examples of this obsessive focus on the individual from some of the South's leading proslavery advocates in several essays on the subject of slavery published in 1852. One essay in particular from the aforementioned former Chancellor of the University of South Carolina, William Harper, claimed that slavery hadn't been responsible for anyone's misery. His reason was that it's the individual who holds that responsibility. Harper explains:

I say *apparently,* for the greatest source of human misery is not in external circumstances, but in men themselves—in their depraved inclinations, their wayward passions and perverse wills.[22]

Reducing freedom to just personal morality, and personal morality to just puritanical thinking, allowed proslavery moralists to disassemble the whole conceptual structure so that they could rearrange the parts in a manner that suited their predetermined purposes. The final result was completely devoid of either morality or freedom (not to mention justice). After the curtain was lifted, the idea of freedom was transformed into a totally individualistic concept in which the person herself bared all responsibility. This prevented existing injustices from being seen as depriving anyone of his or her liberty.

It's clear that the intellect had purposefully created a wall separating itself from any genuine moral accountability for actions (or inactions) affecting other people. Of all the gimmicks used this had the most severe practical implications. Daly sums it up all too well:

> On the contrary, *people were responsible for bearing their own burdens.* They should not seek after "comfort or to mitigate the inconveniences of life" except when comfort comes from curbing desire, facing responsibilities, and building moral character [my italics].[23]

Likewise, this traditional understanding of freedom gave evangelicals a basis for *tolerating almost any form of labor exploitation without blanching* [my italics].[24]

We see that by applying various techniques to confuse the issue, slavery's supporters were able to accomplish their self-serving ideological mission, the final result being that one required tunnel vision to see what freedom was. There was no room for expansion, only perpetual contraction. The concept of freedom didn't relate at all to one's societal status, or material conditions. It was removed from any real overview, moral or otherwise. It was about management science, technical innovation, a prosperous unfettered marketplace, orderliness, and the dominant class's self-serving gaze. It was about irrevocable natural limits placed on individuals as well as societies. It was about character, self-discipline, hard work, and individuals relying on their own private endeavors. The one thing that it definitely wasn't about was the ideal that they feared the most, the one perched on the higher moral plane—namely justice.

When studying the antebellum era you see that Orwell's concept of doublespeak pre-dates twentieth-century totalitarianism. Portraying something as the opposite of itself—war is peace, scarcity is abundance, and for the liberty-loving antebellum South, slavery is freedom—is probably the best defense against exposing the God-awful horrors that you would foist upon others. What's interesting is that the primary purpose is to protect the aggressor from being saddled with a negative image of himself. Since even perpetrators need to believe that they are the good guys possessing noble intent, using artfully constructed deceptive rationalizations to camouflage the true nature of one's action is as essential to the overall strategy as the transgression itself.

This need to distort one's real intentions didn't end with the success of abolition. It continues to be endemic to right-wing thought. As already alluded to, much of the core reasoning used to defend slavery has lived on to be recycled for contemporary purposes. That's why we should fast-forward to the present and take a look at how modern day reactionaries have incorporated this thinking. However, there is an important distinction that must first be addressed. At times I employ the term "conservative" only because of people's familiarity with the word's current-day usage and not because of its accuracy. What is currently said to be "conservative" couldn't be more opposite, since it doesn't pertain to conserving virtually anything—not civil liberties, not voting rights, not antidiscrimination commitments, not regulatory protections, not unions, not lawfully negotiated labor contracts, not public education, not a billowing middle class, not our social safety net, and not even our earth's environment. No, it's really about undoing more than 150 years of American history (i.e., progress); or, in other words, extreme reaction. So my apologies to any genuine conservatives who are still out there; but remember, it's not liberalism that has deceptively appropriated your good name.

That having been said, let's now take a look at an attempt to confuse the issue by narrowing the focus to a specific group of individuals who "just happen" to reside in a purposefully targeted environment. We saw how the proslavery side used this tactic quite effectively. They reduced the concept of freedom to how free the enslaved appeared to be during their playtime on the plantation. The totality of a person's existence was shrunk to just a few moments. By focusing in on this localized reality, proslavery advocates could filter out the broader questions that were too difficult to answer.

A conservative documentary that is making its way around the Internet employs the same strategy. In this documentary, Steven Crowder's "Detroit in Ruins (Crowder Goes Ghetto),"[25] the focus is narrowed by zeroing in on an "urban plantation." The scenes are almost exclusively from Detroit's African American "ghetto." Early in the video the viewer is shown a wall poster with the picture of a black youth on it. Although it is done very subtly, it's clear that minority neighborhoods are being targeted. Only this time the surroundings are showcased as being exactly the opposite as they were supposed to be in the antebellum South. They are now fraught with shortcomings. It is certainly implied (without actually saying it) that given their circumstances the people living there must be, unlike the faux portrayal of enslaved laborers, burdened and unhappy.

Yet the overall purpose is exactly the same. As with plantation life, the facts that lie outside this selected niche (and don't conform to the intended premise) can be safely disposed of. The camera scans a dilapidated environment. The area appears structurally rundown and economically distressed. The viewer can almost feel what a resident's

121

despair must be like. Of course what one observes would never be seen in places with more enlightened social policies such as Canada or Western Europe. Nevertheless, that doesn't matter. The moderator explains that Detroit has had a long history of excessively liberal-leftist politics (i.e., a politics that considers in addition to business interests human ones)—and look at the disaster that liberalism, as well as unionism, has wrought!

I know many people who have seen this documentary and I can personally attest to its effectiveness. To date it has received over two million hits on YouTube. By narrowing the focus to metropolitan Detroit's inner urban area and dismissing the larger outside world (and how it connects to it), this filmmaker has very cleverly convinced lots of people that social policies cause poverty and dislocation while free markets prevent such occurrences.

Yet if we don't exclude the other industrialized areas of our planet and dare to look at the whole picture, we see that the truth couldn't be more opposite. At first glance we observe that the U.S. is by far the most market-oriented country in the "first world." We have a more friendly business climate, less taxes, and a much smaller social safety net than any other advanced capitalist nation. Despite our adherence to market forces, we perform dismally in regards to health care, education, and other important quality-of-life indicators. As of this date the United States is 130 years behind Germany, 70 years behind Britain, and 50 years behind most other countries in insuring its entire population has access to medical care. It's no accident that we have the highest percent of our people in poverty and we rank first in the industrialized world in inequality of wealth and income. To add insult to injury, while spending less on our people we spend more on the military than almost all the other wealthy nations combined.

You would think that conservatives would have a difficult time explaining why the most market-friendly nation does so poorly in meeting human needs. Of course, as we now know, they don't see this as a problem. The documentary maker is able to get around it by presenting one small snippet of life in a gigantic metropolitan region in the same manner as the slavery-friendly visitor once did after observing the slave quarters on an antebellum plantation. The superficial gaze of the partisan observer becomes the whole story.

In both situations, connections to larger forces are severed. In the case of the plantation, the slave trade (forced relocation) and the overseer (forced labor) are removed from the setting altogether. In the case of the modern day "urban plantation," the power centers that shape the larger financial and economic realities might as well not exist. The evisceration of the local infrastructure—not to mention the environment—and the resulting human cost is the sole fault of the people living there (or those who misled them).

What's subtly implied is insidious. After all, how dare these residents think that they deserve health care or vacations, or their children a decent education. Don't they know that the big corporations hold all the cards? Don't they know that they can take their business to a third-world country where they can employ real "slaves" (in all but name)? Don't they know that this is not only allowed but encouraged to happen by a corrupt legal and political system that is in the pocket of "organized money" (not organized labor)? Don't they know that the nation's political and corporate powers reside outside the ghetto and therefore are not obligated to assume any blame? Don't they know that the winners write history, and that means "slaves" must assume all responsibility for their own "slavery"? Of course the questions are rhetorical, and the obvious answers are not intended for the benefit of the mass of people deemed to be disposable. Narrowing the focus in this manner reinforces a self-serving hidden agenda. It also continues to be an effective propaganda tool.

Yet historically, the most successful method of confusing the issue is to narrow the focus to the individual herself. We saw how the proslavery side attempted to deflect attention away from the institution's injustices by arguing that freedom was a moral battle residing within each person and thereby solely dependent on one's own private actions. No matter how unjust the outer world appeared to be it wasn't ever accountable. Therefore, independent of the source of a bad situation, it's the individual who must assume responsibility for any difficulties that may result from it. They said that slaves needed to understand that their situation was all about them coming to terms with the conditions they confronted.

Modern-day conservatives have a similar obsession with individualism and a steadfast conviction that society is not obligated to insure a fair playing field or redress blatant wrongs. This attitude is observed in their opposition to any societal policies that provide protection against adversity. Laws that help the unfortunate are seen as harmful because they supposedly weaken initiative and discourage people from helping themselves. Yet this line of reasoning also includes programs that productive citizens have paid into, like Social Security and unemployment insurance. Given the obvious contradiction, what's really behind such a viewpoint?

Like their antebellum counterparts, they think that acting to make society a better and more secure place violates the cardinal rule of individual responsibility while simultaneously challenging their deeply ingrained belief that the external world is essentially a "given" immutable to improvement. Therefore, a collective engagement that's purpose is to alleviate injustice and improve conditions is seen as violating a "natural order" of sorts. At the core of such thought rests the conviction that only individuals can possess moral responsibility. This means that they see actions that arise out of a sense of social solidarity as devoid of moral worth. Any arrangements initiated because of empathetic concern and meant to benefit the group as a whole are by definition illegitimate. This includes monetary allocations coming out of a common fund rather than from separate individual accounts, no matter the person's contributions to it. They view what's universally distributed as but another name for a giveaway.

Yet like the pre-Civil War defenders of the indefensible, today's Right faces some difficulties in selling its views. How can one claim that there is no entitlement to benefits if they are tied to people's momentary contributions? The answer of course is to subtly change the definition of entitlement. Where have we seen "subtly changing the definition" used before? Remember, the proslavery apologists succeeded in not only redefining the concept of freedom but making its unabridged version a dirty word. In modern times we have seen this trick all too successfully used to alter the true meaning of entitlement. It no longer refers to something that has been rightfully earned, but rather to just another "handout."

We see this attitude carrying over to just about anything that one can imagine—access to good education, housing, nutrition, and at times even criminal justice, to mention just a few. The recent debate over extending access to health care (including life-saving early detection and preventative treatment) is a prime example. If your health insurance is rescinded after you are diagnosed with a serious and costly illness, the problem is solely yours. The insurance company or the rules of the larger society that enable their practices are without blame. If only you had studied harder and gotten a better job you would have had the money to either pay for the costs of care yourself or have had better insurance coverage. You should feel lucky that you have the freedom to decide whether or not to plan in advance for any unforeseen catastrophe that may befall you. Relying on collective action will only take individual accountability (i.e., punishment) out of the equation—and without it how can there be any morality?

Interestingly, moralists of both eras have cared little about individual responsibility and entitlement when their group is in question. In fact, receiving something of value without having to earn it is raised to the highest of principles when it relates to what's believed to be one's legitimate birthright. For this very reason slavery's defenders sought to sanctify the idea that individuals were entitled to receive (for better or worse) their "rightful inheritance." Modern-day apologists for inequality demonstrate a similar proclivity when they insist that inheritance is such a sacred privilege it's virtually a sin to tax it. They pretend that a dead person is the one being taxed (i.e., "death tax"). Of course in the real world the dead don't pay taxes. Living human beings who receive the benefit of this unearned gift are responsible for the taxes. Nevertheless, unlike with tax-paying Social Security recipients, they believe that the beneficiaries of hand-me-down wealth are entitled to get away scot-free without being required to give anything at all back to society.

Yet this is where we see an area where two centuries of liberalism have definitely taken their toll. The question of how those with little or no nest egg awaiting them fit into the scheme of things inconveniently moves to center stage. Or to put it another way, are children entitled to access to life's basic necessities? Unlike their compatriots of yesteryear, today's moralists are actually expected to come up with a meaningful response. Of course they would prefer you don't ask this question, since like their antecedents they have no good answer. The Right of all eras has seen children as their parents' responsibility, not society's. Even when it's admitted that they are a category of human beings whose worthiness isn't totally dependent on their own actions, it changes little. Children are appendages of their parents, and if their parents aren't worthy enough they are just out of luck. In this regard time hasn't made much of a difference, since today's sermonizers still hold (although they deny it) that the sins as well as the blessings of the parent should carry over to the child.

While modern conservatives may feel uncomfortable being associated with the ideological defenders of slavery, past antebellum moralists would feel very comfortable with the gut inclinations of today's Right. Independent of the specifics, their worldview is exceedingly similar. Each of them loves to pontificate on the subject of individual responsibility while possessing little sensitivity for those who fall between the cracks. Each of them defines freedom as having nothing to do with how just or unjust things are but rather one's willingness and readiness to bear any burden. Each of them sees it appropriate that the rewards or misgivings of the parent be passed on to the child, without any societal intervention to guard against injustice.

This leads us to a related as well as essential corollary: underneath it all, most conservatives think of themselves as being on the favored side of the divide. Reformulating the meaning of freedom so it becomes a parochial rather than universal concept is the common denominator. For the moralists of both periods the primarily focus is one's own kind. That's why for such a mindset freedom's main purpose becomes insuring that your group retains as much autonomy (and advantage) as possible while at the same time having little concern for how it affects others outside your world.

However, we aren't done yet, since we still have to address one last and very noticeable comparison. For both groups of moralists, "freedom" is seen as primarily an unbounded and thriving marketplace. We saw how Thomas R. Dew thought that unrestricted economic activity was so important to the advance of civilization that it even included a sacred right to sell one's self (and of course children) into slavery—the natural result of which was an incredibly stratified society that effectively made inequality liberty's most definitive characteristic. Identifying unrestrained market prosperity, and the outrageously disproportionate distribution of wealth and influence that flows from it, as the essence of our freedoms remains at the core of conservative thinking. Although we no longer possess a sacred right to sell ourselves or others into slavery, an eerily similar underlying theme lives on. An undue amount of weight is placed on the demands of market forces and the aggrandizement of a wealthy elite at the expense of the harm it does to the majority of working people or even the planet as a whole. Once again, commerce either trumps morality or becomes indistinguishable from it. While legal slavery is gone, attempts by the owners of society's major means of production and distribution to use their economic and political influence to reinstate many of the deprivations it inflicted on the less powerful continues. A culture where there is little emphasis on fairness and justice, including the abundant number of disadvantages that are passed on to children, is a lingering remnant of times past that still must be confronted.

If all this isn't enough and you require even more direct proof of the historical link between today's moralists and those of the antebellum period, just take a look at how one of the twentieth century's leading conservative thinkers viewed the philosophical legacy of slavery's most esteemed spokesman, John C. Calhoun. In 1953, *The Conservative Mind* by Russell Kirk was published. During the 1950s and '60s this work became the handbook of the intellectual Right. It still remains a very popular reading. No one can claim that Russell Kirk wasn't one of the most prominent conservative thinkers in the latter half of the last century. When Clyde Wilson published his book *The Essential Calhoun: Selection from Writings, Speeches, and Letters,* he asked none other than Russell Kirk to write the forward for it. In his forward Kirk afforded Calhoun great deference as one of conservatism's greatest thinkers. He wrote:

> Calhoun was the best exponent of the idea of political order that underlies both the written Constitution and the unwritten Constitution of the American Republic.[26]

Kirk shows an incredible awe for slavery's most renowned hero. Of course no twentieth-century conservative is going to defend legal slavery. Nevertheless, this fact means little, since Kirk was well aware that Calhoun and his fellow illiberal thinkers proved to be dead wrong on the central question of their day. History had moved beyond the specific issues of that earlier period and Kirk couldn't have done anything about it. Yet he purposefully ignored the fact that the underlying logic that Calhoun used to justify the institution was classical Calhoun and the very same manner of thought that he so admired. Kirk never asked the $64,000 question: In the case of slavery, why did Calhoun's stellar constitutional reasoning turn out to be so wrong?

Instead he advocated using Calhoun's constitutional perspective to defend other injustices. There was clearly a blind spot for the truth. This becomes even clearer when you compare Kirk's view of Calhoun with the view of the highly respected historian, Richard Hofstadter.

Concerning Calhoun, Hofstadter wrote:

> *Not in the slightest was* [Calhoun] *concerned with minority rights* as they are chiefly of interest to the modern liberal mind—the rights of dissenters to express unorthodox opinions, of the individual conscience against the State, least of all of ethnic minorities. At bottom he was *not interested in any minority* that was *not a propertied minority*. The concurrent majority [concept of limiting the power of the majority in order to enhance the authority of the minority] itself was a device without relevance to the protection of dissent,

designed to protect a vested interest of considerable power ... *it was minority privileges rather than* [minority] *rights that he really proposed to protect* [my italics].[27]

The South's foremost guardian of minority rights saw slavery all around him and thought it was a positive good. At least slaveholders like Jefferson and Madison (intellectually) recognized it as the great evil it was. As we have seen, in his 1837 speech Calhoun openly acknowledged that some group of people—not his of course—must be slaves. This doesn't give one too much confidence in Calhoun's judgment regarding minority rights or, for that matter, freedom.

Kirk admired Calhoun because he was a genius at reasoning away the obvious. This is exactly what Kirk wished to do. In contrast, Hofstadter, who Kirk would probably call a liberal, saw Calhoun not as an advocate for minority rights (which Calhoun claimed to be) but as an advocate for minority privilege (which Calhoun was). Hofstadter got it right because he, unlike Kirk, was interested in truth rather than cleverly deceptive rationalizations. Yet most important, the fact that Kirk's assertion that Calhoun was a great thinker whose ideas underlined all aspects of our Constitution speaks volumes about the intellectual connection between the Right of Calhoun's period and the Right of the second half of the twentieth century. Since conservative viewpoints have if anything grown even harsher in the early years of twenty-first century, it also tells us a great deal about today's adherents. They remain the philosophical descendants of the antebellum moralists as much of their thinking is indistinguishable from theirs. Like them they are quick to ignore the reality of slavery. From the glorification of the nineteenth century's leading advocate of the institution, to opposition of affirmative action, to tolerance of the Confederate flag, the significance of the slavery that actually existed is continually downplayed. Yet at the same time they have no problem seeing everything "liberal" as a variation of it.

On the website Daily Kos Susan Gardner writes about how conservatives have viewed public policy over time. She lists all the things that they have compared to slavery. I wouldn't have fully believed her if I hadn't witnessed some of them firsthand, the latest being "Obamacare." Here is her incredible list:

- The national debt
- Obamacare (or any type of national insurance program routine throughout the world)
- Abortion!
- Gay marriage
- Fair Housing Act
- Food stamps
- Public education
- Social Security
- Income tax
- Medicare
- Contraception
- FEMA (Federal Emergency Management Administration)

- Affirmative action
- Illegal immigration
- Climate change
- Gun control
- The TSA (Transportation Security Administration)
- Public employee unions
- Any and all Great Society programs (including Head Start, National School Lunch Program, and of course civil rights)[28]

Gardner then adds:

> Hell, let's go for the whole ball of wax, shoot the moon with one ludicrous overstatement: Liberalism!!![29]

It's absurd, but not that surprising. If like Kirk and his hero John C. Calhoun you view your freedom as being dependent on someone else's bondage this is the distorted picture you get. If we peel away all the fancy words we are left with one amazing oxymoron—just about everything (they don't like) is slavery except slavery itself. Gardner sums it all up nicely by saying:

> Sorry, conservatives. Only one thing compares: slavery.[30]

It doesn't matter if we are in the mid-nineteenth, twentieth, or even the twenty-first century—the differences in interpreting the root meaning of freedom are the same. The conservative worldview is in sharp contrast to the abolitionist understanding of how important the bigger picture is. For the abolitionists and their decedents it's not complicated: when freedom and justice are irrevocably intertwined a better life is achieved for all. For the Right, the well-being of the greatest number of people has always been irrelevant; it's all a game of intellectual argument, the goal of which is to prove one's prejudices to be true. This crucial difference has transcended particular eras in American history; when the two worldviews are put up against one another, their difference couldn't be starker.

Chapter VI

The Idiosyncratic Abolitionist

Believe it or not, Confederate sympathizers actually have a favorite abolitionist. His name is Lysander Spooner and he has become a right-wing icon who is often quoted by today's conservative libertarians. One of the most prominent is Ron Paul. Paul relies on Spooner's contrary opinions of Lincoln to justify his support for the Southern cause. Academic critics of Lincoln and the North's role during the Civil War also fall back on Spooner's views to justify their dissenting opinions. Spooner was about the only leading abolitionist who thought that the South had the right to leave the Union and the North should have let them go. Since his views are adapted for current use by the philosophical descendants of slavery's defenders, it's important that we examine them.

Spooner left a wide body of writings about multiple topics. Just about any side of the political divide can find something in his work to bolster its argument. Leftist revolutionaries can use Spooner to justify their support for violent class war. Socialists of all varieties can quote Spooner to attack corporate capitalism. Yet these aspects of Spooner's ideology are less frequently seen in right-wing circles. A more narrowed discussion of his thinking exists among conservatives.

Since Spooner didn't support Lincoln or the North during the Civil War, libertarian conservatives make what appears to be a small leap in saying that he sided with the South. Yet that sidesteps Spooner's abolitionist commitment. At least in theory he was against slavery. Although known for his highly respected legal analysis opining that the original U.S. Constitution didn't condone the institution,[1] he couldn't have said the same about the Confederate Constitution.[2] So from a practical standpoint, how did he think that slavery should be dealt with?

The answer to this question reveals the real Spooner, not the rightist icon. It begins with the reason why violent leftist revolutionaries can embrace him. Just a few years before the Civil War, Spooner concocted a plan that entailed the enslaved and nonslaveholding Southerners undertaking an all-out guerilla war against their state governments. Of course the nonslaveholders comprised the social class that was just above those enslaved, second from the bottom. Spooner was in fact planning what could best be described as a race–class war. Correspondingly, he plotted with John Brown,[3] a man who would lead the most famous violent insurrection in U.S. history,[4] to engineer such a war. Their connection was so strong that before Brown was hung in 1859 Spooner concocted an aborted scheme to kidnap the Governor of Virginia and exchange him for Brown's freedom.[5]

His admiration for Brown explains his distaste for Lincoln. In contrast to Brown's fiery outrage, he saw Lincoln and his party as both insincere and soft on the issue of slavery.[6] Spooner was just too much of a purist to approve of people concerned with halfway measures and political maneuverings. That's why to better understand his assessment of Lincoln it's useful to take a look at how Lincoln's view of politics differed from Spooner's.

Abraham Lincoln was a practical man who operated on the ground level, playing the "game" by the moment and waiting for the right opportunities to present themselves. During his early years in office, Lincoln the politician proceeded very carefully, since he wasn't certain how deep the Northern antislavery sentiment was, or even if it had majority support. Frederick Douglass wasn't appreciative of the president's cautiousness and consequently was quite vocal in his criticism of him. Douglass didn't meet with Lincoln until after the Emancipation Proclamation was issued. During their first meeting, Douglass criticized Lincoln for establishing a policy of paying black soldiers less than whites. He notes that Lincoln calmly responded to him by saying that allowing blacks in the army was difficult enough for many Northerners to accept. At the time, paying black soldiers the same as whites would seriously compound this problem. However, once black soldiers proved themselves and whites became accustomed to blacks being in the army, their pay could then be equalized without undue resistance. While not necessarily agreeing with Lincoln, Douglass accepted his straightforward response. He seemed impressed with his long-term intentions, i.e., moving in the direction of equality.[7]

During the war Douglass would meet with the president on many other occasions. With this increased exposure— not to mention time and perspective—he would come to a very telling assessment. Some eleven years after Lincoln's death, Douglass summed up his view of him in these words:

> Had he put the abolition of slavery before the salvation of the Union, he would have inevitably driven from him a powerful class of American people and rendered resistance to rebellion impossible. Viewed from the genuine abolition ground, Mr. Lincoln seemed tardy, cold, dull and indifferent; but measuring him by the sentiment of his country, a sentiment he was bound as a statesman to consult, he was swift, zealous, radical, and determined. Though Mr. Lincoln shared the prejudices of his white fellow countrymen against the negro, it is hardly necessary to say that in his heart of hearts he loathed and hated slavery.[8]

In comparison, Spooner was a very academic thinker, who was as much concerned about doing something for the "right reason" as he was about the actual outcome. Although a self-proclaimed abolitionist, he did not have the same commitment to abolition as Douglass had. Douglass expressed his commitment with the following words:

> I am, of course, for circumscribing and damaging slavery in any way I can.[9]

For Spooner, results were often secondary. Unlike Lincoln, Spooner wouldn't ever be seen acting like a politician responding to "a sentiment he was bound as a statesman to consult." In fact he was such a purist (even prima donna) that any kind of real-life politics, which by necessity requires compromise, was anathema to him. And to add insult to injury, he was in the habit of denouncing antislavery politicians who (for practical political reasons) couldn't totally embrace his "infallible" logic.

A good example of this can be seen in his 1864 letter to Charles Sumner. Spooner implies that if only Sumner (and his Republican and antislavery compatriots) had publically adopted his interpretation of the Constitution, the South would have had to agree to abandon slavery, making war unnecessary. Here is an excerpt from his letter:

> The South could, consistently with honor, and probably would, long before this time, and without a conflict, have surrendered their slavery to the demand of the constitution, (if that had been pressed upon them,) and to the moral sentiment of the world; while they could not with honor, or at least certainly would not, surrender anything to a confessedly unconstitutional demand, especially when coming from mere demagogues, who were so openly unprincipled as to profess the greatest moral abhorrence of slavery, and at the same time, for the sake of office, swear to support it, by swearing to support a constitution which they declared to be its bulwark.[10]

This is the side of Spooner that was so enamored with his own "genius" that he actually believed his constitutional

140

analysis (virtually by itself) would have made the slave states see the error of their ways. If only his ideas had been more supported by antislavery Northerners, all would have been perfect (like himself).

Yet genius or egomaniac, just a few years before the Sumner letter, his own actions reveal that Spooner knew that this wasn't true. His flirtation with Brown is proof of this. Since he formulated the plan for abolishing slavery at the time he was plotting with him, Spooner's blueprint was more than just academic. It's also a real-life demonstration of how his exaggerated sense of himself was a perfect fit for Brown's megalomania. Looking at Spooner's plan we see that he justified the use of violence by the enslaved population, saying:

> That so long as the governments, under which they live, refuse to give them liberty or compensation, they have the right to take it by stratagem or force.[11]

OK, so far no problem. But what exactly does he mean by compensation? What additional rights do they possess? Spooner clarifies this point when discussing the responsibilities of nonslaveholding whites:

> Until such new governments shall be instituted, to recognize the Slaves as free men, and as being the rightful owners of the property, which is now held by their masters, but which would pass to them, if justice were done; to justify and assist them in every effort to acquire their liberty, and obtain

possession of such property, by stratagem or force
...[12]

They have a right to seize their owner's property and in this pursuit the right to be assisted by nonslaveholding Southerners. In fact Spooner expects that these whites will be in alliance with the enslaved population. He writes:

> Your numbers, combined with those of the Slaves, will give you all power. You have but to use it, and the work is done.[13]

How will this work in practice? From Spooner's plan:

> To form Vigilance Committees, or Leagues of Freedom, in every neighborhood or township, whose duty it shall be to stand in the stead of the government, and do that justice for the slaves, which government refuses to do; and especially to arrest, try, and chastise (with their own whips) all Slaveholders who shall beat their slaves, or restrain them of their liberty; and compel them to give deeds of emancipation, and conveyances of their property, to their slaves.[14]

And what do the slaves share with their white allies (the social class second from the bottom)? Spooner again:

> They could afford to let you share with them in the division of the property taken. We hope you will adopt this measure. It will not only be right in

itself, it will be the noblest act of your lives, *provided you do not take too large a share to yourselves*; and provided also that you afterwards faithfully protect the Slaves in their liberty, and the property assigned to them [my italics].[15]

What if the nonslaveholding whites cooperate with the slave owners instead? Spooner warns:

> *White rascals of the South! Willing tools of the Slaveholders! You, who drive Slaves to their labor, hunt them with dogs, and flog them for pay, without asking any questions!* We have a word specially for you. You are one of the main pillars of the Slave system. You stand ready to do all that vile and inhuman work, which must be done by somebody ...[16]

If all it took was a good argument to convince the South to free its slaves, why this plan?

History tells us that a suspiciously similar plan was attempted by Spooner's cohort John Brown. Brown and his followers seized the federal arsenal at Harpers Ferry, Virginia. They intended to confiscate the weapons and then gather up supporters, mostly blacks, to join them as they moved south on a military campaign to free the enslaved. They ultimately wished to establish a new country, free of slavery. Brown had already written its constitution. Although the attempted uprising failed, it does offer us a living example of what Spooner's revolutionary theorizing would have most likely led to.

Below are two eye-opening articles in Brown's provisional constitution:

ARTICLE XXXIX.

All must labor.

All persons connected in any way with this organization, and who may be entitled to full protection under it, shall be held as under obligation to labor in some way for the general good; and persons refusing or neglecting so to do, shall, on conviction, receive a suitable and appropriate punishment.[17]

ARTICLE XL.

Irregularities.

Profane swearing, filthy conversation, indecent behavior, or indecent exposure of the person, or intoxication or quarreling, shall not be allowed or tolerated, neither unlawful intercourse of the sexes.[18]

Notice that these articles intrude quite a bit on one's personal liberties. Although it could be argued that there is some merit here, it surely doesn't sound like a society that abhors government intervention into people's lives— in other words, the kind of society that Spooner wrote so elegantly on behalf of. Yet it does remind you of the coercive authority that would most likely emerge from a race–class war. Spooner's support of this type of "civil war" is literally a real-life demonstration of the dangers inherent in the kind of purity of principle that he was committed to.

While Spooner advocated a race–class civil war, he opposed a geographical one. Why so? In regard to the former, Spooner reasoned that since the enslaver was denying those enslaved their natural right to be free, a state of war was already in existence. He saw this as a "just war" (a perpetual jihad, so to speak). Of course this would explain why Spooner thought that nonslaveholding whites were obligated to assist people being held in bondage. Speaking of the party most aggrieved, he writes:

> The state of Slavery is a state of war. In this case it is a just war, on the part of the negroes—a war for liberty, and the recompense of injuries; and necessity justifies them in carrying it on by the only means their oppressors have left to them.[19]

Yet why "in God's name" didn't he support the Northern side during the Civil War? The reason was that he saw geographical war between the states in quite a different light. Spooner reasoned that it entailed a violation of a voluntarily agreed-upon contractual relationship among equals, i.e., the freedom of member states to join or leave the Union as they freely choose.[20] And of course for Spooner just being "the bad guy" (e.g., slave state)

145

doesn't nullify what has been voluntarily agreed to by the parties. If it did so, no contract would have any meaning since no party is without vices.

From the perspective of intellectual symmetry this reasoning may sound good, but there are significant holes in it. As the geographical Civil War progressed, the line between it and a race–class upheaval narrowed appreciably. In response to unplanned contingencies, the nature of the conflict along with the Union itself was continuously changing. The evolving circumstances altered the rules of the game in ways no one could have predicted or engineered. Although Lincoln had not originally intended to employ African American soldiers, by war's end they comprised some ten percent of the Union army.[21]

Most black soldiers were fighting on their own home (Southern) soil; and by Confederate laws they were enslaved persons. Even by Spooner's own reasoning, these African Americans were not bound to honor any violation of their liberties imposed upon them by Confederate authorities. How are these freedmen fighting to remain free any different in principle from the army that Spooner hoped to raise?

At the time of the South's surrender, it was clear that the old arrangement that had existed between the states had exhausted all applicability. The forbears of some four million formally enslaved Southerners hadn't taken part in the original contract that declared them and their progeny to be only three-fifths of a person. By war's end African Americans had earned the right to a new arrangement that fully included them. The previous agreement of 1787 was itself usurpation. The Founding Fathers bypassed the existing Constitution (Articles of Confederation) without abiding by its requirements for amendment because they arbitrarily judged it to be unworkable. The situation that existed on the country's Southern soil in 1865 was far more demanding of such arbitrary action. What was needed was a reconfigured federal–state relationship that would be workable under very different circumstances. Equally important, the will (or consent) of a state could no longer be considered legitimate if it was the product of a political process that excluded forty-five percent—in the South four out of nine million—of its population, not to mention its turning a blind eye to the active intimidation of those among the other fifty-five percent who expressed dissenting opinions.

Putting all this aside, it's important to understand how the war that Spooner wanted would most likely have played out. Let's assume that his race–class war had been a military success. With all the "Vigilance Committees," planned reprisals, and property seizures, there would have been a considerable amount of anarchy. And add to this in the heat of all the upheaval the likelihood of spontaneous vengeance. Normal civil society would have been in shambles. No one could have controlled the resulting chaos. One doubts that a hastily assembled "people's army" would have been better at restoring order than the established U.S. Army under Lincoln. History shows us that to fill the void and insure resumption of some sort of normality the most likely scenario would have been the emergence of a strong, possibility dictatorial central authority. History also shows us that most dictatorial authorities don't just wither away when the chaos that brought them to power subsides.

Next, it's important to ask if Spooner's race–class civil war would have been appreciably less violent than the war that took place. Interestingly, it was exactly this type of civil war that Jefferson and Madison feared most. They saw it as the ultimate catastrophe. As we have seen, they thought if enslaved people were freed they would surely take revenge for the centuries of abuse that they and their kin had endured. This needed to be prevented at literally any cost. For the time being this even included the continuation of slavery, an institution that they claimed to loathe.

One could argue that they may have been right about the nature of this type of civil war; since such conflicts are usually the most violent. Remember they were only thinking of what might result from a voluntary emancipation, not a forced one. Given that the situation in question would have been the latter, were the fears of these Founding Fathers still misplaced? If all the personal grudges of the enslaved population had been let loose in a violent emancipation, would the ensuing carnage have been more preferable to what occurred? On both counts it's quite doubtful.

Legal slavery was eventually dealt with, as most bad situations in history are, through the medium of imperfect politicians and institutions. Yet it could all have worked out so much worse. Two years into Lincoln's first term we had the Emancipation Proclamation, and shortly into what would have been his second term we had the Thirteenth Amendment abolishing slavery everywhere in the country. The very important Fourteenth and Fifteenth Amendments would soon follow. Within about a decade after Brown's unsuccessful coup, legalized slavery had been completely abolished and American jurisprudence had taken a giant step forward in defining, equalizing, and securing basic human rights (at least on paper). A Constitution that retained the wisdom of the Founding Fathers—while adding such improvements as the Thirteenth through Fifteenth Amendments—was passed down to posterity. Would a constitution that emerged from the depths of a race–class war have left us a better legacy than our current one? Judging by a reading of Brown's provisional constitution, it's highly unlikely.

Ignoring all the "what ifs" there is one irrevocable fact that can't be seriously challenged: in the real world, Abraham Lincoln, the politician Spooner rejected, was a good deal more successful in the struggle against slavery than John Brown, the fiery purist Spooner embraced. Unfortunately Spooner's self-centered egomania prevented him from acknowledging the obvious. In fact, he reacted by going in exactly the opposite direction.

In 1867 he wrote an article for the proslavery journal, *DeBow's Review*. While listing all the terrible consequences of the Civil War, he completely ignored slavery's demise, instead lamenting:

The probable desolation of the cotton fields of the Southern section, and the yearly loss to the nation of two hundred millions of dollars in gold from that quarter alone.[22]

In the absence of any antislavery sentiments this is exactly how proslavers thought (i.e., forget abolition, it's all about the cotton fields). Yet this isn't surprising. Following the abolition of slavery, Spooner repeatedly downplayed its importance. Speaking about what resulted from the Civil War, he said:

If it really be established, the number of slaves, instead of having been diminished by the war, has been greatly increased ...[23]

Apparently the end of slavery resulted in a worse situation for the white population! Their supposed loss of "liberty" (to leave the Union) overrode eliminating the injustice of slavery.

If ever a Rawlsian thought experiment were in order it's now. Let's assume that at the time Southern whites were given an opportunity to return to pre-Civil War days. Their choice would have been between the previous society that preached liberty while possessing little concern for justice (i.e., saw virtually no contradiction between freedom and the existence of chattel slavery) and their current one which was actively attempting to balance liberty with a commitment to justice (i.e.: enacting the Thirteenth-Fifteenth Amendments because it's understood that a just society is a perquisite for a free one).Oh yes, and let us not forget one caveat. This time there would be a very real possibility that the roles would be reversed and the whites would wind up as the slaves. Under these circumstances it's very likely that the real truth would emerge. Spooner aside, I put my money on them opting for the more balanced and humane choice: the society that strives to achieve "justice for all."

Maybe the elder Spooner wasn't that different from the race–class warrior version. Both were only half-heartedly connected to reality. When outlining his plan for the abolition of slavery, Spooner wrote:

> … to destroy the security and value of Slave property; to annihilate the commercial credit of the Slaveholders; and finally to accomplish the extinction of Slavery. *We hope it may be without blood* [my italics].[24]

His plan entailed overthrowing state governments, seizing slaveholders' nonslave property, criminalizing and whipping them, and punishing nonslaveholder helpers by saddling them with the most burdensome work. Yet he actually held out a possibility that it could all be accomplished "*without blood*"! It tells you how seriously to take Spooner's (and his neo-Confederate admirers') dubious assessment that slavery could (in reasonable time) have been abolished without the Civil War.

A Frederick Douglass Spooner wasn't. His excessive concern over "proper" intentions as well as the appropriate federal–state relationship blinded him to the importance of what was transpiring before his own eyes. When push came to shove, his support for abolition turned out to be thin. He would support getting rid of legalized slavery only if it could be done without violating what he saw as the logical order of things. As a result, at a crucial point in history he acted like a proslavery apologist, using his intellect to justify turning a blind eye to the interests of people whose liberties were the most violated and deserving of redress.

French existentialist philosopher Jean-Paul Sartre was brilliant man. Yet when Sartre stood on a Paris street corner handing out Maoist pamphlets he publicly demonstrated that understanding reality entails more than a genius intellect. Like the twentieth-century Sartre, Lysander Spooner was also a brilliant man. Yet his assessment that John Brown knew the right path to take and Lincoln's was a dead end is just a nineteenth-century version of that twentieth-century man standing on a Paris street corner.

Chapter VII

The In-between Years

The formal success of the abolitionist cause didn't resolve all the injustices accumulated during 250 years of legal slavery. Nevertheless, passage of the Fourteenth and Fifteenth Amendments would prove crucial. While their passage didn't result in immediate implementation, they were still part of the Constitution and in place to be used when the unresolved injustices of the pre-Civil War period would once again assume center stage. The years separating these two groundbreaking efforts in advancing racial equality are just as crucial. The struggle for justice didn't remain dormant in this time in-between. A great deal would be accomplished in what I call the "in-between years"—the period that began in the late 1870s (the end of reconstruction) and continued until the mid-1950s (the beginning of the civil rights movement). Although many new political and social concerns arose during this era, differences in thinking between opposing sides remained remarkably static. Between the demise of outright slavery and the beginning of the successful battle to end a not-so-subtle vestige of it—legal segregation—the philosophical divide that abolitionism gave birth to permeated almost all the historic struggles for justice. Included are the battles to end child labor, ensure safe working conditions, protect the public against unsafe products, shorten the work week, guarantee a minimum wage, allow labor to organize, and provide some semblance of financial security in old age.

In every one of these struggles there was a tension between two distinct groups. On the one side were reformers who were emotionally revolted by an injustice and campaigned for a social remedy that would serve to better integrate the ideal of freedom with that of justice. On the other side were those who rejected any reforms that they claimed would compromise their individualistic notion of liberty. With this in mind, let's review some of the major struggles for justice during this time.

Women's Rights (aka Suffrage)

Some may argue that women's suffrage was somewhat of an exception since it appeared narrowly focused on just one specific wrong: lack of voting rights. They would claim that suffragists were for the most part not concerned with other societal injustices. Although this may be a popular perception in some quarters, it isn't true. There was a direct connection between women's suffrage and the other justice movements. The movement grew out of and was nourished by the abolitionist cause. The great suffragist spokesperson Susan B. Anthony and most of her early compatriots got their start as social activists in the struggle against slavery. In fighting injustices levied against enslaved persons, many of the movement's founders became sensitive to the injustices that they and their sisters had to endure. We saw a good example of this in Chapter IV. Remember the groundbreaking response of women delegates to being denied the right to speak at the London Anti-Slavery Convention? It led to the first Women's Rights

Convention and the beginning of the larger feminist struggle.

The important point is that the basic concepts of fairness and justice are universal and also contagious. Men can be infected as well. Male abolitionist leaders like Garrison, Phillips, and Douglass were among the suffragists' strongest supporters. In fact, most all the nonfemale signers of the Declaration of Sentiments at the first (1848) Women's Rights Convention in Seneca Falls, N.Y., were male abolitionists.[1] In contrast, during the movement's formative years there wasn't a hint of a women's rights movement coming from conservative or status quo circles of either gender.

In any discussion of the women's suffrage movement, the accomplishments of Susan B. Anthony always make their way to the forefront. With the assistance of another great suffragist-activist, Elizabeth Cady Stanton, she wrote the initial draft of what would later become (after her death) the amendment that would ban discrimination in voting based on gender. In fact, when it was first introduced in the U.S. Senate, it was presented to that body as the "Anthony Amendment."

The most heralded suffragist leader merits a few words about her life. Anthony was born into a Quaker family. Her mother Lucy was in her own right a farsighted person. Just weeks after the groundbreaking Women's Rights Convention in Seneca Falls, Lucy attended a similar gathering held in Rochester, N.Y. She was one of the signers of its Declaration of Sentiments. Susan's father Daniel was a strident abolitionist who understood the significance of his daughter's God-given gifts. Susan was able to read and write by age three.[2] When she was six years old, the teacher refused to teach her long division because she was the wrong gender. Daniel responded by taking his talented daughter out of the school and placing her in a group home school. At this same home school there were women teachers who would provide Susan positive female role models.

By age seventeen, she was actively working against the "gag rule" that prevented the House of Representatives from receiving antislavery petitions. Anthony would later become an agent for the American Anti-Slavery Society. In the process she would also become an accomplished orator. Speaking on behalf of both abolition and suffrage at the ninth National Women's Rights Convention, Anthony told the audience:

> Where, under our Declaration of Independence, does the Saxon man get his power to deprive all women and Negroes of their inalienable rights?[3]

In 1851 she met Elizabeth Cady Stanton, and they would become compatriots as well as life- long friends. The two women traveled together throughout the country spreading the message of the women's suffrage movement. They jointly founded the journal *The Revolution*. Its masthead called for "Men their rights and nothing more; women their rights, and nothing less;" and its aim was to establish "justice for all."[4]

Notice that the ultimate goal of these radical feminist, abolitionist (and also pro-union) women is a good match for the final three words of the Pledge of Alliance. Their journal would soon become one of the most influential voices of the early women's suffrage movement. While for financial reasons *The Revolution* would turn out to have a relatively short life span, its impact would be quite significant.[5]

Extending the movement's reach was what *The Revolution* contributed to the larger struggle. It combined class and race issues with those of gender. In addition to espousing the more traditional goals, the journal advocated empowering working women through the formation of trade unions. [6, 7] During the early stage of the struggle the maltreatment of these low-paid workers was seen as part and parcel of the battle for suffrage. *The Revolution* advocated for the eight-hour day and was even involved in active union organizing.[8]

Equally important, in these formative years the plight of women was frequently compared to that of formally enslaved African Americans. Listen to what Susan B. Anthony had to say about the comparison between racial slavery and the status of women, in her 1871 speech addressing suffrage and the working woman:

> You say the women and the negro are not parallel cases. The negro was a down trodden race, but for the women there is no such necessity for they are lovely and beloved, and the men will guard them from evil. I suppose they will guard their own wives and daughters and mothers and sisters, but is every man as careful to guard another man's

wife, daughter, mother, and sister? It is not a question of safety to women in general. It is simply "Is she my property?" ... [9]

The founding suffragists cared about voting rights as an essential element of a much larger concern: the broader status of women in society. Full equality before the law was an integral part of that overriding concern. What about social justice? As already noted, the early suffragists were just as sensitive to class injustices. This was particularly true in regard to the unfair hardships that working women confronted. The fact that many of the founding suffragists were active in the formation of unions and the struggle to improve both working and living conditions of wage laborers was a reflection of their outrage over the mistreatment they witnessed. Their reaction to naked exploitation was reminiscent of the gut response of the abolitionists. Once again, listen to the concerns raised by Susan B. Anthony in the same speech:

> Now what do women want? Simply the same ballot. In this city, they, the women hat and cap makers, 2,000 of them, made a strike and held out three weeks, but finally they were forced to yield. Their employers said "Take that or nothing," and although "that" was almost "nothing" they had to take it or starve. Until two weeks ago I never heard of a successful strike among women. I'll tell you why this was successful. The employers of the Daughters of St. Crispin at Baltimore undertook to cut their wages down, and the Daughters struck. They were about to be defeated

when the men of St. Crispins came to the rescue and said to the employers, "If you don't accede we will strike," and they carried their point.[10]

Note that Anthony was not averse to women working in conjunction with male-dominated unions to remedy the social injustices confronting both genders. If additional proof is required, you need only read more of what Susan B. Anthony had to say about the plight of working women, men, unions, and strikes. Again from the same speech:

> In '68 the collar laundry women organized into a trades union. Their wages had once been but from $6 to $8 per week, but they gradually got them raised to $11 to $21 per week. You may all say that this is very good wages and so it was, compared with what they had been getting, but they thought they were poorly paid in proportion to the profits of their employers, and struck for an advance. Their employers said they must put a stop to this. Give women an inch and they will take an ell. The women called the men trades unions into counsel. The men said, "Now is your time to make a strike; you are organized and your employers will come to terms." So one May morning in '69 the 1,000 women threw down their work. For three long months these women held out. They exhausted all their money. From all over the United States trade unions sent money to help them … [11]

Anthony glorifies the heroism of low-paid female workers who courageously went on strike. The male trade unions are seen quite favorably as they are considered to be allies in the same struggle. She has more to say on how the power of working men benefits working women:

> No political party can hope for success and oppose the interests of the working class. You can all see that neither of the great parties dared to put a plank in the platform directly opposed. Both wrote a paragraph on finance, but nobody knew what it meant. They did this not because of a desire to do justice to the workingwomen, but simply because of the power of the working men to do them harm ... [12]

Anthony understands there is a "working class" that's being victimized and that both men and women are included. Since the genders share common concerns, they need to join forces in pursuing them. The welfare of all working people is at stake. Unfortunately relations between the suffragists and male-dominated unions were not always cordial. This was to be expected, since women were excluded from joining many of these unions, the result being that the classical labor–management struggle didn't always preclude concurrent hostilities between divergent gender interests. Nevertheless, given a level playing field it's clear what side of the social–economic divide Anthony identifies with. From the perspective of current-day conservatives (like past conservatives), Anthony is actively waging "class war."

If Susan B. Anthony is any authority on the subject, it's obvious from her speech "Suffrage and the Working Woman" that a direct cross-fertilization existed between the early women's suffrage movement and other progressive movements. In fact as late as the beginning of the twentieth century, their leading opponents were still using their advocacy of social justice against them. In 1905, former President Grover Cleveland argued against women's suffrage by saying:

> Woman suffrage would give to the wives and daughters of the poor a new opportunity to gratify their envy and mistrust of the rich … [13]

It is almost certain that Cleveland wasn't the only person who understood that female suffrage would enfranchise a lot more poor women than rich women. Obviously, there was concern over the implications of this fact.

There are a few important points pertaining to Anthony and the women's suffrage movement that require comment. To begin with, I must confess that the history just presented was not as neat as it may seem. For example, the suffrage movement was split over supporting the Fifteenth Amendment to the U.S. Constitution, because this amendment did not specifically include women. Black men were getting constitutionally protected voting rights while women were once again being left out in the cold.

The (male) abolitionist position was that black men's suffrage should come first. One group of suffragists supported this stance and an opposing group (which included Anthony and Stanton) would have none of it. In response they would advocate against the amendment itself. [14] Their opposition rested on a tactical rather than principled position. They thought that a strategy requiring unity of purpose, whereby the disenfranchised (women and blacks) steadfastly supported one another, was the proper path to take. Both would move forward together or not at all.

However, as reality often dictates, the "ground floor" turns out to be a bloody battlefield, encased in unspeakable mess. When black abolitionists like Frederick Douglass threw their support behind the (male) abolitionist position, many women suffrage leaders (like Anthony and Stanton) saw it as a stark betrayal. After all, hadn't they always been steadfast in their support of the rights of black men?

As a result of this fissure some very nasty things were said, and even Garrison was critical of what he saw as racist appeals. [15] Stanton even went as far as to claim that women were more deserving of voting rights than black men. [16] Yet even more disconcerting, it marked the beginning of an unsavory alliance with racist but pro-suffrage elements. [17] The universality of the movement was weakened as both Anthony and Stanton seemed to have become the spokespeople for just white women's suffrage. [18]

Yet if one takes a step back and allows emotions to settle down, a much broader perspective emerges. The positive character of the Fifteenth Amendment (i.e., greater inclusion of the citizenry in the electorate) was not what was being opposed. If at the time a real non-gender-biased universal suffrage was attainable, virtually all suffragists would have supported it. When you look beyond the messiness of all the turf wars, you see that the resulting divisions were primarily questions of when and how, not what.

Elizabeth Cady Stanton's thinking as well as its evolution provides us with a good example of this. At the time of the split she was much more embittered than Anthony. For her, black men had gone over to the enemy side. She didn't hesitate to verbally demonstrate her anger towards them. [19] Unfortunately this included "playing the race card." She implied that enfranchising black men would endanger white women. [20]

Nevertheless, during some real nasty infighting, when harsh words were being thrown every which way, Stanton was still quite willing to change her position if suffrage for women could be assured. In May 1869, during a debate over the Fifteenth Amendment, Stanton said she did not wish to join those on the other side until they demanded "suffrage for All—*even Negro suffrage without distinction of sex ...*" [21]

In other words, as previously said about her side of the divide, Stanton's opposition to the amendment wasn't at its core principled but rather tactical. And despite her nay-saying, she never lost sight of the bigger picture, at least in private. She expressed her thoughts about all the controversy in a letter to a friend:

Our Abolitionists are just as sectarian in their association as the Methodists in their church, and divisions are always the most bitter where there is least to differ about. But in spite of all, *the men and women who have been battling for freedom in this country, are as grand and noble as any that have ever walked the earth. So we will forget their faults and love them for their many virtues* [my italics]. [22]

As an aside, notice that when speaking privately about her longtime comrades, Stanton doesn't describe them as feminists or suffragists but rather as abolitionists. As far as her public proclamations are concerned, we see that with time and distance the real fighter for universal human rights emerges once again. Ann D. Gordon, coeditor of the *Papers of Elizabeth Cady Stanton and Susan B. Anthony*, writes this about Stanton:

When time proved the Fourteenth and Fifteenth amendments inadequate protection for blacks' voting rights in the South, she mounted the biggest suffrage campaign of her lifetime for "National Protection for National Citizens," arguing that the voting rights of all citizens were too important to be left to the states and should be guaranteed by constitutional amendment. [23]

Fundamentally, Anthony, Stanton and most of the other early suffragists were progressives. They contributed to advancing liberalism's goals in more ways than just one. Although actual history may not have been quite so pristine, if you look at what's really important (i.e., actual intentions and outcomes), the foresightedness and courageous undertakings of founding suffragists like Anthony and Stanton improved the lives of people of every race, class, and gender. And it's this deeper reality that's behind the neat picture.

There is one more point that needs to be acknowledged. I am not contending that the women's suffrage movement was always and undividedly in step with a wider progressive vision. What's being claimed is that the movement's original founding mothers came out of the broader liberal tradition. As their "radical" views spread into the larger society, more conservative women would come to embrace them. And in narrowing their scope these converts would afford the radical the respectability required to be successful. This was an important part of the process as well. Yet this doesn't change the fact that without the revolutionary efforts of early visionaries there wouldn't have been a women's movement in the first place. And respectability or not, without the larger liberal community that birthed them, women's suffrage would have been long delayed.

The manner in how "official history" has portrayed "Anthony suffragists" is very similar to its portrayal of "Garrison abolitionists." In both cases the span of their concerns was narrowed. As the abolitionist goal was limited to just the abolition of slavery, the suffragist goal was reduced to just a women's right to vote. Yet the truth is otherwise. For most of the founding suffragists, like the abolitionists before them, (and of course there was a good deal of overlap) were actively opposed to a broad range of injustices.

The Labor Movement

Conservative historians have been less successful in distorting the true nature of some of the other justice movements. The labor movement is a case in point. Given the movement's actions and accomplishments, there is little doubt that it was (and is) very concerned about social justice. The rhetoric and writings of its most esteemed leaders quite clearly encapsulate this ideal. One of the earliest and greatest of these was Eugene V. Debs. He was a major participant in the founding of our first industrial union, the American Railway Union (ARU). As a leader of the ARU he played an important role in the first nationwide strike conducted against a giant corporation, the Pullman Palace Car Company. For his part in this strike, Debs served six months in prison. Afterwards, he would go on to help found the Industrial Workers of the World (IWW), a major umbrella organization of some of the nation's largest industrial unions. Running as the Socialist Party's presidential candidate in 1912, he received nearly a million votes. This was when a million votes was really a significant number. He repeated this feat again in the 1920 presidential election, with the only difference being he was in prison at the time.

In a speech delivered on November 22, 1895, Debs makes it clear that he sees working people—like the slaves of yesteryear—as victims who must endure terrible injustices because of the greed of others. Of course these others are their employers, who—like the former slaveholders,—blatantly violate the golden rule. Debs said in part:

> To wish it otherwise would be to deplore the organization of the American Railway Union and every effort that great organization has made to extend a helping hand to oppressed, robbed, suffering and starving men, women and children, the victims of corporate greed and rapacity. It would be to bewail every lofty attribute of human nature, *lament the existence of the golden rule and wish the world were a jungle, inhabited by beasts of prey that the seas were peopled with sharks and devil-fish and that between the earth and the stars only vultures held winged sway* [my italics].[24]

The more one reads Debs the clearer it becomes that he was driven by his outrage over injustices waged against the most vulnerable and his unshakable desire to rectify them. Like abolitionists of the previous era, he doesn't hesitate to outline the existing wrongs in the starkest of terms. In a piece entitled "A Call to the People" published two years later, Debs's theme is just as forthright. He wrote:

> Under the rule of the money power, labor is plundered until the *starvation* point is reached and

then its *emaciated* body is shot full of holes. It is notoriously true that the American miners have been *robbed* in countless ways, and now that they are *hungry*, it is proposed to *murder* them [my italics].[25]

The very next year, while writing about the Haymarket riot, Debs not only uses the same passionate language but speaks of none other than "emancipation" from—you guessed it—(wage) "slavery."

> ... the present generation of workingmen should erect an enduring memorial to the men who had the courage to denounce and oppose wage-*slavery* and seek for methods of *emancipation* [my italics].[26]

Six years on, in his opening speech as the 1904 Socialist candidate for president, Debs lays out his worldview. Notice his analogies to the injustices of the antebellum period:

> Mr. Chairman, Citizens and Comrades:
> ... Human society has always consisted of *masters and slaves*, and the slaves have always been and are today, the foundation stones of the social fabric.
> Wage-labor is but a name; *wage-slavery* is the fact.
> The twenty-five millions of wage-slavery in the United States are twenty-five millions of *twentieth century slaves*.

This is the plain meaning of what is known as the Labor Market.

... They who buy and they who sell in the labor market are alike dehumanized by the inhuman traffic in the brains and blood and bones of human beings.

... Twenty-five millions of wage-slaves *are bought and sold daily at prevailing prices* in the American Labor Market [my italics].[27]

It is obvious that Debs is once again making a comparison between the struggle to end slavery and what labor is up against. It is also obvious that he continues to be in sync with the appeal that nineteenth-century abolitionists made to one's sense of moral outrage over the unjust treatment of fellow human beings.

During World War I, Debs was convicted of sedition for publically speaking out against the military draft. In addressing the court, Debs presented a justification for his actions based on the very same core values that fueled his life's work. And in doing so, like Garrison before him, when up against a blistering attack, he stands his ground offering no apologies. He said in part:

I am thinking this morning of the men in the mills and factories; I am thinking of the women who, for a paltry wage, are compelled to work out their lives; of the *little* children who, in this system, are robbed of their childhood, and in their early, tender years, are seized in the remorseless grasp of Mammon, and forced into the industrial dungeons, there to feed the machines while they themselves are being starved body and soul … Your honor, *I ask no mercy. I plead for no immunity* [my italics].[28]

Notice that the content, tenor, and consistency of Debs's appeal spans decades. In his repeated use of phrases like "twentieth century slaves," "labor market" (take-off on "slave market"), "verge of slavery," "wage-slavery," "methods of emancipation," and "fetters were upon their limbs," there isn't any question of what previous struggle in history he identified with or how he viewed labor's current struggle. In all his works, we see comparisons between what he is fighting against and what the abolitionists confronted. Remember, the great achievement of the antislavery movement was still fresh in the minds of many living Americans. Therefore, from Debs's speeches we see that he not only saw the abolitionist strategy as the prototype to follow, but also viewed labor's battles as being a continuation of it. Even Theodore Roosevelt saw a comparison (albeit a negative one) between those on the Left advocating more radical measures than himself (a perfect description of Debs) and the nineteenth-century abolitionists (a movement active in his own lifetime). In reviewing Doris Kearns Goodwin's book *The Bully Pulpit* for *The New Yorker*, Nicholas Lemann speaks to Roosevelt's understanding of their similarity:

> But he never cut off relations with the Republican bosses who disapproved of his attacks on the misdeeds of business, and he grew dismissive of

allies who turned from reform to socialism. He liked to point out that Lincoln had accomplished more in the struggle against slavery than the abolitionists had.[29]

Roosevelt's astute observation explains why you could easily envision the abolitionists feeling perfectly at home with both Debs' words and intentions. It's not only the language he uses but also his points of reference and the nature of his appeal that are almost identical.

Yet it doesn't end there. One of the abolitionists' most distinguishing features was their almost total lack of concern about the consequences of shaking up the apple cart. This is why so many people looked at them as reckless and dangerous radicals. It's no accident that Debs was seen in exactly the same light. Like the great abolitionists, he was totally unapologetic for any mess that he stirred up. Both understood that to achieve their goals, things needed to get messy. As far back as 1890, Debs had written:

> Agitation is the order of nature. Nature abhors quiet as it does a vacuum. ... Nature prefers agitation, hence the hurricane, the tornado, the cyclone, the lighting, and the thunderbolt; hence the volcano and the earthquake. Call them evils, it matters not, they are a ceaseless protest against stagnation. Men cry "peace," but there is no peace. The elemental war goes on. Indeed, those who clamor for peace are agitators.[30]

If one didn't know the author, these writings could easily be attributed to William Lloyd Garrison. Correspondingly, you could also say that in Debs's repeated references to slavery, outrage over the treatment of the downtrodden, contempt for the perpetrators of such treatment, blatant appeal to the human sense of fairness and justice, Garrison's works could just as easily be attributed to Debs. The interesting point here is that neither the works of Garrison nor of Debs could ever be mistaken for works by the authors of the Federalist Papers. While the political genre of these two men is strikingly similar, it's equally dissimilar to the classical liberal perspective that preceded it.

Yet it's not only Debs who is associated with the political genre of abolitionists. The entire labor movement embodies their modus operandi. This can be seen when we look at the words of many of labor's other great leaders. One of them was John L. Lewis. For forty years he was president of the United Mine Workers of America (UMWA). In the 1930s Lewis was instrumental in organizing millions of industrial workers. He was one of the first union leaders to successfully make use of the sit-down strike," a tactic that would later prove very useful to the civil rights movement. The formation of the Congress of Industrial Organizations (CIO) and the United Steel Workers of America (USWA) was largely the result of Lewis's efforts. His stature as a labor leader was second to none. Lewis's name was even mentioned in the 1938 movie *Holiday*. The character played by Katharine Hepburn uttered the famous line: "I never could decide whether I wanted to be Joan of Arc,

Florence Nightingale, or John L. Lewis."[31] And it must be said that for America's working people he was the joint reincarnation of both Joan of Arc and Florence Nightingale.

In her work *America in the 20th Century: 1930–1939*, Carolyn Kott Washburne pointed out that:

> One of the most successful of Lewis' organizing techniques was his "crust of bread" speech. He often compared the typical life of a worker—living in a polluted shantytown, in a house with no glass or screens on the windows, and with hungry children running around—to that of a factory owner driving a Rolls Royce to the marina where his yacht is moored. All the workers were really asking for, according to Lewis, was a "crust of bread" to feed themselves and their families.[32]

If this isn't an emotional appeal to one's sense of basic decency nothing is. In this vein most of Lewis' rhetoric targeted human revulsion of injustice and the well-meaning desire to remedy it. I would add another essential component of his advocacy. In pursuing justice he was demonstrably proactive and encouraging of others to be the same. All these essential elements are seen in Lewis's famous Labor Day speech delivered on September 3, 1938:

> The organization and constant onward sweep of this movement exemplifies the resentment of the many toward the selfishness, greed and the neglect   of   the   few.

The workers of the nation were tired of waiting for corporate industry to right their economic wrongs, to alleviate their social agony and to grant them their political rights. Despairing of fair treatment, they resolved to do something for themselves. They, therefore, have organized a new labor movement, conceived within the principles of the national bill of rights and committed to the proposition that the workers are free to assemble in their own forums, voice their own grievances, declare their own hopes and contract on even terms with modern industry for the sale of their only material possession—their labor.[33]

Note that Lewis speaks of the "selfishness, greed and the neglect of the few." He then refers with pride to the proactive steps that labor is taking to remedy the unfairness of their situation. Rankin or the other great abolitionists wouldn't have expressed it any differently. Targeting those who oppose labor's objectives, Lewis precedes to spell out exactly what disturbs them:

Do they fear its influence will be cast on the side of shorter hours, a better system of distributed employment, better homes for the under-privileged, social security for the aged, a fairer distribution of the national income? Certainly the workers that are being organized want a voice in the determination of these objectives of social justice. Certainly labor wants a fairer share in the national income. Assuredly labor wants a larger participation in increased productive efficiency.[34]

He sees that a fairer playing field for workers requires a more equal distribution of both political and material resources. It is no wonder that the owners of great wealth are so resistant to labor's demands. They are the ones who must surrender (some of) their privileges. This places them in a similar position to nineteenth-century slaveholders. Lewis understood that like these past oppressors, they will not surrender anything without an ardent struggle. He was always there to remind people of the need for such an endeavor. In 1947, following one of the worst mining disasters in American history at Centralia Kentucky, congressional hearings were held. In regards to the role of corporate management, Lewis didn't hesitate to lay the blame where it belonged. While the testimony of others has long since been forgotten, his testimony before the congressional committee is still remembered as a masterpiece of righteous outrage as well as an uncompromising demand for social justice. Look at some of the excerpts from Lewis's testimony:

> And, of course, that is the history of the industry, that is the operators' philosophy, "we kill them; you [the union] provide for their widows and orphans. You bury them; we [the operators] just kill them"[35] ... I called the roll of them for a five year period for you gentlemen [Congressmen] a while ago; 300,000-odd mine-made victims, some died more than 6000, some lived, some lived blind, some with twisted backs, lost limbs,

paralyzed bodies, broken bones, the flesh burned from their faces until they are grinning specters of gas explosions ... If we must grind up human flesh and bone in the industrial machine we call modern America, then before God I assert that those who consume coal and you and I who benefit from that service because we live in comfort, we owe protection to those men first, and we owe security to their families if they die. I say it. I voice it. I proclaim it, and I care not who in heaven or hell opposes it.[36]

In this litany of horrors one sees the words, the outrage, and the moral appeal of a Garrison, a Phillips, or a Douglass. The task of opposing this call for justice was essentially the same as it was for the proslavery crowd that argued against these great abolitionists. The bloody truth was their enemy. In speaking to this truth, Lewis makes one want to enlist in the battle to prevent such inhumanity from occurring. Stark images of reality were the most effective counter to conservative intellectualizations that were supposedly neutral but just happened to justify the worst of situations. That's because his words really hit the nail on the head, and on a deep human level this was understood.

A famous quote, in which John L. Lewis sums up his relationship to labor's struggle, is listed on the UMWA web site:

I have pleaded your case from the pulpit and from the public platform—not in the quavering tones of a feeble mendicant asking alms, but in the thundering voice of the captain of a mighty host, demanding the rights to which free men are entitled.[37]

Once again, this could have been easily said by Garrison, Phillips, or Douglass, since it speaks to everything they were about.

Walter Reuther was another great leader whose lifetime work showcases labor's commitment to social justice. Next to Debs and Lewis, he was probably the movement's most potent voice in the twentieth century. Reuther was a founding member of the United Auto Workers (UAW) and served as its president for over two decades. Prior to its merging with the American Federation of Labor (AFL), he was concurrently president of the Congress of Industrial Organizations (CIO). Reuther was one of the most successful union leaders in negotiating benefits for workers. In addition to high wages, UAW members received paid vacations, pensions, and family health insurance. He was also one of the premier liberals of his day. Reuther fought not only for his immediate constituents, but for the betterment of all people. He was a diehard advocate of civil rights and was noticeably present at the 1963 march on Washington and the 1965 march from Selma to Montgomery. Even after medical coverage had been obtained for his own union members, Reuther actively worked to secure universal health insurance for all Americans.[38] During contract negotiations with auto industry management he pushed for lower auto prices for every consumer.[39, 40] The leading conservative political figure of the time, Barry

Goldwater, paid a backdoor tribute to Reuther by saying that he was "a more dangerous menace than the Sputnik or anything Soviet Russia might do to America."[41]

There is one unique factor about Reuther that should be mentioned. He was much more of an insider than either Debs or (somewhat of a prima donna) Lewis. He used his authority as a top labor leader to support and buttress Franklin Roosevelt's New Deal Coalition. This coalition would be in existence until the end of Lyndon Johnson's Great Society. During these three-and-a-half decades the New Deal Coalition was the dominant political force in the country. For much of this time labor had a strong voice in the halls of power, and Reuther was an integral part of its success story. This may explain why we see in him less of an appeal to righteous outrage then we see in Debs or Lewis. Yet his rhetoric elegantly reflects his vision of—as well as his striving for—social justice. In fact, the pursuit of a more just society is what Reuther's life was all about. A famous quote of his sums up what he saw as his calling to be:

> There is no greater calling than to serve your fellow men. There is no greater contribution than to help the weak. There is no greater satisfaction than to have done it well.[42]

Reuther fully understood that liberty was meaningless without justice and frequently said as much. Look at these excerpts from his 1958 Labor Day address:

> The free world labor movement is effective because it acts in the knowledge that the struggle

for peace and freedom is inseparably tied together with the struggle for economic and social justice … Industrial stability in a totalitarian society is possible but in a free society, sound labor management relations must be based upon elementary, economic and social justice.[43]

Economic and social justice is what makes freedom possible. The reverse is just as true, freedom makes justice possible; they are "inseparably tied together." What specifically does Reuther think constitutes justice, and what does labor wish to achieve? Once again from Reuther's Labor Day address:

We need to overcome the serious deficit in education, which is denying millions of our children their rightful opportunity to maximum growth. The American labor movement is proud that it was among those who pioneered for free public education.[44] … We need to wipe out slums and build decent wholesome neighborhoods. We need to provide more adequate medical care available to all groups. We need to improve Social Security so that our aged citizens can live their lives with a fuller measure of security and dignity. We need to provide all our citizens without regard to race, creed or color, equal opportunity in every phase of our national life.[45]

We see such concerns as quality free public education, decent housing, adequate medical care, security for seniors, and ending all vestiges of racial discrimination making Reuther's to-do list. In other words, in the broadest sense, he is calling for the betterment of the entire society. And just as crucial, this objective requires that we improve the everyday lives of ordinary citizens. In this vein, what does Reuther think is the ultimate standard that we will be judged by?

> America will be judged not by its economic wealth or its productive potential. We will be judged by a sense of social and moral responsibility by which we commit our national resources and our productive potential to basic human needs and practical human fulfillment.[46]

If you read the address's entire text, what stands out the most is Reuther's global appeal. Narrow concerns of auto workers are hardly mentioned. It is literally all about striving for a more just existence for everyone. In an age when labor's star was continually on the rise, much of its energies were diverted into making the world fairer. And this wasn't just highbrow talk. During the time when Reuther was labor's most successful spokesperson, labor used its role as a leading player in the New Deal Coalition to successfully create or improve such programs as Social Security for the aged and disabled, Medicare for senior citizens, a minimum wage for all Americans, elimination of child labor—as well as other protections effecting (everyone's) children—and much more. The millions of people who directly benefit from just these enumerated accomplishments far exceed the nation's total union membership. Just as Anthony was far more than an advocate for women's suffrage, Reuther was far more than a labor activist. He shares responsibility with other progressives for improving the lives of all Americans, union members or not. Reuther's contribution to the America we live in today is immense.

The Battle for Social Security

While women's suffrage and labor constituted some of the most progressive movements during these "in-between years," there were others as well. One of the most crucial is hardly known about now. Yet its success has had monumental consequences for Americans living today. Social Security is its legacy.

Great achievements in social justice have been brought about by broad-based progressive coalitions, and the creation of Social Security was no exception. Yet there was one movement in particular that was solely focused on the plight of seniors and expended all its energy on alleviating their distress. This movement took shape during the depths of the Great Depression and was known as the "Townsend movement." The name came from its founder, Francis Townshend, a retired physician.

The Great Depression was economically devastating to millions of older Americans. Most of them had lost their life savings, and there were few jobs available. Motivated by his horror over the plight of an old woman scavenging through a garbage dump, Townsend wrote a letter to the editor of his local newspaper, proposing a national pension plan. What happened next has no parallel in American history. From Townsend's empathic concern for the elderly and a simple letter to the editor proposing a proactive solution to their predicament, a mass movement involving millions of people was born virtually overnight. Thousands of "Townsend clubs" sprung up spontaneously throughout the country. Members wrote millions of letters to their elected officials demanding that they support Dr. Townsend's plan.[47] In just a few years' time, these grassroots clubs sponsored the largest mass meeting in human history: there were more than twenty million participants filling some five thousand auditoriums![48]

In his piece "A Man and His Plan" for *The American*, Robert McHenry speculated on the relationship between Townsend and the movie *Meet John Doe*. He wrote "Just add an ambitious newspaperwoman (Barbara Stanwyck) and a plutocrat with fascistic dreams of power (Edward Arnold), and you have Frank Capra's *Meet John Doe* (1941), in which some homespun thoughts on neighborliness from 'John Doe' (Gary Cooper) inspire an eerily similar national movement."[49]

The only difference was that the Townsend movement, like Townsend himself, wasn't the creation of any Hollywood scriptwriter; it was as real as you and me. Yet reality was just as in the movie: the consciousness of the nation was awakened by a genuine grassroots movement. The president and Congress were forced to respond quickly. They come up with their own plan for a national pension system, called "Social Security." Of course their plan was far less generous than Townsend's plan. The Townsendites demanded better. In response to continued pressure from them and other reformers, four years after its passage, Congress would amend the original Social Security Act to improve its benefits and advance the implementation date.

It should be noted that in remaining proactive and causing the powers that be to move up Social Security's start date the Townsend movement quite possibility made a major contribution to saving the program. The original date would have come due soon after Pearl Harbor, during all the chaos that accompanied America's unplanned entry into WWII. If Social Security had not already begun operations, it's highly probable that because of the ongoing national emergency the program's implementation would have been put off for an unspecified time period. If so, during the early postwar years when the nation's politics turned to the right, Social Security would not have had the protection of being an established entity in American life.

It must be said that Townsend's specific plan was complicated and somewhat convoluted. And Townsend himself was a little naïve and—like a few of the early suffragists—prone to making unfortunate political alliances. He even rejected the actual Social Security Act. It wasn't his plan; it was a false and incomplete substitute. Yet this is not the real story. What are most important are Dr. Townsend's sincerity and the fruits of his efforts. There is a statement appearing on the History section of the Social Security Administration web site that addresses the situation quite nicely:

In his autobiography we can see the forces and values that shaped and motivated Dr. Townsend. What we see, I think, is a very sympathetic character [who] is well-meaning and sincerely motivated to do good. It was an irony of history, apparently lost on the good Dr., that his Townsend Plan would have its greatest impact on the well-being of the elderly by serving as a prod to the adoption of Social Security.[50]

In regards to the significance of the Townsend movement, Edwin Amenta in his book *When Movements Matter* says that:

Politicians of both parties feared the Townsendites and began to think of the aged as a group whose demands and wants were deserving of respect and attention. The Townsend Plan also demonstrated the value of mobilizing the aged and was soon copied by all manner of organizations.[51]

Without the existence of the Townsend movement there would have been much less incentive for politicians to address the concerns of the elderly. The bottom line is: no Townsend, most likely no Social Security. It should also be added that "all manner of organizations" with a social grievance, aged individuals, or otherwise would learn important lessons from what was ultimately accomplished by his movement.

Putting aside Townsend's foibles, he still has important things to tell us. In his 1943 autobiography, *New*

Horizons, he explains what the generic concept of Social Security is all about:

> This book is dedicated to the proposition that all men are created with certain inherent rights among which is the right to live above the status of poverty … [52]

Human beings have inherent rights, and included among them is the right to live in dignity. This right allows for the well-being of the society as a whole. Nevertheless, opponents at the time (and today as well) argued that it was wrong to give the elderly "something for nothing." There is no better answer to these naysayers than the one Townsend gave:

> They just didn't think old folks ought to have "something for nothing" as they termed pensions—*just as though sixty years of useful work in the community were "nothing"* [my italics].[53]

I think that it's crucial that we digress for a moment and explore why the values of the Townsend movement are so important. The best place to begin is with the rationale underlying public education. The institution fosters the greater development of every citizen. This has the effect of advancing human dignity while at the same time benefiting society as a whole. This is why childless adults are required to contribute to the education of future citizens. Without this societal commitment, we would have an illiterate and uneducated population. The social mobility that allowed for the building of the nation would be almost nonexistent (to say nothing of the democracy).

Since justice is a core human value, most people think that children are entitled to a fair chance in life. Fortunately this perspective would contribute to public education being seen as a de facto "entitlement" that shouldn't be dependent on a parent's ability to pay. Mandating universal childhood education (including progressively advancing the boundaries), and correspondingly providing for it, has contributed immeasurably to society and every individual in it. This is a perfect example of why liberty when moderated by justice inevitably produces even greater liberty, in this case by significantly expanding life's opportunities.

Now let us get back to how the Townsend movement fits into this picture. You might say that free public education was our first "social security" system. As our children's access to this de facto "entitlement" fundamentally changes the nature of society, Townsend understood that the same was true for how we deal with people at the other end of life. These two extreme sides of the spectrum, our development and our demise, are the stages of existence where we human beings are the most vulnerable. Therefore, they both raise the basic question of human dignity. This matters because you cannot separate the well-being of the society from that of the individuals in it. In promoting a more just society, Social Security, like free public education, expands our life opportunities. Both young and old are in a much better position. For younger people, the burden of having to worry about caring for their elderly parents, at a time when they need to be focused on the needs of their own children, is much reduced. For the elderly, their financial dependency is lessened and their horizons are enlarged. By shrinking economic worries and enhancing human dignity, Social Security affords everyone a bit more free space in which to live their lives.

Yet at rock bottom, it's really a question of the kind of world we choose for ourselves and our posterity. Should George Orwell's book *Animal Farm* be the model for how the elderly are treated? The old horses that had outlived their usefulness were shipped off to the glue factory (in our case it would be the garbage dump). Interestingly *Animal Farm* was originally intended to be a harsh parody of life under (Stalinist) communism, yet it can just as easily be a description of life under (libertarian) capitalism. Neither has much affinity for those deemed to have outlived their usefulness. However, it doesn't matter whether it's communism or capitalism; the fundamental question remains the same: Do we want our children to inherit a world where they are desired so long as they are thought to have productive potential but discarded when it's presumed to be gone—in other words, a world that prizes them only for their utility and not as human beings with human life spans? Do they cease being our children when they are old and vulnerable? Do they cease having any merit when no longer of industrial use? Separating the supposed interests of the young from the old is but another way of separating ourselves from our own phases of existence and thereby cheapening the value of our lives. We become no more than pieces of machinery or any other disposable market commodities. Or do we want them to inherit a world where they are treated with dignity and respect for whatever time they have on this earth—in other words, a world that acknowledges their full human worth? For Townsend the answer was clear. We must reject a "what have you done for me lately" society and respect the contributions of people whose shoulders we stand on. In doing so, we honor and respect our own personage; and in the process we enrich the value of everyone's life, young, old, and middle-aged.

The people agreed with Townsend because on a deep level they understood the principle of justice that Social Security embodied. They saw the plight of the elderly as decidedly unfair. The vivid language and imagery used to highlight their situation encouraged people to open their eyes and look at what was happening. It wasn't long before they saw the distinction between what was actually occurring and their innate sense of what was just. In bringing both empathic concern and vivid reality to the national consciousness, the Townsend movement, like those of the suffragists and labor, followed the blueprint that the abolitionists left their descendants.

Chapter VIII

Bookends

This chapter is named "Bookends" because the parallels between the fight to end the remnants of legal slavery (e.g., legal segregation and racial discrimination) and the struggle to abolish slavery itself serve to confirm the premise of this book: that the same two competing philosophies have been persistent throughout our history, and this hasn't yet subsided. I will show that even after the passage of a hundred years' time, the core arguments and conceptual divide between the two opposing sides remained fundamentally unchanged. This means that the basic philosophical differences forged during the abolitionist period are with us today—I say today, because the ideological battles of the 1960s have yet to be resolved.

If this premise is true it also shows that during the "in-between years" the philosophical wars of the antebellum period were lurking underneath the surface. They were still there while all the struggles for gender and social justice were taking place. It may be an historical irony that the truth about contemporary thinking would be uncovered by the emergence of a movement that seriously challenged the vestiges of legal slavery. And it's just as ironic that this truth would turn out to be not so contemporary after all.

This takes us to one of the most important destinations on our journey: the civil rights era. It's named after a movement for racial justice that was the direct descendant of nineteenth-century abolitionism. In the mid-twentieth century, America's original justice movement was reactivated in a more modern form. The unresolved issues left over from that period were being addressed seriously once again. What's amazing is that like the protagonists who fought over the issue of slavery a century earlier, both the supporters and opponents of civil rights claimed to be fighting for freedom. And as with the antislavery debate, they not only had diametrically opposite views of what freedom was, but their contrary opinions paralleled the differences of the previous struggle.

To understand this period we need to take a look at both Martin Luther King Jr.— the twentieth century's greatest American—and the civil rights movement he dedicated his life to. However, I will first digress for a moment. On the subject of civil rights the nation deserves a good deal of credit. Despite all the injustices in our history, we have shown a capacity for growth and fundamental change. This is why we see "bookends" in the birthdays we honor: the most important nineteenth-century birthday is that of Abraham Lincoln,[1] and for the twentieth century it's Martin Luther King Jr.'s.

Both of these men have come to symbolize their century's great eras of progress in racial justice. So a hand of applause—we got this right. And it should be added that in the case of King's birthday we got it even more right. For once it wasn't a president, politician, or someone with formal credentials who received the honor; it was a person who fought the battles that needed to be fought, not from a residence on high, but in the bloody fields and trenches below. King was a hero of the highest order, one who earned his place in history by proactively forging change and not just by favorably responding to events that others initiated.

In King's short thirteen years on the national scene (1955–1968) he, along with fellow civil rights activists, profoundly advanced the course of justice. Only our first justice movement—abolition—is comparable in importance. An African American born in Atlanta, Georgia, at a time when segregation and Jim Crow were in full swing meant that King grew up under dismal circumstances. Yet his immediate surroundings were quite the opposite. He had loving and nurturing parents, with his father being a Baptist minister and stellar member of the community.

He was a brilliant student, graduating from Morehouse College at the young age of nineteen. Three years later, in 1951, he received his divinity degree, and in 1955 earned his PhD from Boston University. At age twenty-five he became pastor of the Dexter Avenue Baptist Church in one of the most segregated cities in the country, Montgomery, Alabama.

We know that when King was first appointed pastor (or very soon thereafter) he was already eyeing the bigger picture and preparing to challenge an unjust system. Just a year after his appointment, there was a legal case involving a young African American woman who had been arrested for violating Alabama's segregation laws. She refused to surrender her seat to a white person on a public bus. King contemplated using the resources of his church in support of making this a test case challenging the state's segregation laws. However, since the woman was pregnant and not married, the impetus to move forward fizzled.[2, 3] A defendant who could easily become the focus of personal attacks was not what was desired.

Yet at this point King and his colleagues were waiting for a case they could back for this purpose. That case would come only months later, when an unquestionably respectable woman named Rosa Parks was arrested on a Montgomery bus for the exact same offense. That was on December 1, 1955, and what would follow set the country ablaze. A boycott of Montgomery's public buses immediately emerged as a protest to Ms. Parks's arrest. African Americans would sacrifice and if need be walk miles to work before they would allow themselves to be treated as second class citizens on city buses. The young twenty-six-year old pastor of the Dexter Avenue Baptist Church would quickly become the Montgomery bus boycott's leading spokesperson. Before the boycott's end, King's house would be set on fire and he would be arrested by authorities.[4] Yet during all the turmoil his voice would rise above the fray and his cry for justice would be heard around the world. The boycott wouldn't stop until more than a year later, when a U.S. District Court ruling ended segregation on all Montgomery public buses.

This was the first major blow against segregation in nearly a hundred years. Although the Supreme Court had previously decided that segregation in public schools was unconstitutional (1954), it was a legal decision that, like the Fourteenth Amendment itself, didn't immediately desegregate much of anything. The Montgomery bus boycott was an act of civil disobedience on the part of ordinary people who picked up the ball that the court had thrown them and ran with it. Amazingly, they actually scored; measurable results were finally achieved. It was clear that the courts and legalities alone would be ineffective without activating the grass roots. And now that process had begun.

In 1957, civil rights activists founded the Southern Christian Leadership Conference (SCLC) to harness the capacity of African American churches to help plan, organize, and effectuate nonviolent protests along the lines of the successful Montgomery bus boycott. Until his death, Martin Luther King Jr. would be SCLC's leader. While SCLC and King were not the only organization and leader working for civil rights and racial justice, they were the most upfront and prominent during this period.

Their aura of leadership would carry over to the methods they employed. SCLC's use of nonviolent (passive) resistance would come to be associated with the entire civil rights movement. From the inception of SCLC, both civil rights and nonviolent resistance would be the lead items in the mass media of the planet's premier superpower. Throughout the world, Martin Luther King Jr. would become the most prominent spokesperson for these values. This was openly acknowledged in 1964, when he was awarded the Nobel Peace Prize.

King's acceptance of the world's most revered award for promoting peace merits some words on his pacifism. His commitment to nonviolence ran deep. In addition to King's own insights, his understanding of this concept was derived from Jesus's Sermon on the Mount,[5] Thoreau's essay "On Civil Disobedience,"[6] Gandhi's achievements,[7] the works of Niebuhr,[8] Tolstoy,[9] and Tillich,[10] as well as Quaker compatriots.[11] It is almost certain that King's pacifist convictions, along with his disdain of imperialism, played a significant role in his ardent opposition to the Viet Nam War.

The central point is that King, like the great nineteenth-century abolitionists, was fully committed to taking the moral high ground. His appeal, like theirs, was always addressed to people's consciences and sense of fairness. When human beings are thought to have "better angels of their nature" (as Lincoln said in his First Inaugural Address) to guide them, violence becomes counterproductive. You might say that nonviolence is the only philosophy that recognizes human worth in all its aspects. King was a civil rights leader who understood that violence itself was a violation of a person's civil rights and being freed from it was an essential element of being free.

Along with nonviolence, King's commitment to civil rights included the other essential elements of being free. And for all of them, human dignity was the core ingredient. There could be no genuine or lasting freedom without it. This is why justice was so important. It was the one ideal that was broad enough to encompass everybody's well-being. Therefore, in practical political terms, all King's strivings were directed towards building a society where there would be, in addition to liberty, "justice for all."

The injustice that King and the civil rights movement battled against included racial discrimination in education, public accommodations, housing, employment, and civic life, as well as the nation's voting booths. While it was true that African Americans were the most aggrieved group and benefited more than others from the advancement of justice, many whites were also uplifted. Discriminatory practices like the poll tax and (phony) literacy tests originally designed to prevent African Americans from voting also (as an added "benefit" for the powers that be) denied many poor whites representation in the halls of government. Their elimination opened up the political system to poor people of all races.[12]

Yet there is no better example of King's commitment to "justice for all" than his efforts to obtain a fairer playing field for people of every race, religion, and gender. Social justice was just as important to King as any other variant of the ideal. Two of the demands of the historic 1963 March on Washington were an increased minimum wage (for all workers) and a public jobs program.[13] So it is no surprise that following this famous march King would address with ever increasing frequency social concerns such as unemployment and poverty.

In 1967 he began organizing a Poor People's Campaign to fight for economic justice. The formal campaign was to commence with a march to Washington D.C. scheduled for May 2, 1968. As we now know, King wasn't able to be there because he was assassinated a month earlier. His absence was certainly reflected in the campaign's lack of success.

However, it is important to look at what King had hoped to accomplish. The end goal of the campaign was the attainment of an "economic bill of rights" for all Americans.[14] Yes, all those positive freedoms that are in line with a truly just society—adequate employment, income, education, housing, access to what's necessary to meet basic human needs—were deemed to be just as important as the traditional negative (political) freedoms. Conservatives may have seen Lyndon Johnson's War on Poverty as a radical redistribution of wealth, but King saw it as just a bare beginning of what was needed to be done.

If there is any doubt about King's credentials as a full-blooded liberal, one only needs to look at the final chapter in his life. After two sanitation workers in Memphis, Tennessee, were accidently killed on the job, their fellow workers demanded union representation. This was denied them and they decided that their only recourse was to strike.[15] King felt that supporting their strike was a vital part of the Poor People's Campaign.[16]

Labor's right to organize and bargain collectively with their employers was seen by King as an essential requirement for obtaining economic justice. Unfortunately, King would be murdered in Memphis. Yet it's no accident that Martin Luther King Jr.'s last campaign was in support of striking workers.

King's concept of and commitment to justice is liberalism in its finest hour. Many of his great speeches spoke to its importance. In what many think was his greatest oration (in sea of great ones), the "I Have a Dream" speech delivered at the 1963 March on Washington, the ideal of justice rings loud and clear. In speaking to the marchers King said:

> I have a dream that one day even the state of Mississippi, a state sweltering with people's *injustices*, sweltering with the heat of oppression, will be transformed into an oasis of freedom and *justice* [my italics].[17]

We see that what's being opposed is injustice and the ultimate goal is to achieve freedom via its natural remedy, justice. Yet you needn't believe me; you can see for yourself how King interpreted it. But first, I think it's important to say that King's interpretation of how justice fits into the scheme of things is the best articulation of the liberal viewpoint that could ever be found. A little background is also needed. King, along with the entire civil rights movement, was heavily criticized for fermenting discontent and disorder, which was feared to have the potential for violence, even if unintended. King answered this charge in his response to other pastors who had written him a critical letter. It is now known as the *"Letter from a Birmingham Jail," since King wrote it while in jail for his active engagement in passive resistance.*

In his letter, King elaborates on the concept of justice. He addresses the injustice of preserving the peace when achieving real justice meant that some turmoil was required. In other words, as with abolitionism and other previous justice movements, he understood that making a mess was necessary. A portion of King's response reads as follows:

> I have almost reached the regrettable conclusion that the Negro's great stumbling block in his stride toward freedom is not the White Citizen's Counciler or the Ku Klux Klanner, but the white moderate, who is more devoted to "order" than to justice; who prefers a negative peace which is the absence of tension to a positive peace which is the presence of justice; who constantly says: "I agree with you in the goal you seek, but I cannot agree with your methods of direct action"; who paternalistically believes he can set the timetable for another man's freedom; who lives by a mythical concept of time and who constantly advises the Negro to wait for a "more convenient season." Shallow understanding from people of good will is more frustrating than absolute misunderstanding from people of ill will.[18]

Notice that his response is about far more than the need to stir things up. King explains why justice is at the core of it all. He says that there are two types of "peace"—a "negative peace which is the absence of tension" and a "positive peace which is the presence of justice." Of the two, it's understood that the only one that has any real meaning is the positive peace with justice. The negative peace without justice is vacuous. It's the presence of justice that gives meaning and therefore is what's most important.

One could easily substitute the word freedom for peace and you wouldn't have missed a beat. On this I have no problem going out on a limb and claiming that King would not only have consented to this substitution but that it speaks as much to King's own idea of freedom as it does to his idea of peace. Therefore for a person of the liberal mindset real freedom is more than just the absence of restraint; it requires the presence of justice. This means that any claim of liberty that is bereft of it is meaningless. Therefore to remain viable freedom must be a positive force that proactively engages in the pursuit of justice. This is liberalism in its purist form, stripped down to its bare essentials.

There is one added point that I cannot resist mentioning. When King talks about the person "who paternalistically believes he can set the timetable for another man's freedom" he supplies history with its best retort to Jefferson's and Madison's anemic opposition to slavery and their hostility towards those who were actively resisting it.

The civil rights movement of the 1950s and '60s would make our country a far fairer place. While Lyndon Johnson's War on Poverty would be cut short, the passage of the 1964 Civil Rights Act and the 1965 Voting Rights Act would have long-lasting consequences. The '64 Act would almost completely end legal segregation. Unfortunately, it would have less of an impact in the public schools than in other areas such as public accommodations and higher education. Yet the nation's formal commitment to racial justice would have a profound effect. This time around, justice in law would initiate an all-important process of cultural change.

Equally important, it was the first effective step since the passage of the Nineteenth Amendment toward a national commitment to gender equality. In banning discrimination in employment, Title VII of the '64 Act would also include the category of gender.[19] Building on this provision, Title IX would be added eight years later. It would be responsible for a more equal allocation of funds between the genders in school athletic programs.[20] So the next time you are watching women's sports on television, remember that the 1964 Civil Rights Act began a process that in large part is responsible for the United States frequently being in the top tier of women's international athletic competition.

The 1965 Voting Rights Act opened up the political system to all Americans. The long-term political implications of the legislation have been immense. They are still with us today, nearly fifty years later. The emerging political power of minority voters is a confirmation of this fact, and there is no sign of any letup (unless reactionaries succeed in once again preventing minorities from voting). This reshaping of the electorate has already lasted longer than the New Deal realignment.

Looking back on the core elements of the movement, we see that African American civil rights protesters were not hesitant to vividly describe their terrible experiences, including the social and economic deprivations endemic to a segregated society. They claimed that unfair and unequal treatment plus degraded living conditions was injustice—not consistent with freedom—and reason enough by itself to fight against it. This is how they justified the turmoil, and it was their rational for reaching out to the broader population. They asked those not directly affected to take the moral high ground and identify with their plight. Since they saw their fight against injustice as a fight for freedom, and they lived in a national state that supposedly revered freedom, they demanded that the federal government take positive actions to eliminate these injustices.

Doesn't all of this sound familiar? We have all the components of abolitionism. There was an appeal to empathic concern, outrage over injustice, determination to take the moral high ground, willingness to make a mess, and a conviction that genuine freedom couldn't be devoid of justice or removed from redressing the gross inequities in real-life conditions. Every one of these characteristics was as important as it was a century before. This leads us to our next but equally essential point of inquiry: how did the passage of a hundred years' time impact the Right's understanding of what was transpiring?

The Right Reacts: The Story of Justice's Enemies

Before we look at the position of King's conservative opposition, a point of order needs to be addressed. Neither mainline nor libertarian conservative viewpoints have substantively weakened or moderated since King's time. Although some conservative thinkers have reported a change of mind about particular issues of that period, they have never altered their fundamental concept of liberty or failed to apply it to other post-civil-rights-era situations. In fact if anything in the last fifty years, right-wing ideology has hardened and grown much more aggressive. It is less apologetic and its propensity for ideological purity is stronger today than ever before.

We should now take a look at the leading conservative thinker and publication of the civil rights era, namely William F. Buckley Jr. and his magazine, the *National Review* (*NR*). Together they provided conservatives with a platform on which to oppose Martin Luther King Jr. and the civil rights movement. During the greater New Deal era, the conservative worldview was out of favor and somewhat marginalized. Buckley's *National Review* carried the torch for beleaguered conservatism. It was upon this base that conservatism got its message out and battled against the liberal thinking of the day. Anyone who was recognized as a legitimate thinker within conservative circles had written something for the *National Review*.

Buckley appeared repeatedly on radio and television as the spokesperson for the conservative viewpoint. When PBS was looking for an esteemed intellectual to host a show with a conservative bent, it was none other than William F. Buckley Jr. who was chosen. Buckley would go on to have a very popular show on PBS, "Firing Line," which lasted many years. The successful growth of conservative ideology, the results of which we see today, was in large part built upon what Buckley began back in 1955 (the *NR*'s beginning year). As King's works best represent liberal thinking, Buckley's writings as well as the opinions expressed in his magazine were seen at the time by conservatives as best representing their perspective.

So how did Buckley and likeminded conservatives respond to the civil rights movement? For one thing, they were almost totally unaffected by emotional appeals, rage against injustice, or any type of empathic inclinations. You might say that they prided themselves on their hard rationality. In fact, in their blindness to the injustices perpetrated against "other people" we see strong comparisons with the nineteenth-century proslavery apologists. In a November 11, 1961, *NR* article entitled "Can We Desegregate, Hesto Presto?" Buckley said that:

> There are others who know that some problems are insoluble. These last are for the most part conservatives; and I am here to defend them.[21]

He then proceeded to add:

> Should we resort to convulsive measures that do violence to the traditions of our system in order to remove the forms of segregation in the South?[22] … [referring to the previous question] I say no.[23]

If Buckley's primary concern wasn't ameliorating gross injustices that were in clear view of any sighted person, what was it? In the same piece he clarifies what it was:

> … when Negroes have finally realized their long dream of attaining to the status of the white man, the white man will still be free; and that depends, in part, on the moderation of those whose inclination it is to build a superstate that will give them Instant Integration.[24]

Buckley's primary concern was the freedom of white people and avoiding the creation of a "superstate" that would endanger it. Note that the existence of freedom depended on whether or not whites lived in a country that placed too many restrictions on them. The fact that for nearly a century (legally free) African Americans had been subject to laws that significantly limited their life opportunities was not seen as a major impediment to the society's freedom.

This is of course is not unexpected. When your concept of freedom contains no understanding of justice, the sole question becomes "what's in it for me" (or for the people I identify with). Unfair treatment that takes away or restricts the freedom of others (those I don't identify with) is not seen as a significant concern. This is eerily similar to antebellum proslavery advocates who saw no contradiction between a society being free and at the same time having a large slave population.

There are so many other examples of Buckley's lack of sensitivity to the plight of his fellow human beings it's difficult to choose among them. So let us start with the supposed happiness of oppressed people. Remember how enthused proslavery advocates were when they observed how "carefree" the enslaved population appeared? They claimed that those "crazy" abolitionists didn't speak for the slaves. We see a version of this in Buckley's writings. Buckley was quick to picture prominent African Americans who were critical of the status quo as especially bitter and hostile people. They were of course not representative of ordinary blacks who weren't all that upset by their circumstances. The vocal and progressive African American author James Baldwin was often characterized as an example of such an aberration. There were others, including Louis Lomax and even (on multiple occasions) Martin Luther King Jr. Here is an example taken from his November 11, 1961, *NR* article:

> A distinguished New York Negro told the audience of the television program "Open End" that he did not know three white people in all New York with whom he felt genuinely comfortable, such is the prevalence of prejudice even in this cosmopolitan center. *Louis Lomax may be more sensitive, and hence bitter, than the*

average New York Negro, and so unrepresentative of the state of Negro serenity in the North; but then, too Dr. Martin Luther King is more sensitive, and so more bitter than, the average Southern Negro, and hence unqualified as a litmus of the Southern Negro's discontent [my italics].[25]

Another similarity is an expectation of revenge. We saw how fearful Jefferson and Madison were of freed blacks taking revenge on whites. This fear of African Americans getting even with whites was widespread throughout the antebellum South and, as with these two Founding Fathers, often used as a justification for maintaining the status quo. In a column entitled "The Issue at Selma" written just months before the passage of the 1965 Voting Rights Act, Buckley warned against:

> … a suddenly enfranchised, violently embittered Negro population which will take the vote and wield it as an instrument of vengeance, shaking down the walls of Jericho even to their foundations, and reawakening the terrible genocidal antagonisms that scarred the Southern psyche during the days of Reconstruction.[26]

Fear of legally freeing the enslaved population is now transferred to fear of (more) fully freeing them (e.g., permitting them to vote). And what is the fear based on? Same as under slavery, that they want revenge!

Like the highly intellectual defenders of slavery, Buckley was quite successful at sounding very knowledgeable with an in-depth understanding of both the classics and the affairs of the larger world. His arguments on behalf of the segregationist status quo appeared so exceptionally well informed that opponents could very easily become intimidated, and as a result appear foolish when they challenged him. Here is an example of his supposedly broad-based knowledge written in a *NR* editorial, appropriately entitled "Why the South Must Prevail":

> It is not easy, and it is unpleasant, to adduce statistics evidencing the median cultural superiority of White over Negro: but it is a fact that obtrudes, one that cannot be hidden by ever-so-busy egalitarians and anthropologists. The question, as far as the White community is concerned, is whether the claims of civilization supersede those of universal suffrage. The British believe they do, and acted accordingly, in Kenya, where the choice was dramatically one between civilization and barbarism, and elsewhere; the South, where the conflict is by no means dramatic, as in Kenya, nevertheless perceives important qualitative differences between its culture and the Negroes', and intends to assert its own.[27]

Note that like our antebellum "friend" Chancellor Harper, who showcased his knowledge of the Roman Empire's slave culture, Buckley highlighted his astute awareness of the British Empire's racism.

What about the idea that freedom is derived from individual character and therefore is to be achieved by one's own effort? Take a look at this excerpt from Buckley's June 3, 1961, *NR* editorial entitled "Let Us Try at Least to Understand":

> That is what they feel, and they feel that their life is for them to structure; that the Negro has grown up under generally benevolent circumstances, considering where he started and how far he had to go; that he is making progress; that the coexistence of that progress and the Southern way of life demand, for the time being, separation.[28]

Buckley and other *NR* writers believed that it was up to the people dissatisfied with their lot in life to earn their fair place in society, not by any collective action but by their own personal endeavors. They thought that white people had achieved an advanced culture by relying on individual initiative and thus were entitled to their privileges; but, on the other hand, the "Negro" hadn't advanced nearly as much and therefore was not entitled to be in an equal position with whites. This inequity between the two groups wasn't based on the restriction of anyone's freedom but was instead a reflection of important differences in temperament and character. Although Buckley intermixed racial advancement with the concept of individual advancement, the basic tenant of his argument was the same: those who demanded more freedom must first earn it, via their own solitary efforts. Any inequity in the society wasn't contrary to the concept of freedom; in fact the society was quite free. This was right out of the playbook of proslavery moralists.

How did Buckley view those on top? In the same editorial he talks about the reason why whites are so hostile to the Freedom Riders (biracial groups of people traveling through the South trying to integrate buses). He says:

> Jim Crow at the bus stations strikes us as unnecessary, and even wrong, [but] irrelevant [because it] does not strike the average white Southerner as wrong.[29]

Like the obvious but unstated opinion (it didn't need to be stated) of proslavery ideologues, those on top must have either earned their position or be representative of societies best "stock," and therefore it's their perspective that is central to any discussion. For this reason Buckley was contemptuous of the moral outrage being displayed by those challenging the established social order. In his 1959 book *Up from Liberalism*, he comments on the ruthlessness and "Righteousness" of such people:

> Consider first: the response to the Southerners' refusal to integrate their schools. To the extent that the Liberals have influence with the Executive and the Congress, that influence is being used to encourage a ruthless resolution in the teeth of Southern resistance. There to harden this resolution, of course are the fires of Righteousness.[30]

How about the antebellum tactic of narrowing (or changing) the definition by subtly adding erroneous qualifiers? In the same book he modifies the meaning of democracy by reducing its reach. Consider this passage:

> Democracy's finest bloom is seen only in its natural habitat, the culturally homogenous community. There, democracy induces harmony. Harmony (not freedom) is democracy's finest flower. Even a politically unstable society of limited personal freedom can be harmonious if governed democratically, if only because the majority understand themselves to be living in the house that they themselves built.[31]

Like with proslavery supporters, if one is forced to admit that a specific injustice really does hamper a person's freedom, you just move the goalposts and change the wording so everything sounds good. It's not freedom that we strive for, but democracy, and as we all know, "Harmony (not freedom) is democracy's finest flower." So like with Rev. James Thornwell's "order and regulated freedom" we now have from Mr. Buckley "democracy"-induced "harmony."

Yet if pressed to the point that any reasonable person would have to concede that harmony wasn't the same as democracy, Buckley's rational argument breaks down and reveals itself for the self-serving illogical prejudge it is. Once again from "Why the South Must Prevail":

If the majority wills what is socially atavistic, then to thwart the majority may be, though undemocratic, enlightened. It is more important for any community, anywhere in the world, to affirm and live by civilized standards, than to bow to the demands of the numerical majority.[32]

As any claim to be speaking on behalf of freedom or democracy withers away we see the goalposts on the move once again. Even if "undemocratic," it is "enlightened," and that is what's required for "civilization." Or in other words, for Buckley freedom was purely a parochial concept that pertains to his (civilized) group alone. And it is shockingly close to the view of the South's leading defender of slavery, John C. Calhoun, since it's also dependent on another group's lack of freedom.

It is clear that Buckley's opposition to civil rights was but a subcategory of his ambivalence about—if not outright distaste for—democracy itself. In the same article he writes:

> Rather, it is whether the White community in the South is entitled to take such measures as are necessary to prevail, politically and culturally, in areas in which it does not predominate numerically? ... The sobering answer is yes—the White community is so entitled because, for the time being, it is the advanced race ... [the South] perceives important qualitative differences between its culture and the Negroes', and intends

to assert its own ... [of which Buckley approves].[33]

As an aside, I must say that if you had any lingering doubts about my previous assessment of Buckley's views concerning the appropriate position and status of the respective races, this article should now put them to rest. The piece is just as telling in regards to Buckley's views on democracy. He had absolutely no difficulty dissing the "majority" if the "minority" is considered to be more "civilized." Since this is coming from a "proud" anticommunist cold warrior who claimed to be a fighter against human tyranny, one would think that he would have been somewhat embarrassed by the inconsistencies in his argument. Yet this wasn't even close to being the case. Universal suffrage was just too much of a sticking point (i.e., dangerous). Buckley had to find a way around it without being too obvious or acknowledging any flaws in his reasoning. Condescending language and subtle ridicule would serve this purpose. He belittles the desirability of a fair playing field by insinuating that universal suffrage is just a numerical majority and therefore not of the highest importance. An intelligent person wouldn't take cold mathematics all that seriously. To do so would be to show your ignorance. If one still lacks a viable argument after all the pretense and purposefully misleading intellectualizations, one falls back on a passive–aggressive attack. What's so frightening is that the battle for universal suffrage is still being waged. While continuing to claim to be freedom's defenders, today's conservatives (including the modern

NR) haven't abandoned their search for devious ways to limit the voting rights of minorities.

Yet in this very pursuit, Buckley—unlike today's conservatives—didn't attempt to hide his suspicion of democracy and the fact that his distaste for liberalism resulted in large part from his associating democracy with it. His book *Up from Liberalism* reads like a better title would have been *Up from Democracy*. The work is an artful attempt to use linguistic subtlety, as he does with his dissing of numerical majorities, to mock the liberals' commitment to democratic values. He condescendingly writes:

> It follows, of course, that to harbor an undemocratic thought is to be guilty, under the law of liberalism, of the highest form of treason.[34]

A page later he is more direct when speaking of his own commitment to such values:

> The democracy of universal suffrage is not a bad form of government; it is simply not necessary nor inevitably a good form of government.[35]

This speaks best to Buckley's understanding of freedom; it needn't be for everyone. Could it be that Buckley's mindset was indicative of just one idiosyncratic conservative? To dispel this impression here is more of the same from other *NR* writers.

A July13, 1957, *NR* article by Richard Weaver, entitled "Integration is Communization" (shades of Rev. Thornwell again):

'Integration' and 'Communization' are, after all, pretty closely synonymous. In light of what is happening today, the first may be little more than a euphemism for the second. It does not take many steps to get from the 'integrating' of facilities to the 'communizing' of facilities, if the impulse is there." ... In a free society, associations for educational, cultural, social, and business purposes have a right to protect their integrity against political fanaticism. The alternative to this is the destruction of free society and the replacement of its functions by government, which is the *Marxist dream* [my italics].[36]

A September 7, 1965, *NR* article by Will Herberg entitled "Civil Rights and Violence: Who are the Guilty Ones?" accusing Martin Luther King Jr. and the civil rights movement of fermenting violence (Los Angeles race riots have just taken place and the people fighting against racism are seen as being responsible):

For years now, the Rev. Dr. Martin Luther King and his associates have been deliberately undermining the foundations of internal order in this country. With their rabble-rousing demagoguery, they have been cracking the "cake of custom" that holds us together. With their doctrine of "civil disobedience" they have been teaching hundreds of thousands of Negroe ... particularly the adolescents and the children—that it is perfectly all right to break the law and defy constituted authority if you are a Negro-with-a-grievance; *in protest against injustice* ... And they have done more than talk. They have on occasion after occasion, in almost every part of the country, called out their mobs on the streets, promoted "school strikes," sit-ins, lie-ins, in explicit violation of the law and in explicit violation of the public authority. They have taught anarchy and chaos by word and deed ... [my italics].[37]

But most disturbing is the fact that excerpts from many of these *NR* articles are once again appearing on far-out right-wing and racist websites (e.g., *American Renaissance,* Alternative Right.com) for the stated purpose of castigating the current-day *NR* for lowering its profile on questions of race. Highlighting the magazine's historical position on the civil rights movement is a clever way to provide them with the necessary cover for their own extremism. This tells us a good deal about the *NR*'s level of discourse at a time when the nation was confronted with a defining moral choice. Look at this representative sample of six *NR* articles in an ocean of likeminded ones, relied on as a source by modern-day purveyors of the worst imaginable in an attempt to appear intellectually legitimate.

A 2012 *American Renaissance* article quoting a July 2, 1963 NR editorial on what is all the fuss (over civil rights) about:

> The Negro people have been encouraged to ask for, and to believe they can get, nothing less than the evanescence of color, and they are doomed to founder on the shoals of existing human attitudes—their own included.[38]

A 2012 *American Renaissance* article quoting a June 2, 1964, *NR* editorial commenting on the tenth anniversary of the Supreme Court's decision declaring segregation unconstitutional:

> But whatever the exact net result in the restricted field of school desegregation, what a price we are paying for Brown! It would be ridiculous to hold the Supreme Court solely to blame for the ludicrously named "civil rights movement"—that is, the Negro revolt ... But the Court carries its share of the blame. Its decrees, beginning with Brown, have on the one hand encouraged the least responsible of the Negro leaders in the course of extra-legal and illegal struggle that we now witness around us ... Brown, as *National Review* declared many years ago, was bad law and bad sociology. We are now tasting its bitter fruits. Race relations in the country are ten times worse than in 1954.[39]

A 2012 *American Renaissance* article quoting a March 9, 1965, *NR* article by Russell Kirk (author of *The Conservative Mind* and our John C. Calhoun devotee) on the 1965 Voting Rights Act, mixed with opinions on the importance of whites maintaining power in South Africa:

> [Black voting rights in U.S. is a] theoretical folly [but in South Africa] if applied, would bring anarchy and the collapse of civilization ... In a time of virulent "African nationalism," ... how is South Africa's "European" population ... to keep the peace and preserve a prosperity unique in the Dark Continent? ... to govern tolerably a society composed of several races, among which only a minority is civilized.[40]

A 2012 *AlternativeRight.com* article quoting a September 28, 1957, *NR* article by James J. Kilpatrick (federal troops had recently been sent to Little Rock, Arkansas, to uphold a court order that directed the desegregation of public schools):

> Conceding, for the sake of discussion, that the Negro pupil has these new rights, what of the white community? Has it none? [Whites are seen as the victims of desegregation].[41]

A 2012 *AlternativeRight.com* article quoting another article by Kilpatrick dated September 24, 1963, giving reasons why what would become the 1964 Civil Rights Act should be rejected by Congress:

I believe this bill is a very bad bill. In my view, the means here proposed are the wrong means ... In the name of achieving certain "rights" for one group of citizens this bill would impose some fateful compulsions on another group of citizens.[42]

A 2012 *AlternativeRight.com* article quoting still another article by Kilpatrick dated April 20, 1965, asking "Must we repeal the Constitution to give the Negro the vote?"[43] and attacking supporters of the 1965 Voting Rights Act for "perverting the Constitution":

Over most of this century, the great bulk of Southern Negroes have been genuinely unqualified for the franchise ... Segregation is a fact, and more than a fact; it is a state of mind. It lies in the Southern subconscious next to man's most elementary instincts, for self-preservation, for survival, for the untroubled continuation of a not intolerable way of life.[44]

This rendition of the arguments as well as the contemporary applications pertaining to the works of Buckley and the other *NR* writers of the period is a good indicator not only of how they viewed the situation when the unresolved issues of the abolitionist era resurfaced, but more fundamentally their core hostility to justice (i.e., redressing wrongs done to others). In later years the magazine supposedly purged its white supremacist contributors (for obvious self-serving reasons) and stopped engaging in overt racism. Its current editors even express regret about its past positions on civil rights (which of course is still of use to others on the Right). Nevertheless the modern-day publication chooses to ignore the institutional racism that continues to exist and remains quite hostile to other people's struggles for justice. The *NR*'s shameful past has not really disappeared, but instead has just been covered over; its antagonistic attitude towards justice is unapologetically the same.

However, if you don't believe the data presented or think that I stacked the deck, you can go online and read almost all of Buckley's works at Hillsdale College's "Buckley Online." You can also go to *National Review* online. That being said, we should hear a less liberal opinion than mine on Buckley, the *NR* and conservative thinking of that era. William Voegeli is the senior editor of the *Claremont Review of Books*. He is the author of *Never Enough: America's Limitless Welfare State*. The book's title gives you some idea how (non-) liberal Mr. Voegeli is. *Wikipedia* notes that "Many consider it [the *Claremont Review of Books*] a conservative intellectual answer to the liberal *New York Review of Books*."[45] In an article written for Claremont's 2008 summer issue, Voegeli makes some good observations concerning the Right's mindset during the civil rights struggle. He writes:

> This opposition to Big Government engendered conservative opposition to every milestone achievement of the civil rights movement. *National Review* denounced Brown v. Board of Education (1954), calling it "an act of judicial

usurpation," one that ran "patently counter to the intent of the Constitution" and was "shoddy and illegal in analysis, and invalid as sociology." It opposed the 1964 Civil Rights Act and 1965 Voting Rights Act on similar grounds. A Buckley column dismissed the former as a "federal law, artificially deduced from the Commerce Clause of the Constitution or from the 14th Amendment, whose marginal effect will be to instruct small merchants in the Deep South on how they may conduct their business."[46]

For the Right it was all about keeping the powers of the federal government at bay. Like slavery's supporters, who were adamant in protecting the prerogatives of slave states, conservatives were adamant in protecting the right of segregationist states to preserve the last (legal) remnants of slavery. "Proper" institutional relationships trumped human rights. If one goes deeper, it wasn't even a question of individual liberty. During that period many deep Southern states had laws against integrated public accommodations.[47] A retailer that chose not to discriminate would have been arrested and charged with a crime. Although formally it didn't approve of such laws, the *NR* didn't appear to be all that outraged by them, as evidenced by their low priority on its political to-do list. You would have been well advised not to hold your breath waiting for the *NR* to make the constitutionality of these state laws—long notorious for violating individual rights—a central theme. The irony of it all is that states' rights, or the prerogatives of a political entity legally defined as the state, superseded an individual's rights almost every time.

On a similar point in his discussion of Buckley, Voegeli really hits the nail on the head:

> The single most disturbing thing about Buckley's reactions to the civil rights controversies was the *asymmetry of his sympathies*—genuine concern for Southern whites beset by integrationists, but more often than not, perfunctory concern for Southern blacks beset by bigots [my italics].[48]

This "asymmetry of sympathies" permeated conservative thought. It ran so deep that it affected their perception of events not only at home but also abroad. After virtually the entire world supported levying sanctions against South African apartheid, Buckley and other leading American conservatives—including such notables as George Will and William Safire—remained ardent opponents of any actions taken against that country.[49, 50] Their efforts to read any concept of justice out of the equation meant that they had to downgrade the importance of the victim the same as they did the violation. On both accounts, their task was similar to that of the proslavery apologists: it was immense. What existed in both the U.S. and South Africa were not ordinary slices of life where logic dictated that you were being naïve and going too far in trying to rewrite every injustice at the expense of a system that in practice worked well. No, these were extraordinary conditions that were more analogous to what Holocaust deniers attempt to explain away.

In these situations it wasn't a trivial injustice that was at the center of the controversy but a colossal one—one so large, in fact, that any product of logical reasoning, no matter how good it looked on paper, that ignored or minimized the importance of such horrific injustice, should have led a person who truly valued freedom to seriously question the conclusion reached. Unfortunately, this irrational (and self-serving) "asymmetry of sympathies" proved to be up to the task. It provided the Right with an excellent pair of blinders. Without even flinching, they were able to claim to be speaking on freedom's behalf while simultaneously ignoring the victims of some of its worst violations. Observe how similar this is to John Patrick Daly's description in *When Slavery Was Called Freedom* of the attitude prevalent among antebellum Southerners: "Likewise, this traditional understanding of freedom gave evangelicals a basis for *tolerating almost any form of labor exploitation without blanching* [my italics]."

One would have hoped that conservative thinking had gone in exactly the opposite direction, making Buckley's opinions on civil rights responsible for diminishing his influence in right-wing circles. Unfortunately, this is not what happened. An ever-widening audience would see him as their voice.[51, 52] This shows us that Buckley's views were not isolated or idiosyncratic ones but rather were embraced by the larger segment of the conservative community. Although William Voegeli was refreshingly frank about the Right's failure during the civil rights era, his article doesn't explain why it occurred. This is because he doesn't really see how the failure he admits to is part and parcel of a much broader theme. He casts civil rights as a stand-alone issue bypassing any generic concept of justice. Voegeli offers no explanation for the Right's asymmetry of sympathies (i.e., lack of appropriate empathy) or its inability to comprehend the magnitude of the injustice involved other than that it was trying to prevent what he sees as government intrusions such as future affirmative action programs. In fact Voegeli even uses this weak excuse in an attempt to somewhat mitigate what he admits are Buckley's awful positions.

Unfortunately, this is where we see a facsimile of Lysander Spooner's idea about how the end of slavery made conditions worse for white people (i.e., the majority of the population); if we had left well enough alone everything still might have turned out all right. The real world need not prioritize the concerns it confronts since its true nature is perfectly flush without rough edges. The historical existence of slavery and segregation in a society that supposedly reveres freedom should have told Voegeli otherwise. But most important, despite his honesty about the specifics of the situation his lack of any viable rationale for Buckley's escalating popularity leaves us with the most bottom-line and obvious explanation. And that only further confirms that, stripped down to its bare essentials, this was in its purist form the mindset of a community that still more than half a century afterwards sees no need to give the ideal of justice its proper due.

We have now reached a critical crossroads where a most important question needs to be asked: What are the odds that those who believe in a substantive concept of liberty, one that actually matters, would be so blind to so many outrages? No matter how you cut it, the evidence supports a harsh answer. The fact that Buckley along with most prominent American conservatives was oblivious to some of history's worst infringements of human rights indicates that either they knew nothing about the genuine item or their concept of liberty was a total perversion. Doesn't this all sound familiar? It should, since their harsh, empathy-free, and self-serving intellectualizations were analogous to the arguments employed by antebellum defenders of slavery's status quo. Their understanding of the meaning of freedom was also almost identical, and it doesn't take a pre-Civil-War-period expert to see it. Attempts on both their parts to thwart human progress confirm that any concept of freedom which is devoid of justice is really not freedom at all but prejudicial inclinations masquerading as such.

In fairness to Buckley, it should be noted that while he never apologized, many decades later it was reported by Bloomberg.com in a March 31, 2006 article by Heidi Przybyla and Judy Woodruff that he had at least somewhat recanted on civil rights. The exact report reads: "Buckley said he had a few regrets, most notably his magazine's opposition to civil rights legislation in the 1960s. 'I think that the impact of that bill should have been welcomed by us,' he said."[53] Assuming the accuracy of this report, it appears that Buckley begrudgingly conceded that the actions of the federal government were not only effective but desirable. However, this was at best a (quite peripherally and softly articulated) personal recant. There was no effort to encourage others to do the same, and in conservative quarters there was no audible cheering.

More important, this doesn't alter the fact that the lack of concern for the "other" underscores the Right's thinking. For obvious self-serving reasons, the Right has made it a point to showcase likeminded African Americans. During the last few decades more of them have been seen in conservative circles than ever before. This likely had some effect on Buckley's attitude towards African Americans. It is quite possible that for Buckley they became less of an outside group, and as a result his stance softened. A similar scenario appeared to happen with gay people, when those in his social circle "came out."[54] It is too bad that he didn't get to know more people who were struggling economically, or were without health insurance. Their absence in his inner circle may explain why he didn't change his mind about policies that negatively affected those less financially secure than him.

At its core it's not about the specific group that's classified as the outsider, but rather the need for such groups and the tunnel vision that gives rise to them. Despite progress in racial justice, the Right's need for someone to blame has only intensified over the last forty years. Governor Romney's comment implying that 47 percent (a number progressively on the rise as years pass by) of the population lives off the other 53 percent was no accident. He knew his audience of diehard GOP contributors, and what he said appears frequently on right-wing websites. It's unfortunate that due to the need for a people to target—along with the inability to identify with—individuals outside their comfort zone, conservatives remain unconcerned about the well-being of a large number of their fellow human beings.

In the beginning of this chapter I stated that the core disagreements between anti- and proslavery advocates were reenacted again in the mid-twentieth century. I have presented evidence to show that the driving force and philosophical perspective of the civil rights movement paralleled the nineteenth-century abolitionist cause and its conservative opposition paralleled the mindset of abolition's opponents. I think I made a strong case for this, but it's up to individual readers to judge for themselves. I also asserted that the ideological divide of the 1960s is still with us today. If both these claims are true, it suggests that our contemporary political divisions go all the way back to the birth of our first justice movement.

Chapter IX

Bookends with Blinders

The struggles for abolition and civil rights were entangled efforts across time, jointly sharing responsibility for shaping much of what our nation has become. As already stated in the previous chapter, they can be said to be America's historical bookends. By including in this picture, the intransigence of right-wing thought, we gain an even greater understanding of what's really behind today's political controversies. In fact it is their persistent world outlook that supplies the crucial evidence supporting my claim that the roots of our current philosophical differences go all the way back to abolitionist times.

I will show that from an ideological standpoint conservatives haven't come to terms with the changes brought about by the Civil War let alone the more recent ones of the civil rights era. Since active opposition to the achievements of the latter struggle would once again stir up too many disconcerting truths—not to mention a political hornet's nest—a number of modern-day right-wing theorists choose instead to address the fundamental disagreements of the antebellum period. In doing so, they not only reveal the truth about themselves but unintentionally expose the broader link that connects the Right's past- and present-day thinking.

At the time when William F. Buckley Jr. supposedly softened his position on civil rights, the ideology of the fastest-growing conservative subgroup, (capitalist) libertarianism, was on the rise within that community as well as the general society. One of its biggest heroes is the previously mentioned former Texas congressman and repeated presidential candidate, Ron Paul. Paul's assessment of the civil rights movement is totally in line with Buckley's original view. Paul is theoretically opposed to the landmark civil rights legislation of the 1960s. Yet for the reason just stated Paul, has more to say about the philosophical battles of the pre-Civil War period than the ones during the civil rights era. In fact, Paul's current views make the bond between proslavery ideology of the antebellum South and modern conservative thought even clearer than Buckley's did a half a century earlier. Therefore we should take a close look at them.

Paul says that 600,000 Americans died senselessly in the Civil War.[1] And who does he see as primarily responsible for these deaths? The answer is President Lincoln and his supporters.[2] In espousing these ideas Paul both relies on and publicly acknowledges the work of historian Thomas DiLorenzo. Paul frequently tells people to read DiLorenzo.[3] To date DiLorenzo has written two books on Lincoln, *The Real Lincoln* and *Lincoln Unmasked.* I doubt that Mr. DiLorenzo would disagree with me when I call him Lincoln's severest critic. Since Paul's ideas about this period in American history are, by his own admission, based on DiLorenzo's scholarly work, and are essentially the same, I will unless otherwise noted address Paul's positions as "Paul/DiLorenzo."

For Paul/DiLorenzo, Lincoln not only bears responsibility for the Civil War, but is also faulted for not getting rid of slavery! The reasoning goes that since every other country in the world abolished slavery without war, the United States should have done the same. They say that if Lincoln had used diplomacy to end slavery he could have avoided a military conflict. [4, 5] Paul/DiLorenzo believe that Lincoln was determined to go to war, that it was his plan all along.[6, 7] From their perspective, the institution of slavery offered Lincoln a golden opportunity to initiate a war for the purpose of rejecting the notion that the "consent came from the people."[8] In other words, they see Lincoln using the Civil War to get rid of the original intent of the Republic.[9, 10] — putting it in Paul's direct words, "to cancel out opportunity of choice."[11] In addition to his being responsible for the Civil War, Paul/DiLorenzo think that Lincoln's policies have had harmful and long-lasting consequences. They even claim that his actions continue to plague us today. Ron Paul in speaking about their effect said "unfortunately that is what we have had to live with for so many years and has given us so many problems."[12]

Since the views of Paul/DiLorenzo are associated with a living and fast-growing political movement, I think it's of prime importance that this chapter centers on exposing their claims for the fiction they are. So let's begin with DiLorenzo's last book on Lincoln, *Lincoln Unmasked*. In it he shows his true colors by falling back on a common argument used by neo-Confederate apologists to support their claim that the North didn't oppose slavery any more than the South did. DiLorenzo says that after slavery was abolished in their states, New England slavemasters used this as an opportunity to sell their slave property to southern plantation owners for a rewarding monetary gain.[13] He goes on to say that New England abolitionists opposed slavery because they wanted to abolish "the presence of black people from their midst."[14]

Of course it's not difficult to answer these weak arguments. No one is claiming that New England slavemasters were any better than their Southern counterparts. The important point is that in terms of their influence and ideology slaveowners were in a much weaker position in New England than in the South. As far as accusing Northern abolitionists of being "racists," the answer is even easier. Has DiLorenzo ever read any prominent abolitionists? Since I have read his books, I know that he has. I have also read the works of the leading abolitionists and I know how ridiculous his charges are. Therefore the only other explanation is that he knowingly distorts the Northern abolitionist sentiment by selectively quoting (and out of context) only those sources that support his contrived position while purposefully ignoring overwhelming evidence to the contrary. You can Google Rev. John Rankin's *Letters on American Slavery* and read online what the leading abolitionists had to say; then judge for yourself.

DiLorenzo also reveals his true leanings in his first book on Lincoln, *The Real Lincoln*. In this work he refers favorably to one of the leading libertarian conservative economists, Friedrich Hayek. DiLorenzo characterizes him as "one of the great defenders of capitalism during the twentieth century."[15] This isn't surprising. As with Paul, the underlying thinking behind DiLorenzo's historical analysis is based on a right-wing libertarian worldview. And this perspective is broader than just having an opinion about centuries-old historical events; it's an all-encompassing reactionary outlook.

In keeping with their reactionary leanings, Paul/DiLorenzo think that if the slave states had won the Civil War, things would be wonderful today.[16] A perfect libertarian constitution that is a near copy of the original Constitution could still exist in North America. If so, millions of people wouldn't have to endure the tyranny of programs like Social Security and Medicare, not to mention child labor, worker safety, or environmental protections; the Founding Fathers never mentioned them. I should note that I am being a bit presumptuous about their specific wording, but believe me, not much.

Of course, as already implied, slavery would have disappeared without a war. The victory of the slave states would have insured this. Think of the misfortune that could have been avoided if only the free states and the trouble making abolitionists understood that there was no need to struggle against slavery; it would have simply gone away by itself, poof. After all, didn't the slave states fight aggressively to preserve the institution, so it could vanish overnight? Paul/DiLorenzo try to solve these inherent contradictions by blaming slavery (and later segregation) on the people who actively battled against it rather than those who fought to perpetuate the evil. Even the crimes of the Ku Klux Klan are their fault. DiLorenzo writes:

> Had the Republican Party not been so determined to recruit ex-slaves as political pawns in its crusade to loot the taxpayers of the South, the Ku Klux Klan might never even have come into existence.[17]

Note that the "ex-slaves" are presented as just pawns, not historical agents in their own right. They can also be seen as responsible for the Klan—if only they hadn't allowed themselves to be duped. Whether it is nineteenth-century freed slaves or twentieth-century workers, this downplaying of the role of grassroots victims (and activists) is endemic to Paul/DiLorenzo's ideology; but more about that later.

DiLorenzo has written that slavery's demise would have been certain due to the progression of enlightenment ideals. Yet he not only ignores the role that historical (human) agents must play in advancing new concepts but sides with the group that was most estranged from them (to confirm this one need only read the writings of Confederate scholars; see Chapter V). Most significant, Paul/DiLorenzo claim that since Southern slavery was destined to become unprofitable it would have ended anyways due to economic self-interest. Interestingly, these two believers in "ideas" chose to minimize the importance of people's belief systems. For 250 years the Southern population had been immersed in a culture that justified slavery. Race had become so primary that even their (non-white) children were "barricaded" behind the color line. Nevertheless, they think that economics would have been determinant, and relatively quickly. Wow, they are right-wing Marxists! Unfortunately, as twentieth-century left-wing Marxists would discover, it doesn't work like that; human attitudes and culture don't change that fast or that easily. But most absurd, in the absence of a scintilla of objective evidence, they like to pretend that slaveholders were willing to free their slaves for monetary compensation. If you read what the proslavery side had to say, hell would freeze over before you would find this option mentioned even once. Their ridiculous speculations aside, to paraphrase Martin Luther King Jr., what gives them the right to put a timetable (and a murky one at that) on another human being's freedom! Unfortunately this is what results when one sees liberty as self-centered individualism, devoid of any commitment to justice.

Yet even beyond the question of slavery, what about citizenship rights (Fourteenth Amendment) and voting rights (Fifteenth Amendment); would they also have shortly followed? I guess there is no way of knowing what exactly would have occurred if the South had won the day. Yet there are a few things that we do know with absolute certainty.

We know that unlike Paul/DiLorenzo's view that slavery was summarily doomed even if the South had prevailed, segregation and denial of full citizenship rights weren't. They didn't just go away by themselves. We know that the former Confederate states never voluntarily granted African Americans the right to vote. We know that for at least one hundred years following the Civil War the former Confederate states had yet to recognize African Americans as real (or equal) citizens, opting instead to marginalize their existence by every legal (and illegal) means possible. We know that a century after slavery's abolition was forced upon the South, the former Confederate states fought the federal government tooth and nail to prevent the "abolition" of a condition of "semi-slavery" that had been instituted when full-fledged slavery was no longer an option for them. We know that it wasn't until there was direct intervention on the part of the "tyrannical" federal government that "Lincoln helped to create" that African Americans achieved any substantive improvement in their situation, including the right to vote.

It doesn't end there. We know that the legislature of one of the most Confederate of the former Confederate states, Mississippi (the home state of Jefferson Davis), didn't ratify the amendment abolishing slavery (Thirteenth Amendment) until 1995. And even then it took the state an additional eighteen years to make it official (i.e.; the U.S. Archivist wasn't formally notified until 2013!).[18] We know that it wasn't until African American members of the state legislature became aware of this situation that any action was taken—130 years after the Civil War's conclusion.[19] We know that the passage of the Fourteenth Amendment, which granted former enslaved persons citizenship (a step beyond the abolition of slavery), was one of the major consequences of the defeat of the slave states in the Civil War. We know that, three decades prior to 1995, Congress passed major civil rights legislation that in large part drew its constitutional authority from this Civil-War-era Fourteenth Amendment. We know that this legislation contained game-changing voting rights provisions. We know that as a result of these voting rights provisions, African Americans living in Mississippi were by the mid 1990s well represented in the state legislature. We know that without this law their presence would have been highly unlikely. And even without knowing for sure, we can be almost certain that absent this African American representation, Mississippi would still today not have ratified the amendment abolishing slavery.

In this regard there is an additional piece of information that should be known. In his writings DiLorenzo praises (what he thinks are) the improvements made by the Confederate Constitution. Yet he conveniently fails to mention that the Confederate Constitution specifically prohibited Congress from outlawing slavery.[20] Mississippi aside, since the Confederacy, unlike the Union, was composed of only slave states, a successful Southern succession would have made it a lot more difficult to garner a supermajority to amend the Constitution and lawfully abolish the institution in North America.

Oh yes, and let's not forget there are few more interesting facts that we know. We know that in every country that abolished slavery with or without war, there was at least a metaphorical battle waged between two opposing sides. We know that in every case, including ours, the proslavery side used every means at their disposal to resist abolition. And given our unique federal system and slavery's geographic distribution, the proslavery side in the U.S. had a good deal more political means at their disposal (i.e., states' rights and eventually succession). You can also add to this list the fact that unlike most other nations our republic was founded in large part by slaveholders who were quite cognizant of their long-term interests. It was no accident that obtaining racial justice was hindered by multiple constitutional provisions that required supermajorities. Now look at DiLorenzo's list of the countries that abolished slavery without war:

- British Empire
- Brazil
- Cuba
- Puerto Rico
- Argentina
- Colombia
- Chile
- Central America
- Mexico
- Bolivia
- Uruguay
- French and Danish colonies Ecuador

- Peru
- Venezuela[21]

What's even more crucial, we know that not one of these nations ever experienced, following formal abolition, a one hundred year period of denial of basic human rights, including racial segregation, terrorism, and lynching. Unfortunately, this dismal situation was unique to the American South. You might call it an American exceptionalism that you don't want to brag about; and this time you can't blame Abraham Lincoln. Nevertheless Paul/DiLorenzo still try to, but they can't shirk the fact that we are looking at the span of a century. During most of this period (after 1877) the rest of the nation kept its hands off of the South, allowing the region a considerable (even undue) amount of internal autonomy. One hundred years is certainly enough time to expect the perpetrators and apologists for Jim Crow to take responsibility and not try to pass it on to people (like Lincoln) who weren't even alive during the nearly ten decades of post-Civil War atrocities.

We know because of these and numerous other historical facts that even with the defeat of the slave states in 1865, a "God-awful" long struggle for justice ensued. And we know that that even today the goals of this struggle are vigorously resisted by a good number of former Confederate states. Many of their legislatures, along with some Northern ones controlled by like-minded sympathizers, have recently passed bills with the intention of suppressing the vote of African Americans and other minorities. We know all this for certain—until enough time passes, memories fade, and a future DiLorenzo comes along and tries to convince us that it wasn't George Wallace or Ross Barnett (two Deep South governors who actively opposed racial integration) who slowed down the demise of segregation, but instead it was Lyndon Johnson (who reportedly liked to tell racially-charged jokes) and Hubert Humphrey (whose rabid manner offended the South) who were the real culprits in allowing legal segregation to last for so long.

Unfortunately for the Paul/DiLorenzos of the world, this time hasn't yet come. Therefore it's no wonder that they choose to focus on the 1860s rather than the 1960s. The fact that legal slavery exists only in textbooks means that for most people the historical details of the antebellum era have long been forgotten. The same cannot be said about segregation and racial discrimination; they remain a believable reality. Memories of conservative resistance to redressing these injustices are still too fresh. As a result, the denier's ability to stretch the truth is restricted. However, most important is the possible reason behind William F. Buckley Jr.'s reported recanting. An all-too-recent civil rights history attests to the fact that federal intervention to safeguard the rights of citizens can be both necessary and successful. This has been witnessed firsthand by too many people alive today and is exactly opposite of the "snake oil" that Paul/DiLorenzo are peddling. Yet despite their efforts to ignore the more recent struggle and instead focus on the earlier one, the truth won't go away. The two eras cannot be separated, because they are not just discrete points on a timeline but rather part of the same ongoing continuum. The battle against slavery and its lingering properties wasn't completely won in 1865 or for that matter in 1965. It has been a battle that has been fought in stages with partial victories here and there. And yes, after a while (150 years or so) those partial victories begin to add up. Yet the complete elimination of slavery's ugly appendages—such as de facto segregation, denial of voting rights, and all other policies designed to reinstitute through the back door shards of the original institution—has not only been a particularly long struggle in the Unites States but to date is still a work in progress.

In light of the obvious, I suggest that Paul/DiLorenzo reconsider their ludicrous claims and apologize to our sixteenth president for their statements about him going to war instead of just getting rid of slavery, poof. Unfortunately, don't expect an apology anytime soon. Their disparaging of Lincoln is likely to continue. Therefore, it's important that some of their attacks on him be examined. The primary reason is not because he has to be defended as an American icon, but that the specific nature of the attacks reveals much more about the detractors than it does about Lincoln.

Paul/DiLorenzo fault Lincoln for not being a strong enough opponent of slavery and disliking African Americans.[22, 23] The fact that he once said he favored keeping slavery if it would preserve the union is used to bolster their argument that Lincoln wasn't really against slavery.[24, 25] They also say that because he didn't believe that African Americans could ever be equal in America, and thought it best to deport them back to Africa, shows that Lincoln was hostile to African Americans (or was racist).[26] This is essentially selective character assassination, as they hold him to standards that they conveniently fail to apply to many of his contemporaries. Interestingly, they choose to compare Lincoln to the small number of exceptional people who possessed an abolitionist mindset; a group from which they themselves are for the most part estranged. It is true that Lincoln wasn't a "radical" abolitionist, but instead a more moderate opponent of slavery who wanted to stop it from expanding into the territories. The people who opposed slavery's expansion rather than its immediate abolition were also averse to the institution. However, like Jefferson and Madison, they knew that the South would never accept complete abolition without a bloody war. To avoid such a catastrophe they moderated their position and for the time being focused instead on just containing the evil. Although many of them, including Lincoln, had views on race that were far from exemplary, those views didn't prevent them from engaging in some type of broad based antislavery activity other than just an improbable deportation. Robert E. Lee, the antislavery Confederate about whom Paul/DiLorenzo have virtually nothing bad to say, couldn't be said to meet the same standard.

Nevertheless, to bolster his allegation that Lincoln wasn't really against slavery, DiLorenzo likes to point out that the abolitionists were very critical of him. While true that abolitionists thought he was too accommodating to the South, I don't think that the people actively fighting slavery (by then Lysander Spooner wasn't included) would have been comfortable replacing Lincoln with anyone that Paul/DiLorenzo would favor. The abolitionist criticism centered on the fact that the president's policies weren't different enough from the historical figures Paul/DiLorenzo side with. For individuals who minimize slavery by minimizing the difficulty of abolishing it to criticize Lincoln for being soft on the institution is like a bystander who witnesses a crime and refuses to identify the perpetrator, yet blames the police for not solving it. It's nonsense through and through.

Paul/DiLorenzo may be right in claiming that Lincoln could have prevented war (for a short while), but they have the diplomacy part backwards. In the period between Lincoln's election and inauguration an informal peace conference was held.[27] Based on the discussions, it appears that there was some possibility that Lincoln could have (temporarily) avoided war if he had agreed to insure slavery's existence (virtually) forever through a constitutional amendment that would once and for all protect the institution and require unanimous agreement to change.[28] If Lincoln had chosen diplomacy, slavery could have won the day without even a fight. In saying no to the proposal (i.e., behind the scenes he did everything he could do to stop it),[29] Lincoln revealed that he had a genuine bottom line in regards to this issue. Of course this real Lincoln runs totally counter to Paul/DiLorenzo's "real Lincoln."

The real Lincoln who rejected this proslavery amendment may have saved our Constitution. For if we had tainted it forever with the yoke of slavery, a future generation would have been forced to toss it in the trash, like our founders did with the Articles of Confederation (which was deemed unworkable because it also required unanimous agreement to change).[30] Unfortunately, the rejection of a constitutional amendment protecting slavery meant that war was inevitable, either right then or soon thereafter. With the African slave trade gone, a large runaway population would have been exceedingly costly to the South. Under these circumstances, the two resulting countries would have shared an expansive border that would have likely been as tense as the cold war era's Berlin Wall. This wasn't a prescription for long-lasting tranquility. When all is said and done, Lincoln was essentially right: we (this contiguous area of North America) couldn't have endured (peacefully) much longer as half slave and half free, whether made up of one or more nations.

Was Lincoln racist? Like those of most white people of the time, his views on race would not have stood up to today's much higher standards. Racist ideas were rampant throughout the country, both North and South. Southern defenders of slavery along with their Northern apologists often fell back on the all-too-common racism of that period to justify the institution. Yet unlike so many other white people living then, Lincoln's opinions about race didn't diminish his distaste for slavery.

If anyone thinks that he was an awful racist, I suggest they read the transcripts of a few Lincoln- (Stephen) Douglas debates. Then I suggest that they evaluate how Lincoln comes off compared to Douglas. Keep in mind that Douglas was anything but the kind of hard-core proslavery advocate that the South loved. In fact, he was seen as so soft on slavery that in 1860 Southern states refused to support his presidential candidacy. They got behind their own candidate instead. That's why Lincoln was elected: Democrats were divided.

Having said this, how does Lincoln look in relation to Douglas? I think that any decent person would be shamed by Douglas's racist language and blatant appeal to prejudice. On the other hand, an imperfect Lincoln still makes one proud to be an American. We should look at few excerpts from their debates. To set himself apart from his opponent, Douglas volunteers his opinion of the nature of our government and the "negro" race at the fourth debate held on September 18, 1858:

> I say that this *Government was established on the white basis*. It was made by white men, for the benefit of white men and their posterity forever, and never should be administered by any except white men. I declare that a *negro ought not to be a citizen,* whether his parents were imported into this country as slaves or not, or whether or not he was born here. It does not depend upon the place a negro's parents were born, or whether they were slaves or not, but upon the fact that he is a *negro, belonging to a race incapable of self-government, and for that reason ought not to be on an equality with white men* [my italics].[31]

Later in the same debate we see Douglas using race-baiting in regards to the audacity of the "negro" Frederick

Douglass and the fact that Lincoln is connected with a "negro" who doesn't know his place:

> In the northern part of the State I found Lincolns ally, in the person of *FRED DOUGLASS, THE NEGRO*, preaching Abolition doctrines, while Lincoln was discussing the same principles down here … I witnessed an effort made at Chicago by Lincoln's then associates, and now supporters, to put *Fred Douglass, the negro*, on the stand at a Democratic meeting, to reply to the illustrious General Cass, when he was addressing the people there. They had the same *negro hunting me down*, and they now have a *negro* traversing the northern counties of the State, and *speaking in behalf of Lincoln* [my italics].[32]

Now compare Lincoln's tone with Douglas's at the same debate:

> The other way is for us to surrender and let Judge *Douglas and his friends* have their way and *plant slavery over all the States*; cease speaking of it *as in any way a wrong; regard slavery as one of the common matters of property, and speak of negroes as we do of our horses and cattle* … I have ventured the opinion, and I say to-day, that we will have *no end to the slavery agitation* until it takes one turn or the other. I do not mean that when it takes a turn toward ultimate extinction it will be in a day, nor in a year, nor in two years. *I do not suppose that in the most peaceful way ultimate extinction would occur in less than a*

hundred years at least; but that it will occur in the best way for both races, in God's own good time, I have no doubt [my italics].[33]

This is the essential Lincoln: end slavery without war by taking small piecemeal steps, the first being containment. The ultimate goal is the complete abolition of slavery at some unknown future date. Although both Jefferson and Madison said that they had the same long-term goal, unlike Lincoln they didn't have any effective short-term strategy. It should be noted that this core position of Lincoln is consistent with both his statement that he wouldn't free a single slave if it would preserve the Union (Lincoln didn't want the nation to undergo a bloody civil war even if it meant that slavery would continue in the areas where it was already established) and his rejection of a constitutional amendment that would enshrine the institution and make it permanent (once it was contained, Lincoln didn't wish to hinder a future generation's efforts to eliminate slavery entirely).

Throughout the debates, Douglas continuously baited Lincoln over the issue of slavery. On this concern Lincoln had no apologies, as witnessed by his response during the seventh debate on October 15, 1858:

At Galesburgh the other day, I said in answer to Judge Douglas, that three years ago [the time of the Dred Scott Decision] there never had been a man, so far as I knew or believed, in the whole world, who had said that the Declaration of Independence did not include negroes in the term "all men." I reassert it to-day. I assert that Judge

Douglas and all his friends may search the whole records of the country, and it will be a matter of great astonishment to me if they shall be able to find that one human being three years ago had ever uttered the astounding sentiment that the term "all men" in the Declaration did not include the negro. Do not let me be misunderstood. I know that more than three years ago there were men who, finding this assertion constantly in the way of their schemes to bring about the ascendancy and perpetuation of slavery, *denied the truth of it*. I know that Mr. Calhoun and all the politicians of his school denied the truth of the Declaration. I know that it ran along in the mouth of some Southern men for a period of years, ending at last in that shameful though rather forcible declaration of Pettit of Indiana, upon the floor of the United States Senate, that the Declaration of Independence was in that respect "a self-evident lie," rather than a self-evident truth. But I say, with a perfect knowledge of all this hawking at the Declaration without directly attacking it, that three years ago there never had lived a man who had ventured to assail it in the sneaking way of pretending to believe it and then asserting it did not include the negro. I believe the first man who ever said it was Chief Justice Taney in the Dred Scott case, and the next to him was our friend, Stephen A. Douglas.[34]

How do they come off in a one-on-one exchange over the exact same concerns? Let's look at the fifth debate held on October 7, 1858:

Douglas says:

I tell you that this Chicago doctrine of Lincoln's—declaring that the negro and the white man are made equal by the Declaration of Independence and by Divine Providence—is a monstrous heresy. The signers of the Declaration of Independence never dreamed of the negro when they were writing that document. *They referred to white men, to men of European birth and European descent, when they declared the equality of all men.* I see a gentleman there in the crowd shaking his head. Let me remind him that when *Thomas Jefferson wrote that document, he was the owner, and so continued until his death, of a large number of slaves* [my italics].[35]

Lincoln responds:

And I will remind Judge Douglas and this audience, that while *Mr. Jefferson* was the owner of slaves, as undoubtedly he was, in speaking upon this very subject, he used the strong language that "he *trembled for his country when he remembered that God was just;*" and I will offer the highest premium in my power to Judge Douglas if he will show *that he, in all his life, ever uttered a sentiment at all akin to that of Jefferson* [my italics].[36]

I think then an objective assessment of all the debates supports my opinion of how well Lincoln comes off at a time when the nation confronted its most defining moral dilemma. I suggest you read them and decide for yourself.

Now imagine: if Douglas resorted to race-baiting and demeaning black people as a way to embarrass Lincoln, how do you think the proslavery advocates sounded? The most virulent racist politicians, philosophers, and ideologues were proslavery and later pro-Confederacy. Yet Paul/DiLorenzo seem to have little interest in highlighting how their racial opinions linked up with their hatred of Lincoln or their support for the Southern cause. After all, attacking Lincoln for his racist attitudes presumes that racism is seen as an important concern. Yet once we get off the subject of our sixteenth president, Paul/DiLorenzo show virtually no evidence of such concern. While they are accusing Lincoln of being so terrible, let's take a look at the racist views that they choose to ignore.

A good way to see the worst racism of that period is to once again look at what was printed in the influential Sothern magazine *DeBow's Review*. Its editor was James Dunwoody Brownson DeBow, one of the South's most respected publishers as well as its leading statistician. He was a former head of the U.S. Census.[37] The South's racial perspective can be seen in an unattributed staff article that appeared in the magazine's December 1860 edition. The *Review*'s writer refers to the work of Dr. J. H. Van Evrie (acknowledged to be a Northern sympathizer of the Southern viewpoint). The substance of his reference to Dr. Van Evrie's views reads as follows:

> the negro is naturally inferior—a separate and distinct race or species of the *genus homo*; hence being a different and inferior being, he must occupy an inferior position to the white man. This being his natural or normal position, it cannot be one of slavery is an unnatural condition or a *wrong* deprivation of a man of his rights, but this is *not* that, for the negro enjoys all the rights he is rightly entitled to, *ergo*, his condition is not one of slavery.[38]

The article goes on to note that one of the South's leading authorities on race, Dr. Samuel A. Cartwright, commended Dr. Van Evrie for his opinion. Dr. Cartwright's approval carried considerable weight since he was an esteemed contributor to the magazine and its de facto expert on "racial science." Cartwright was best known for his "discovery" of "drapetomania," a "mental disorder" characterized by the desire to escape slavery.[39] Dr. Cartwright labeled this "illness" a form of madness.[40] "Whipping the hell" out of a slave was both cure and prevention (!) for the "disease."[41] This sounds even worse than the suspect psychiatric practices that existed under totalitarian communism.

Unfortunately for Southerners, Dr. Cartwright's views were far from isolated. Dr. Josiah Nott was one of the region's leading physicians.[42] He was a founder of the Medical College of Alabama and was also a Professor of Surgery there. During the Civil War he served as a surgeon and staff officer in the Confederate Army. Outside of his writings on racial matters, Nott's medical opinion was highly respected throughout the nation. In 1844, writing about his belief that Africans and Caucasians are not the same species, he said:

> Now it will be seen from this hasty sketch, how many points of resemblance Anatomists have established between the Negro and Ape.[43]

Once again we see that the enslaved population wasn't even regarded as human! These opinions of the South's educated elite infiltrated all segments of Southern society, from the top political leadership to the man on the street. What was to be the Confederacy was the "intellectual" epicenter of the worst of American racism.

The real point here is that, like with Buckley, the tell-tale signs of a self-serving hidden agenda are an "asymmetry of sympathies." In turning a blind eye to the most egregious filth, Paul/DiLorenzo more than qualify as being guilty of such an attitude. Not only do they attempt to downplay pro-Confederate racism, but after he quotes passages from the Lincoln–Douglas debates (to belittle Lincoln), DiLorenzo's supposed concern over it doesn't even merit an unkind word about Stephen Douglas. Why is this so? To do such would expose too much of the truth. Instead, Paul/DiLorenzo try to deflect attention away from it by focusing on the imperfections of one of the period's least racist politicians (least—even in relation to Douglas).

This "asymmetry of sympathies" sheds very little light on the real Lincoln. Equally important, it reveals almost nothing of the magnitude of injustice that was perpetrated against enslaved Americans. However, it has a lot to say about who Paul/DiLorenzo really are. When you peel away the fancy intellectualizations and the self-serving arguments, their understanding of freedom is little more than the freedom of the jungle, where unprincipled predators presume a natural right to take advantage of their unfortunate prey.

Yet there is still more to understand about how Paul/DiLorenzo's historical perspective connects to their current-day libertarian thinking. Since the devil is in the details, we need to go back in time and observe the nature of their distortions. We know that Paul/DiLorenzo try to ignore the bigger picture by claiming that slavery was just a minor issue. This lie must be exposed before we can unravel the hidden agenda that underlies all their positions.

Antebellum slavery was a minor issue like an atom bomb in a school locker. Slavery was the one point of contention that required a major sea change to resolve. Even Jefferson, who talked about ending slavery in the entire country, wasn't in fifty years' time able to end it at Monticello. Nor was Madison at Montpelier. Their financial security was too dependent on slavery. Forty years later, the Southern elites—as well as their entire economy—were even more dependent on the institution. While the North had gravitated towards industrialization and free labor, the South went in exactly the opposite direction.

However, this wasn't the whole story. For even when the North was much more rural, slavery was never as embedded there as it was in the South. That's why of all the disagreements of that period it had the least margin for compromise. All the rest—tariffs, fiscal policy, internal improvements and the like—were normal run-of-the-mill debates that all political systems confront in one manor or another. The vast majority of times some middle ground is reached. Slavery on the other hand was a fundamental ethical and emotional divide that after fifty years of progressively escalating tensions had no end in sight. As evidenced by the existence of the quite extraordinary "gag rule" (see Chapter VII) it had become a great moral crusade that transcended ordinary business as usual politics.

To confirm this assessment you only need to take another look at the Lincoln–Douglas debates. Here again we see why the proslavery side insisted upon a "gag rule." The question of slavery dominated all seven debates. Douglas was constantly attacking the abolitionists and doing his best to associate Lincoln with them. He bemoans the fact that the nation no longer has two national parties. Why is this so? It is because Lincoln's party (a much different Republican Party of a much different era) corrupts the nation's politics by being a sectional party that has succeeded in dividing the union over the issue of slavery. In other words, it's unfortunate that slavery has become the country's central focus.

Look at this excerpt of Douglass speaking, taken from the fourth Lincoln–Douglas debate held on September 18, 1858:

> Every one of those questions which divided Whigs and Democrats has passed away, the country has outgrown them, they have passed into history. *Hence it is immaterial whether you were right or I was right on the bank, the sub-treasury, and other questions, because they no longer continue living issues.* What, then, has taken the place of those questions about which we once differed? *The slavery question has now become the leading and controlling issue*; that question on which you and I agreed, on which the Whigs and Democrats united, has now become the leading issue between the *National Democracy on the one side, and the Republican or Abolition party on the other* [my italics].[44]

What about the opinion of a leading Southern political figure on this topic? Alexander H. Stephens was one of the Founding Fathers of the Confederacy as well as its vice president. As far as his positions were concerned, he was one of the most moderate of the Confederate founders. Unlike most of the others he urged compromise and opposed succession, right up until it was virtually a done deal.[45]

Despite his original opposition to it, when succession occurred he came around and proudly acknowledged its true objective. In a speech delivered in Savannah, Georgia, on March 21, 1861, he spoke about the new

Confederate nation and its Constitution. When first comparing the old U.S. Constitution to the ideas behind the South's new Constitution, he said:

> Those ideas, however, were *fundamentally wrong.* They rested on the assumption of *equality of races.* This was an error. It was a *sandy foundation*, and the government built upon it *fell* when the *"storm came and the wind blew"* [my italics].[46]

Sure sounds like the Confederacy's first V.P. saw the Union falling apart over "racial equality issues," African American slavery being the foremost one at that time. But what did he think about the new Confederate government?

> *Our new government is founded upon exactly the opposite idea*; its foundations are laid, its corner-stone rests, upon the great truth that the *negro is not equal to the white man; that slavery subordination to the superior race is natural and normal condition* [my italics].[47]

Slavery was viewed as a "corner-stone" principle by this Confederate Founding Father in a speech that one doubts got too many (if any) boos. But he has even more to say on this issue. Speaking about the Confederate belief in racial inequality and slavery, Stephens says:

> This, our new government, is the first, in the history of the world, based upon this great physical, philosophical, and moral truth.[48]

In other words, the Confederate States of America's claim to fame is to be the first nation–state in history to be founded on the premise of inequality and slavery. Unfortunately this is as true as it is uninspiring. Yet Stephens goes even further with this love of inequality:

> I cannot permit myself to doubt the ultimate success of a full recognition of this principle throughout the civilized and enlightened world.[49]

The person chosen to be the Confederacy's second-highest official saw the new nation as having a mission to spread (by example) its ideology of racism and slavery throughout the entire "civilized and enlightened world." It's highly doubtful that these opinions were isolated or limited to just this more moderate Confederate founder. When you read what pro-Confederate leaders had to say, you get absolutely no sense that slavery was seen as either a minor issue or one that would be gone any time soon. By the start of the Civil War, one of the most brutal forms of slavery in human history had existed in this country for nearly a quarter of a millennium. At that time, the slave states were more intent on continuing this institution intact than they had been prior to the invention of the cotton gin nearly a century earlier. In fact, by 1860 Southern support for slavery was at its highest peak.

In pushing this historical revisionism, what are Paul/DiLorenzo really trying to achieve? The short answer is that they wish to diminish the accomplishments of history's real heroes—the grassroots justice seekers who have courageously challenged the arbitrary and unjust abuses of the oppressive regimes that have embraced their ideology. The long answer is that this is done to set the stage for their fictionalized worldview. What exactly is this view? From their vantage point, history is a top-down phenomenon where the doings and viewings of the shakers and makers are what count. The run-of-the-mill work-a-day grunts are at best just extras in a script written for the stars. It is right out of an Ayn Rand novel.

Such manner of thinking is disposed to valuing the individual because "he" is envisioned as a rugged loner who rises above the ordinary hordes. Therefore, they see "men" of great wealth and power as much more likely to be representative of humanity's best. Even if not self-made, they are the product of the fair fight that preceded them and wouldn't remain on top if they didn't belong there. For this reason the powerful are usually seen as more deserving than the "jealous masses." And accordingly, when there is conflict between the two, those on top should receive the benefit of any doubt.

This parallels the writings of the previously alluded to economist Friedrich Hayek. During his lifetime, the battle for justice was centered on social evils. Hayek would come to believe that individuals who pursue the broadest ideals of justice were liberty's greatest enemies. Attempts to fix flaws in the system would only lead to liberty's death by a thousand cuts.[50] Of course those who benefit the most from these flaws are those who resist both change and justice—in other words, the people who are usually on top. The implication of such an ideology is obvious: one needn't worry too much about injustices (flaws) or be overly sympatric with their victims; disregarding this dictum will only dismantle the whole thing. For the Paul/DiLorenzos of this world it is but a small step to see another people's slavery as just one more minor flaw in a system that they are otherwise partial to.

Yet to sell such a distorted perspective entails downplaying the role of the genuine freedom fighters who have improved living conditions for the overwhelming majority of their fellow human beings. After all, the well-being of the overwhelming majority is not where it's at. As said earlier, minimizing the contributions of the grassroots victims along with their progressive allies is endemic to Paul/DiLorenzo's (right-wing) libertarian ideology. In his foreword to Ralph Raico's *Great Wars and Great Leaders*, subtitled *A Libertarian Rebuttal* (and published by the libertarian Ludwig von Mises Institute, a think tank Di Lorenzo has been associated with), Robert Higgs states the libertarian case quite accurately. In criticizing non-libertarian academics he says:

> They tend to see society as divided between a small group of oppressors ... and *a conglomeration of oppressed groups, among whom nonwhites, women, homosexuals, and low-wage workers* receive prominent attention and solicitude. When the historians write about the economy, they usually view it th[r]ough quasi-Marxist lenses, perceiving that investors and

employers have been (and remain) the natural enemies of the *workers,* who would never have escaped destitution except for the *heroic struggles waged on their behalf by labor unions and progressive politicians.* When they write about international affairs, they elevate the "democratic" wartime leaders to god-like status, especially so for *Abraham Lincoln,* Woodrow Wilson, Winston Churchill, and Franklin D. Roosevelt ... [my italics].[51]

Therefore it's no surprise that the nineteenth-century abolitionists who fought slavery as well as the Confederate South—and by extension their twentieth-century counterparts who did the same against attempts to retain as much of the old institution as possible (e.g., segregation, denial of voting rights, etc.)—are also to be written off. To downplay their achievements they have to minimize the horrific injustices that they battled against. So they say that they would have disappeared anyways (no big deal). These injustices were just peripheral to the important political questions of the time, not leading factors in themselves.

If we update what they are doing, a comparable position would be claiming that although the Holocaust wasn't good it was just one part of a bigger picture. After all, following World War I Germany was treated unfairly, being subjected to chaotic politics along with terrible economic disruptions. With the Nazi ascendency, national self-respect was restored and economic conditions improved. This semi-apologetic scenario would clearly be seen as a backdoor attempt to minimize the Holocaust's significance. With relation to slavery, segregation, and denial of basic rights of citizenship, Paul/DiLorenzo are doing exactly the same thing, except they are more odious, since their true inclinations are veiled behind the language of freedom.

As an aside, it's appropriate that I comment on using the Holocaust example. In *The Real Lincoln*, DiLorenzo lashes out at his detractors for relying on Hitler comparisons. He calls them "most absurd."[52] As a social activist who has fought (and is continuing to fight) for all Americans to have a right to health care, I have frequently been accused of being a totalitarian Nazi by those on the same side of the ideological divide as Paul/DiLorenzo. Even on a leadership level we see books by prominent right-wingers with such titles as *Liberal Fascism* by Jonah Goldberg. DiLorenzo himself doesn't hesitate to engage in such extremist rhetoric and comparisons. In *Lincoln Unmasked* he has chapters entitled, "Lincolnite Totalitarians" and "Pledging Allegiance to the Omnipotent Lincolnian State" (chapter to be discussed soon). If those who advocate for universal health care are labeled as Nazis by the libertarian Right, then I have no reservation about comparing people who defend slavery's defenders—and even claim that they were freedom fighters—to Hitler apologists. If there is any absurdity, it's all theirs.

Prior to connecting the dots, there is one last aspect that remains to be scrutinized: the practical side of all the nonsense that they spout. A close-up of this distorted ideology in action is called for. If we look at the antebellum states that Paul/DiLorenzo have sympathy for, we see that about *45 percent* of the human population was literally *(not figuratively)* enslaved, and in many of them the other *55 percent* risked arrest if they publically spoke out against the *official "state" ideology of* (you guessed it) *slavery*. Civil War historian Gordon Rhea gives a good description of what "freedom" was like in the antebellum South. He writes:

> Controlling the slave population was a matter of concern for all Whites, whether they owned slaves or not. Curfews governed the movement of slaves at night, and vigilante committees patrolled the roads, dispensing summary justice to wayward slaves and whites suspected of harboring abolitionist views. Laws were passed against the dissemination of abolitionist literature, and the South increasingly resembled a police state. A prominent Charleston lawyer described the city's citizens as living under a "reign of terror."[53]

Here we see the self-serving ideology of Calhoun, where minority rights are really minority privileges. Most important, it once again shows what liberty looks like in the absence of justice. Yet this is the side of the divide that Paul/DiLorenzo think was fighting for freedom! These two men offer us a narrowed and intellectually contrived perspective, totally devoid of any connection to a meaningful freedom which, as Martin Luther King Jr. said about peace, requires the presence of justice. Theirs is a concept so convoluted that it's unable to distinguish the genuine item from history's worst atrocities. With friends like Paul/DiLorenzo claim to be, freedom needs no enemies. Where in American history have we seen this before? The answer is quite easy, since Paul/DiLorenzo would likely agree with me: the antebellum South.

Given that we have finally reached some point of agreement, I feel compelled to compliment Thomas J. DiLorenzo. He single-handedly proves two of my central points. In conceding that the "real union" ended in April 1865 (with a Lincoln victory),[54] and correspondingly acknowledging his loathing for what replaced it, DiLorenzo admits that he and his right-wing compatriots detest the America of the last 150 years! He only confirms what I have always suspected. Those who hate our country are the ones who overcompensate by burying themselves either in the flag or in constitutional interpretations that mimic a fundamentalist Bible study. Remember that chapter I promised to discuss soon. In it DiLorenzo parrots Ron Paul's contempt for the Pledge of Allegiance and confirms what I have said about it representing "liberal"—i.e. "Lincolnian"—values.[55] So what does this tell us about Paul/DiLorenzo's current ideology? The answer is simply that right-wing libertarianism is stuck in a time warp—a time, to quote John Patrick Daly's book title, *When Slavery Was Called Freedom.*

One hundred fifty years after the Civil War and fifty years after the civil rights movement, the issues of both periods are still a subject of debate for the Right. Paul/DiLorenzo's insensitivity to the atrocities of the antebellum South is reminiscent of the *National Review* (*NR*) downplaying the injustices that were fueling the civil rights movement. Remember, during that era the *NR* would view segregation in the same light as Paul/DiLorenzo view slavery, as just a peripheral and not a central concern. And as with the *NR*'s lack of outrage over Southern laws that mandated segregated public accommodations, Paul/DiLorenzo demonstrate a similar attitude towards slave state laws that criminalized free citizens for advocating the abolition of slavery. The conceptual symmetry between the mainline conservative response to civil rights (represented by the *NR*) and the current views of libertarian conservatives (represented by Paul/DiLorenzo) is striking. It's clear that both branches of right-wing ideology are susceptible to the same blindness to injustice and tendency to minimize violations of other people's freedom. Fifty years ago it was the *NR* that carried the Right's banner of resistance. Today it's the libertarians who are front and center. Nevertheless, the war remains ongoing and the thinking behind it hasn't changed.

Before this chapter ends, some additional words need to be said about what is happening right now. Unfortunately, too many people believe that Paul/DiLorenzo's manor of thought is but an esoteric argument without practical implications. They haven't been following current events. Today we see in right-wing dominated state legislatures growing movements that even have the support of some of the governors to openly challenge the authority of all branches of the federal government. Cries for nullification of federal laws, court rulings, and regulations are entering the political debate in an increasing number of states. Some political leaders in these states have even brought up the possibility of succession. It is no fluke that most of the states involved are in the South. Correspondingly, it's also no fluke that it's occurring at the same time that the ideology of Paul/DiLorenzo is on the rise. After a century and a half we are headed right back to the same ideological divide over the meaning of freedom that was voiced so loudly and clearly during the abolitionist era— the only difference being the "loudly and clearly" part, since this divide in one form or another has been with us throughout most of our history. It has shown itself in all our struggles for justice as well as in the dichotomy between liberal and conservative thinking. It's now becoming a controversy that dares to once again show its true face.

Chapter X

Logic of the Emotions

We humans make history, and without us no historical journey would be possible. That's why our travels with this book must include a destination that is a bit more abstract—one that takes a closer look at the species that has underwritten the entire expedition. This entails looking at the internal forces that shape our perceptions and bear responsibility for our actions. By now you might have surmised that the best place to begin is with an age-old inquiry that humanity has long struggled to answer. I am of course referring to the question of the proper alignment between our reason and our passions.

As far back as Plato and the dawn of Western philosophy, reason has been thought of as the human race's most distinguishing feature. Our rationality is seen as not only separating us from the animal kingdom but also the key to mastering the world. In contrast, its opposite, our emotive side, must be subordinated to reason, and failure to do so will lead to the most awful consequences. It is thought that rational thinking can moderate the worst of human actions if only our emotions are placed under its control.

Many great thinkers have embraced this world outlook. In a recent interview, the premier leftist intellectual of our times, Noam Chomsky, said that despite agreeing with Martin Luther King Jr. he is unable to listen to his speeches. The reason is that King appeals too much to emotions;[1] Chomsky prefers a rational argument. The topic of the interview was propaganda, and it was clear that he thought today's versions of this phenomenon were particularly insidious because they encourage people to rely on their gut instead of engaging their rational faculties.[2] Due to the potential harm this could cause, Chomsky, similar to most of the eighteenth-century liberal thinkers, is wary of any appeal to passions. He sees human reason as our species' best salvation.

Of course this perspective is exactly opposite of my contention that an emotive inclination for fairness and justice is at the root of modern liberalism and the leading force behind positive social change. Obviously, it isn't a coincidence that the one individual in American history I see as the best representative of the liberal ideal is the very person Chomsky can't listen to. I focus on Chomsky not because I wish to be critical of him or his convictions. In fact, I very much admire the man and his body of work. I mention him because I think that it shows how ingrained traditional Western thought is when even a progressive as esteemed as Noam Chomsky remains wedded to this concept.

Yet in spite of rationalism's impressive list of supporters, I say unapologetically that it's time for a reevaluation of our belief in it. And there is no better place to start than with Chomsky himself. In a 1988 interview with Bill Moyers, Chomsky opined that (true) democracy is a positive good in and of itself.[3] He implied that it's a fundamental value that doesn't need to be defended; or in other words democracy is its own justification.

I agreed with him then, and I agree with what he said now. I see it as highly doubtful that any amount of intellectual discourse could alter Chomsky's belief in democracy or any of his deeply held values. If so, how could he see democracy as a value in and of itself? Asking whether an antisocial Noam Chomsky born without a capacity for human empathy—but possessing exactly the same incredible intellect—would be the Chomsky the world knows, is an easily answered question. Would one really expect such a person to be one of the twentieth century's greatest justice seekers?

If you peel away the outside layers of a person's thinking you come to an inner core that cannot be reasoned away. Most of us have a human center that speaks more to who we are than what we think. Calling it our emotional underbelly is as good a description as any. Even for history's great minds, it was their emotional underbelly that set the parameters of their thought and was most responsible for its direction. This is the same for both liberals and conservatives. Despite his strongly enunciated preference for rational argument, Chomsky's faith in democracy does appear to be an integral part of his emotional underbelly.

Given Martin Luther King Jr.'s core values, his manner of appeal was no fluke. Even more crucial, his impact was directly related to his ability to reach the emotional underbelly of so many people. Without this attribute I think it doubtful that American history would have had any great justice movements. The underlying truth is that the interrelationship between human intellect and emotion is central to the existence of justice.

The work of cognitive linguist George Lakoff lends much credence to the necessity of reevaluating the role that rational thought plays in public debates. He applies his professional expertise to uncover the factors responsible for our current political disagreements. Lakoff finds that we humans have an emotive logic that is not only ingrained but also quite separate from the formal or classical one held dear by Chomsky and eighteenth-century liberalism.[4] In fact he points to a multitude of psychological studies showing that people respond more to how something is presented than to any logically intended meaning.[5]

Lakoff's investigation has led him to conclude that at the deepest emotive level we humans associate the workings of the larger society with an environment that only incidentally interacts with our rational faculties. To be precise, he finds that the individual's view of the world is primarily shaped by early family experiences. This is because people think in metaphors, and a natural metaphor for societal authority is familial authority.[6] He notes that there are two contrasting versions of the nuclear family that bear responsibility for two very different world outlooks.[7] Of course he discusses their idealized versions which, as theoretical models, provide for an overall point of reference. In actuality these models overlap, yet the overlap tends not to be exactly even, and this can make for substantive differences.[8]

Since Lakoff's models can be very informative, we should examine them. To simplify things, I will refer to their idealized versions. But first, it is important to note that what I believe to be the impetus behind America's great justice movements (see Chapter I)—empathy—Lakoff sees as being the bedrock of liberal thought.[9]

He thinks that the "nurturant parent" family encourages and nourishes empathic inclinations. Looking at this family's basic characteristics, we observe the following:

The parent (or parents) can be of either gender. They understand the importance of teaching by example, because this is how children best learn right from wrong. Parents know that morality is not always carved in stone, and therefore it's seen as part of a process of personal growth. You might say that childhood development is viewed as just the beginning stage of a lifelong journey. That's why it's important that children be encouraged to question the world around them, and authority figures are no exception.

Objective knowledge and the ability to think independently are deemed to be necessary requirements for a good life. Their development depends on engaging in an honest intellectual give and take. Therefore in many situations parents have an obligation to explain themselves and justify their demands.

Searching for personal fulfillment is also important to the life experience, yet it is equally important that children understand that other people have the same opportunity to realize it. When parents show respect for others and are concerned for their welfare, they convey a powerful message to their children. They learn that helping people and valuing fairness are essential ingredients to good character. In the "nurturant parent" family children come to see that the world isn't perfect, bad things can happen even to good people, and it's up to us to help set things right.[10]

If you haven't recognized it by now, this fits exceedingly well with the important roles that empathy, outrage over injustice, and a moral mission to redress unfair treatment have played in all our historical justice movements. If we begin with our first one, we see that for the abolitionists morality entailed treating our fellow humans with respect and being concerned about their welfare. And when they saw innocent others being outrageously violated, they thought that they as moral people had an obligation to do everything in their power to help redress this injustice. That's why when battling wrongs their moral outrage led the charge. The other likely concerns—such as how am I affected ("what's in it for me") or giving authority and tradition the benefit of the doubt ("whom am I to say")— weren't what dictated their response. For the abolitionists as well as those of all the other justice movements, morality wasn't about pretty words or over — intellectualized rationalizations, it was about being on the front line; it was leading by example.

A poem from an unidentified woman published on August 20, 1831, in William Lloyd Garrison's newsletter, *The Liberator*, gives us a good idea of how well this mind-set matches up with the idealized values of the "nurturant parent" family:

> How can you eat, how can you drink,
> How wear your finery and ne'er think,
> Of those poor souls, in bondage held,
> Whose painful labor is compelled?

> Gird up your loins, be firm, be strong,
> Support the right; condemn the wrong,
> So shall the Lord your ways approve,
> And save you by redeeming love.[11]

The message is quite clear: you should be aware of what's happening to others, and why aren't you doing something about it? An individual who thinks she has a moral obligation to both recognize injustice and act to redress it possesses the kind of values that would be developed and nourished in a "nurturant parent" family. While all the people who battled for justice probably weren't raised in the ideal version of this family, the actions they undertook were certainly indicative of the belief system that individuals from such an environment would be encouraged to adopt.

It is interesting that Lakoff himself draws a connection between those who battled for and against America's great justice movements and what he understands cognitive science to be telling us. In his book *Don't Think of an Elephant!* he points out that the liberal mode of thought has historically overcome the resistance of its conservative detractors. In speaking about the failures of these naysayers, he says:

> This is the model that the best in American values has defeated over and over again in the course of our history ... from the emancipation of the slaves to women's suffrage, Social Security and Medicare, civil rights and voting rights acts, and *Brown v. the Board of Education* and *Roe v. Wade*.[12]

But what is the model of the detractors and from what kind of breeding ground do they emerge? In this vein Lakoff sees the "strict father" family as the "nurturant parent" family's direct opposite. Looking at this family's basic characteristics we observe the following:

Only the male parent is the lawgiver. As you might have guessed, strictness is at the core of things. The "strict father" understands the importance of laying down the law right from the get-go. He holds that children need to be taught (told) right from wrong when they are young or they risk never learning proper values.

Since morality is thought to have very little ambiguity, it's not important that children think too deeply about the finer points. What's important is that they know what the bottom line is and they adhere to it. Obviously, asking problematic questions is not encouraged. Children can certainly be rewarded for good behavior, but when they transgress (and all children do at some time) they must know that punishment is certain. It's up to the father to teach his children the "truth" about the world—that it's a tough and even dangerous place.

Yet children should know that despite this it's a place where you will most likely get back what you put into it. Metaphorically, life can be seen as running the gantlet, where the worthy survive and the unworthy succumb. The "strict father" has an obligation to prepare his children for what lies ahead. Having a strong character is the best bet a person has to triumph over adversity. Since strong character requires self-reliance and discipline, anything that endangers their development—such as permitting laziness and excess to dominate one's life— is to be resisted at all costs. [13]

What can be deduced from this viewpoint is that the individual is what's most important and the rules of the surrounding world are essentially a given. By the result of one's own efforts, a person will most likely receive his or her "just" rewards. This notion that justice (for the Right often indistinguishable from freedom) is a product of an individual's actions is seen in many conservative writings. We certainly see it in the antebellum proslavery arguments as well as in the more modern works of William F. Buckley Jr. Remember, Buckley thought that the solution to segregation's injustices was the "Negro race" attaining greater individual achievement.

Although this world outlook doesn't in itself justify wrongs done to people or mean that the individual will never recognize or oppose injustice, it certainly gives the established rules of the game, as well as the authority behind them, a presumption of legitimacy. In contrast, demands to modify established rules or to empathize with those who hold the "short end of the stick" require a much higher standard of evidence for the grieving parties to make their case. Buckley gave the Jim Crow laws (rules of the game) and the Southern state governments (normal authorities) the benefit of the doubt, in large part because they had been in place and in charge for such a long time. It was feared that change would not only stir up a local mess but that the disruption could also impact other longstanding aspects of the status quo.

These inclinations are not only in Buckley's writings but are generally abundant in conservative circles. The proslavery advocates, those opposing remedying social evils (i.e., improvements in dangerous working conditions, child labor, consumer protections, etc.), as well as both current mainline and libertarian conservatives have all shown a decisive tendency to sympathize with established authority and minimize its transgressions against the less powerful (i.e., an asymmetry of sympathies). From an historical perspective the personality characteristics associated with the "strict father" family have been fundamentally in sync with the people in history who were suspicious of or hostile to America's great justice movements; and it remains true to this day.

Although it's fascinating to observe how well Lakoff's understanding of what fuels today's political battles matches up with our historical journey, it needn't be one-hundred-percent accurate. For even if particular differences in opinion fail to correlate perfectly with two distinct types of families, the observational evidence remains striking. The specific concerns underlying both liberal and conservative thought have been as cohesive as they have been consistent for a relatively long time.

That's why what modern-day science can tell us about what lies beneath the attitudes we have about the world is so interesting. We are now able to study brain activity more thoroughly than was previously possible, and the findings are nothing short of revolutionary. Neuroscience is discovering that factors other than rationality bear much of the responsibility for what is seen as normal behavior. In fact, all the evidence suggests that the conscious portion of our mind comprises an exceedingly small part of its total mental capacity.[14, 15, 16] Even more shocking, it appears that our rational faculties are ultimately subordinate to the much larger, unconscious portion.[17, 18]

The fact that science is discovering holes in the traditional Western perspective has forced us to reopen the entire debate. We now know that emotions play an exceedingly important role in human decision making. There is one human emotion, already discussed, that appears not only crucial but also hardwired into our brains.[19] That attribute is what George Lakoff identifies as the origin of liberal thinking, namely empathy. This ability to place oneself in the position of others allows for the emergence of empathic concern, which entails caring about their welfare. As alluded to in earlier chapters, it's empathic concern that allows one to identify with the plight of the people being unfairly treated.

Although there is a difference of opinions on the exact relationship between empathy and social morality, many neuroscientists see our ability to identify with others and be concerned with their welfare as the origin of ethical standards and harmonious civilization.[20] If true, it would mean that this hardwired attribute has been responsible for moral codes in human societies, including the ones that preexisted today's religions. It also suggests that it's not rational thought but the capacity to both care for and connect with others that bears the lion's share of responsibility for higher-level social organization. Interestingly, this is all very consistent with studies suggesting that human beings possess an inborn inclination to treat others fairly. Remember, in Chapter II we saw that reputable experiments found that we begin developing a basic sense of fair play as early as age three, and by age eight we firmly understand that other people are also entitled to the same "just" treatment as we are.

We learn much about our humanity when we look at how unique our capacity for high level social morality is. In 2012, the findings of a study undertaken by the Max Planck Institute for Evolutionary Anthropology appeared in the *Proceedings of National Academy of Sciences* (PNAB). Our closest evolutionary relatives, chimpanzees, were studied in an attempt to find out if a nonhuman species can possess a sense of social morality. To what extent do chimpanzees hold fellow chimpanzees responsible for their behavior? Through the use of a trapdoor, which the chimps knew how to operate, they were given the opportunity to punish other chimps openly caught stealing, by denying the thieves the fruits of their crime. Researchers were looking for answers to some very specific questions. Would chimps show an interest in holding a member of their group accountable when a third party was being victimized? Would their responses in situations involving issues of group morality and retributive justice have any similarities to the way humans respond?

What was discovered was that for the most part the chimps only used the trapdoor when they were personally being victimized and not when a fellow chimp—even a relative—was being taken advantage of.[21] A developmental psychologist at the Max Plank Institute, Katrin Riedl, summed up the findings, saying that the study suggests that the practice of punishing thievery and crimes committed against others is a uniquely human trait.[22] We can safely conclude that with only the most minimal sense of social morality the chimps lacked any inclination—or at least one that they would act upon—for the attribute's more advanced aspects, such as a uniform standard of justice.

If this experiment is verified by similar ones it will mean that the deeper concerns that evolve out of a sense of justice are limited to our species and very much at the core of what it means to be human. And even if future studies uncover a more advanced sense of social morality in a particular group of nonhuman animals, the inclination to redress unfair actions will still be, in relation to other species, one of humanity's most uniquely evolved features. If current scientific findings tell us anything at all it's that our ability to recognize unjust actions and seek redress is at least as distinct and central to what it means to be human as our rationality is.

Yet aren't the classical thinkers still correct in thinking that we would be better off with more reason and less emotion? This brings us to the one caveat in these findings. When testing individuals with a long history of antisocial behavior, it has been discovered that some of them appear to lack a capacity for empathy.[23, 24] They appear to react only minimally to emotionally charged material.[25] When shown a picture of a people in distress they exhibit a diminished emotive response.[26] Their heart rate and other signs of emotional reaction are reduced.[27] In other words, the involuntary physiological responses that make most people unable to fool a lie-detector test appear to be absent or significantly lessened in these individuals. Such scientific testing in conjunction with documented behavioral history has led credence to the existence of a classification of individuals known as "sociopaths."

There is some controversy concerning the intelligence level of sociopaths vs. nonsociopaths. This probably results from the difficulty in gathering a proper sample and inexactness in categorizing the two groups. Yet some mental-health sources claim that sociopaths score high on IQ tests.[28] The brain region responsible for rational thought is shut down when the region responsible for emotions is active.[29] Therefore, lacking an emotive capacity, sociopaths rely almost exclusively on the brain's analytical facilities.[30] Since a sociopath isn't diverted by emotional stimuli, it's not unreasonable to conclude that his rational brain activity is likely to be more active than that of the normal population. Although we have a group of people who may be above average in intelligence, with what appears to be a highly activated rational capacity, the overall results are not very promising. Their problem-solving abilities are used solely for their own gain without regard to how their actions affect fellow human beings. In other words, what we appear to reap from this situation is much more clever criminals.

This attests to the importance of the attribute they lack, empathy. This attribute plays a significant role in determining the destiny not only of the individual, but also of the entire society and by extension the species itself. We learn that without empathy our ability for high level rational thought goes from being a constructive force to a destructive one. This is why without a positive interaction between emotion and reason there can be no real justice.

However, what about the conservative side? In addressing this question I think that this is where things start to become a little more complicated. With every passing year, we are seeing an increasing amount of neuroscience research that focuses on the differences between liberal and conservative brains. As you already know, the human ability to empathize has been identified with liberalism. In contrast, the source of conservative thinking has been associated with our sensitivity to dangers, or in other words, our capacity for fear.[31]

Yet this is where we need to be exceedingly cautious. There is a natural tendency for scientists to try to make everything explainable. And when studying human beings the best way to accomplish this is to reduce our degrees of freedom so as to make us more predictable. It is just too easy to identify liberals as people with an inborn preference for empathy and conservatives as individuals with especially hyper-fearful brains. Even if there are differences between liberal and conservative brains, I doubt that this is the real story.

Both empathy and fear are for the most part generalized, not localized, attributes. Almost all of us possess a capacity for empathy as well as an inborn alertness to dangers. The situation is more reminiscent of St. Augustine's view of the human condition. For Augustine the dichotomy between good and evil was better represented by a common spectrum, not two distinct entities.[32] This perspective leads one to view the human situation as a battle between the good and evil that exists within each individual, not a battle between good and evil people. It's foolhardy to divide the world up into two genetically predetermined and permanently fixed camps: people with liberal versus conservative brains.

More important, modern neuroscience also tells us that the human brain is for the most part a plastic rather than a steel structure. Input from our environment plays a leading role in shaping and reshaping our neurological circuitry.[33, 34, 35] This is consistent with Lakoff seeing considerable overlap in liberal and conservative thinking. Most people are not, as in Ayn Rand's novels, one-hundred percent one way or the other. Although cognitive psychology tells us that our cultural knowledge is physically encoded in the synapses of our brains, and therefore we do not get new worldviews overnight,[36] that doesn't mean that new ideas can never take root; it's just not easy. What one hears, sees, and is exposed to over a sustained period of time is crucial. That's why a progressive cognitive linguist like George Lakoff emphasizes the importance of making sure that positive liberal messages are part of any political discussion.

Over the years there has also been a good deal of respected social-science research that has focused on how particular group settings alter individual opinions. A good example of such a study is contained in a 2008 article by Susan T. Fiske for the Greater Good Science Center at the University of California at Berkeley. Fiske noted in part that:

> These findings are part of a long line of research supporting what's known as the Contact Hypothesis, which states that under the right conditions, contact between members of different groups can reduce conflicts and prejudices … Pettigrew and Tropp have found that school integration can in fact reduce prejudice among students from different groups … We must also try to help them share common goals, on which

they must cooperate to succeed; ensure that they're treated as equals and have positive, noncompetitive interactions with one another … The more of these factors in place, the more likely people are to overcome their biases. This has proven to be true not only in schools but in a variety of other social institutions, from the military to public housing projects. *Our biases are not so hardwired after all, given the right social engineering* [my italics].[37]

It does appear that the preponderance of research data—whether it be from cognitive psychology, neuroscience, or sociology—points to the importance of environmental influences on the formation of individual attitudes. Yet as impressive as this is, the validity of any research study is based not so much on the findings themselves or the reliability of instruments used but on their ability to explain what in fact happens when one leaves the laboratory and returns to the real world. We must remember that our actual history is the best commentary on the value of any laboratory result. In this light we know that if political and social attitudes were that hardwired, the human race would never have experienced the social progress that it has. This fact is attested to by the attitudinal changes that many of us have observed in our own lifetimes. For this reason, the abovementioned student study is an exceedingly fitting one, since it focuses on the results of racial integration.

The fact that a half century has passed since the last great push for racial justice affords us a golden opportunity to utilize the ultimate social-science laboratory—the one existing in real time in the real world. After all the shouting, all the accusations, and all the passionate disagreements that the civil rights struggle ignited, how did it all turn out? When we proactively try to remedy injustice and change minds, what legacy are we left with? What do real-life results tell us about the human capacity for positive growth and change?

To answer these questions we first need to backtrack a bit and take a look at the impediments that had to be overcome. Even on an issue that involved such obvious inequities, those battling for civil rights faced a daunting challenge. They had to awaken the human being's "innate" sense of fairness at a time when many people feared and were even hostile to undergoing any kind of change. During the heyday of the civil rights movement, even the supposed nonracist conservative "experts" assured us that it was only when individuals had a change of heart that the situation would change. They said that government was the wrong vehicle to deal with any social problem, especially one that involved racial disparities. When I was growing up, I heard them say over and over again that "you can't legislate morality." If I was given a dollar every time this was uttered, I would have had quite a pile of cash.

Yet they still insisted that they were opposed to racial injustices. It was just that they understood that government intrusion into people's private lives (i.e., prejudices) would only make a bad situation worse. Not only did their arguments sound sincere and well-thought-out, but the very fact that this was the case afforded frightened or racist individuals a well-worded excuse to hide behind.

Nevertheless, despite the cleverest of rationalizations, justice seekers succeeded in reaching out and convincing enough people of the necessity—as well as the desirability—of undertaking proactive remedies to alleviate the existing disparities. The outcome of these actions is now clearer than ever. A good indicator is the effect it has had on today's politicians. Despite the prevalence of so many aggressive GOP rightists in both Congress and the statehouses there are practically no calls for repeal of the 1964 Civil Rights Act (as there are with "Obamacare"). And the reason for this is not because they like it.

In 2010, Senate candidate Rand Paul (Ron's son) caused an uproar when he appeared on the Rachel Maddox show and expressed his philosophical opposition to the section of the '64 Act that prohibits racial discrimination in public accommodations. In an attempt to quell any rumblings, he assured everyone that he isn't actively pushing for repealing this law.[38] Of course by following up with this stance, he covertly acknowledged the success of this landmark achievement of proactive liberalism.

If the legislation was a proven failure, why not actively work to repeal it? Had the act caused the disaster that the libertarian Right predicted, Paul wouldn't have hesitated in calling for decisive action against it. Remember on this very point it was reported that even William F. Buckley Jr. had (somewhat) acknowledged that the government was right in undertaking the actions it did and that he had been wrong in opposing civil rights legislation. By implying that he favored leaving it well enough alone, Paul indirectly admitted the same thing; but unlike with Buckley's meek recanting, he chose to exit the fray by taking the coward's way out. This was evident in his failure to own up and honestly admit the truth, even though he very much understood that taking his position to its logical conclusion would reveal it for the nonsense it was. The folly he chose to avoid is all too obvious. For everyone today recognizes that what resulted from the passage of the 1964 Civil Rights Act was the birth of an era of unparalleled progress in racial justice. The doors of society were opened up much wider for all Americans. And the specific section that Paul took issue with was the guts of the legislation. It ended over three centuries of racial discrimination in retail stores, hotels, eateries, and other public places. Those who can't admit the truth try to downplay it. And that truth is that the followers of Paul's ideology were proved to be dead wrong.

Although the government may not have been able to legislate morality, it was able to act decisively to redress injustice and improve the lives of its citizens. Equally important, its actions did have a profound effect on changing people's perceptions. The election of Barack Obama in 2008 would have been thought impossible at the time I cast my first vote for president in 1972.

The advance in racial justice that has taken place over the last fifty years shows us that the human capacity to change, grow, and under favorable circumstances bond with those formerly thought of adversaries is the real human story. It is a good indicator that our opinions and prejudges are not hardwired into our brains. We can make this assertion with a good deal of certainty since our laboratory is far bigger than just a few groups of school children. Human history and modern day social science and neuroscience reinforce each other in informing us that changing society for the better will also change individual attitudes for the better.

All this good information notwithstanding, we are still left with an unanswered question: How does positive change equate with the traditional dichotomy between reason and emotion? Remember, this is the divide that the classical liberal thinkers, including many Founding Fathers, envisioned as being a central theme in political thought. Yet does it really pertain to political arguments?

I think that the totality of the evidence shows us that the real dichotomy isn't between reason and emotion, but between positive emotions such as a desire for fairness and empathic concern versus negative emotions such as runaway fear, distrust, and selfishness. It is this basic emotive core that determines our rational side's direction and purpose. Underneath all our clever intellectualizations rests a powerful and very opinionated subconscious mind that possesses its own agenda. This explains how we can see such elaborate and seemingly rational arguments defending—in the name of freedom nonetheless—the worst of injustices (i.e., slavery, child labor, segregation, and much more). The ability of the human brain to rationally justify its preconceived emotional prejudices is one of the great wonders of the world.

It is amazing that those involved in our justice movements were able to reject the accepted rationalizations of their time. And it is just as amazing that in doing so they showed a deep visceral insight into the real underpinnings of human nature. In contrast, Enlightenment intellectuals were blind to the importance of our emotive core. This allowed Founding Fathers like Jefferson and Madison to use rational argument to justify their self-interest under the cover of being against slavery.

Yet even within the bounds of their rationalizations, history has been quite different from what these two followers of classical eighteenth-century liberalism might have expected. Both men would have been shocked to discover that the rabble-rousing abolitionists turned out to be history's agents in the elimination of slavery. What's more, their bewilderment wouldn't have ended with the issue of slavery. The very same abolitionists who had so irresponsibly succumbed to raw passion would also be the driving force behind the passage of Fourteenth and Fifteenth Amendments. These constitutional amendments advanced the legal side of racial relations beyond what these two rational Enlightenment thinkers could have ever thought. They would have been just as flabbergasted over what all the other great justice movements—such as women's rights, worker's rights, social security, and civil rights—accomplished by appealing to our innate sense of fairness and outrage over injustice. Unfortunately, they were more comfortable seeing the moral outrage of the infant abolitionist movement through eighteenth-century rationalist spectacles. The truth that cannot be denied is that their rational faculties failed them on this one. On the question of slavery, they would have fared much better in history if they had chosen to rely on the "better angels of their nature" instead of the slave-owning class's all too self-serving justifications.

By placing the scientific research alongside the historical record we gain deep insight into the mind. What emerges is an understanding that underneath the political battles there is a contest between the two contrasting sides of our being. What's involved is a logic that is specific to the human psyche—a logic of the emotions. We are learning that this logic can take us to great heights as well as great lows. We also now know that since the inner struggle takes place on a dynamic rather than stationary battlefield, our historical experience resembles a feedback loop. We change the world and then the world changes us.

This is why it's crucial that the change we make takes us up a notch, instead of back into an old rut. We mustn't allow any ideology to separate itself from real-life outcomes or conditions. If a theory condones or contributes to grave injustice, we should immediately hold it accountable for horrors it enables, no matter how clever or intelligent it sounds. The heroes involved in our justice movements didn't need any social- or neuroscience studies to be aware of this truth. In our time, proactive liberalism must once again rise to the occasion and battle the forces that are only concerned about their own selfish ends. We mustn't permit them to strangle the very qualities that I think, if they could return back today, Jefferson and Madison would wish they had been more sensitive to: the "better angels of our nature."

Chapter XI

Loose Ends

I am certain that the journey the reader has just taken has left her with some unanswered questions. This is to be expected, since all historical accounts contain loose ends. Here are the two that I think need to be addressed:

- Since Founding Fathers like Jefferson and Madison were hostile to the abolitionists were their ideals the same as those of contemporary conservatives?
- Although this book clearly sees Libertarianism as an enemy of justice some of its beliefs appear to be consistent with liberal ideals. How can this be explained; or in other words is any part of libertarianism liberal?

Conservative Founding Fathers?

Does the thinking of the Founding Fathers match up nicely with modern-day conservatism? I have claimed that two of the most influential founders, Jefferson and Madison, were anything but enthused by the emergence of an aggressive abolitionist movement. Their understanding of the proper relationship between the different levels of government seemed to be more in line with the thinking of constitutional traditionalists. You can also add to the list a mutual distaste for too much social change. Therefore, am I also implying that today's conservatives are as in sync with these founders as they claim to be? This question speaks to the fact that for some things the old adage "beauty is in the eye of the beholder" has broader meaning than just physical attractiveness. Having said this, I do not think that conservatives are compatriots of the Founding Fathers.

But before elaborating any further, it's important to refer back to what I said in Chapter III: namely that all Americans are indebted to the nation's original founders. In real life these heroes were revolutionary and dynamic thinkers. They were able to open their minds to some of the most radical opinions of their age. Most of them were capable of lifelong learning as well as significant changes in attitude. Most important, on the whole they understood that their take on the issues of the day wouldn't be the last word.

They didn't give their predecessors final say and they didn't expect future generations to afford it to them. The idea that one's elders were gods who spoke eternal truths was abhorrent to the founders, and they hoped that future generations would view it the same way. In fact, not to do so would be a complete abrogation of everything that these great men stood for. There is a quote (paraphrase) of Jefferson's, which is on the Jefferson Memorial in D.C. (panel 4), that speaks to this very point. The original, taken from a July 12, 1816 letter to H. Tompkinson, reads as follows:

I am certainly not an advocate for frequent and untried changes in laws and constitutions. I think moderate imperfections had better be borne with; because, when once known, we accommodate ourselves to them, and find practical means of correcting their ill effects. But I know also, that *laws and institutions must go hand in hand with the progress of the human mind*. As that becomes more developed, more enlightened, as new discoveries are made, new truths disclosed, and manners and opinions change with the change of circumstances, *institutions must advance also, and keep pace with the times*. We might as well require a man to wear still the coat which fitted him when a boy, as civilized society *to remain ever under the regimen of their barbarous ancestors* [my italics].[1]

Jefferson couldn't have been clearer when he spoke of "barbarous ancestors." He thought that in a free society new ideas would ultimately trump the beliefs of even the most enlightened thinkers of yesteryear, who would be seen as "barbarous" by their descendants. And frankly that is exactly how I see Jefferson's and Madison's anemic views on questions of slavery and justice. Yet I think it quite possible that if Jefferson could be teleported ahead to our time, he might very well agree with my opinion on this. That's because inherent in Jefferson's worldview is the notion that real progress is going from a barbarous state to a less barbarous one as each generation follows the next.

It's sentiments like this that make some people claim that Jefferson, if alive now, would be a liberal. However, the truth is that nobody really knows what Jefferson would be today. Yet we do know what he most likely wouldn't be. And the same can be said of many of the other Founding Fathers. The Right's lifeless caricatures frozen in time do little justice to the genuine items. As previously said, our founders most certainly wouldn't be men who never change their view of things, particularly in a world that changes at an ever-accelerating pace. This is just as true if we toss aside their personal histories and look at it from an even broader perspective.

What is this more expansive view that I refer to? The answer to the question is all around you. Most of us are aware of friends and acquaintances who broadened their horizons due to life experiences. Speaking for myself, I know intelligent people who were resistant to the women's and gay rights movements when they first began but, with time and information that they either hadn't been aware of or not thought much about, had a complete change of mind. They grew as the world turned and their awareness expanded. To expect anything less from the most cutting-edge thinkers of their day borders on the preposterous.

By 1900, after the last of the founders were long gone, the industrial revolution had already reshaped the planet immeasurably. Yet that was before two bicycle mechanics built the first airplane, before motion pictures, radio, TV, nuclear weapons, computers, men landing on the moon, space stations, MRIs, CT scans, CDs, DVDs, cell phones, smart phones, and much more. Equally important is that almost all of the nation's major political-social events—the Civil War, passage of the Thirteenth-Fifteenth Amendments, universal male suffrage, women's suffrage, the populist movement, labor movement, civil rights movement, women's movement, environmental movement, Cold War, gay rights, etc.— emerged in an ever-evolving world that was long past the time of our founders.

Nevertheless, despite such hyper-escalating change, it is assumed by modern-conservatives that the Founding Fathers would remain impervious to any of it, as they are with personal growth, or virtually any of the human qualities that so distinguished their flesh-and-blood counterparts. Yet this needn't matter, since conservatives hold that the founders left us eternal truths that will always remain the same despite the fact that the real world couldn't be more opposite.

If we look again at Thomas Jefferson, the Founding Father the Right most associates itself with, we see what nonsense this is. The real Jefferson didn't think that contemporary political opinions could ever be thought of as absolutes. To believe such would run counter to his most deeply held ideals. There was no certainty for Jefferson, even on much deeper concerns such as the existence of God.

His correspondence on the topics of religion and science speaks to his position on some of the most fundamental questions of any era and as such provides us with an opening whereby we can examine his broader thinking.

Jefferson scholar Professor Tom Jewett, in the Summer-Fall 2009 edition of the *Early America Review*, tells us that:

> In Jefferson's view, duty toward God was a matter of personal experience, not to be dictated or promoted by thoughts of others. He explained his belief, grounded in the tenets of the Enlightenment, to a young friend ...[2]

Jewett then proceeds to quote Jefferson:

> "*Do not be frightened from this inquiry* by any fear of the consequences. *If it ends in a belief that there is not God, you will find incitements to virtue* in the comfort and pleasantness you feel in its exercise, and the love of others which it will procure you. If you reason to believe there is a God, consciousness that you are acting under his eye, and that he approves you, will be a vast additional incitement; if that there be a future state, the hope of a happy existence in that increases the appetite to deserve it; if that Jesus was also God, you will be comforted by a belief of his aid and love. In fine, I repeat, *you must lay aside prejudices on both sides*, and neither believe nor reject anything ... *Your own reason is the only oracle given you by heaven, and you are answerable, not for the rightness, but the uprightness of the decision* ... " [my italics].[3]

For Jefferson, it was not only appropriate to question God's existence but most important to do so. And what's more, the conclusion may not be the same for everybody; and that's just fine. In the very same letter that Jewett has quoted, dated August 10, 1787, his young friend (and nephew) Peter Carr is advised to:

> Fix reason firmly in her seat, and call to her tribunal every fact, every opinion. *Question with boldness even the existence of a god*; because if there be one, he must more approve the homage of reason, than that of blindfolded fear [my italics].[4]

The real Jefferson believed that reason was the most important human attribute. This meant that everything should be up for grabs, and that encompasses what contemporary man perceives as being eternal truths. When he say's "question with boldness" he means exactly what it sounds like. He doesn't endorse any concept of truth that relies on a prescientific medieval approach to knowledge. Therefore, any appeal to authority alone, no matter how prestigious it may be, is unacceptable. If even God is included in this, Jefferson himself isn't excluded. Openness in thinking—not certainty—is what Jefferson was about. He would see present-day conservatives as being intellectually lazy for shutting the door on new ideas and instead succumbing to a form of ancestor worship, whereby reverence for the past is so shielded from objectivity that it becomes indistinguishable from religious revelation. Jefferson thought that such a mindset was stultifying. He was a proud and open son of the Enlightenment.

If one still doubts the high esteem in which Jefferson held the scientific method or how it relates to politics, take a look at this 1813 letter that he wrote to John Adams; in it he couldn't be clearer:

> One of the questions … on which our parties took different sides was on the *improvability of the human mind* in science, in ethics, *in government,* etc. Those who advocated reformation of institutions, *pari passu* with the progress of science, maintained that no definite limits could be assigned to that progress. The *enemies of reform, on the other hand, denied improvement, and advocated steady adherence to the principles, practices and institutions of our fathers,* which they represented as the consummation of wisdom, and acme of excellence, beyond which the human mind could ever advance…you predict that [freedom of inquiry] will produce nothing more worthy of transmission to posterity than the principles, institutions and systems of education received from their ancestors … [but] *You possess, yourself, too much science not to see how much is still ahead of you, unexplained and unexplored. Your own consciousness must place you as far before our ancestors as in the rear of our posterity* [my italics].[5]

It's important to note that Jefferson is referring not only to ethics and science but also to government when he concludes that we must place "our ancestors" in the "rear of our "posterity." Jefferson himself refutes the conservative image of him as a father spouting an unchanging absolute truth. That's because as a scientist he understood that science knows no intellectual closure. An idea is accepted only until a new one with a better explanation comes along. This entails an eagerness to know and a willingness to accept new discoveries about human beings and their world. Needless to say, these qualities usually do not receive top ranking on the list of virtues of most conservatives. Yet for Jefferson they were of primary importance.

Writing in 1800 to one of the world's most famous scientists, Joseph Priestley, Jefferson reiterates his strong belief in the necessity of open-mindedness and change as well as the dangers of believing that our ancestors are the final word:

> The *Gothic idea that we are to look backwards instead of forwards* for the improvement of the human mind, and to *recur to the annals of our ancestors for what is most perfect in government*, in religion & in learning, is worthy of those *bigots in religion & government*, by whom it has been recommended, & whose purposes it would answer. But it is not an idea which this country will endure ... [my italics].[6]

Note that once again Jefferson places government in the same category as religion and learning when he disparages looking backwards instead of forward for the proper path to peruse. When this founder addresses his long-term philosophical concerns rather than his short-run political positions we see a much deeper side of him.

This is the person whose quote is contained on the fourth panel of the Jefferson memorial, i.e., the man of the Enlightenment, the real deal. This Jefferson will never be reconciled with any pile of mummified remains that have the "everlasting wisdom" of a bygone era written on them. The flesh-and-blood version believed in no such thing!

Yet this corpse is the "Jefferson" used by today's conservatives to provide comfort and assure them that they live in a world of easy answers and few doubts. It's no accident that these are the same people who, when objective facts challenge their fantasy world (e.g., global warming and for some even evolution), readily choose to ignore the very scientific method that Jefferson so believed in. Our third president, the man who thought that if there was a Supreme Being it would favor people who questioned its existence over those who accepted blindly, would have been totally out of place in such company.

No, I don't think that today's conservatives have a special claim on Jefferson or any of the other real Founding Fathers, not even close. Yet I am not claiming that we liberals do either. Speaking for myself, I have a big problem with the founders' reliance on the rational at the expense of the human. However, this doesn't change the fact that much of their thinking was just as incompatible with the views of those on the right. And there are two other exceedingly important points to remember. First is that the real founders had many varied opinions, often disagreeing among themselves. Second—and the most crucial—is that it doesn't matter! We live in a much different world than they did, and we face problems that none of them could ever have imagined. And what's more, we have knowledge that they never had, including two hundred plus years of additional history.

The best we can do to keep faith with them is to emulate their best qualities—energetic thinking, receptiveness to new and far-reaching ideas—and steer away from deifying those who came before us or encouraging the young to deify us. And one more thing: each generation should pay tribute to the founders by making the country better, as Jefferson so elegantly expressed it, continuing the progression towards a less barbarous society.

Is Any Part of Libertarianism Liberal?

Because of its extreme rejection of any societal commitment to altruistic goals, libertarian ideology merits a discussion when observing a civilization's degree of barbarousness. Since the most popular and well-known libertarian is Ayn Rand, we should begin with her. Randian libertarianism has been seen by some as an ideology that doesn't fit into the usual left vs. right divide, possibility explaining its appeal to both a select number of self-identified liberals as well as conservatives.

Pure Randians are in principle opposed to virtually all societal controls that are based on religious beliefs or humanitarian ideals. Therefore they see any attempt by government to place limits on the right of an individual to control her own body, sexual practices, or drug ingestion as tyranny. This is appealing to some liberals. However, any attempt to limit the individual's choice in the socioeconomic sphere, such as mandated social programs or limits on business and market practices, are also viewed as tyranny. Restrictions placed on a person's prejudices, like antidiscrimination laws, can be added to the list as well. These aspects have appeal to many conservatives.

Ayn Rand believed that naked self-interest was life's driving force and was behind all that was good.[7] She was highly suspicious of any overarching social agenda and thought that one should be wary of individuals or groups that appeared to be acting selflessly in the interests of others. They were most likely parasitical and self-aggrandizing frauds with a concealed purpose in mind. [8] For Rand, it simply wasn't natural for individuals to place other people's interests above their own. People were responsible for handling what belonged to them and should expect nothing from anyone else. Consequently, Rand was a fierce proponent of extreme individualism and an equally strong opponent of almost any kind of communitarianism. In regards to religion she was a staunch atheist.[9, 10] Yet personally Rand was not as libertarian as the general ideology she popularized. In fact, at ground level she was very conformist (favoring conservative grooming, i.e., she didn't like facial hair),[11] sexist (men should be in charge),[12] homophobic (gay sexuality disgusted her),[13, 14] and when old and ill she relied on the "nanny state" (i.e., received Social Security and Medicare).[15] Despite this, many people are enamored with her generic views and choose to ignore her individual prejudices and inconsistencies. That's why Rand's philosophy is even popular among particular groups of gays, feminists, and hippie-looking free spirits.

Yet the fact that hers is an idiosyncratic ideology doesn't negate its right-wing underpinnings. Ron Paul's views could be seen as comprising a branch of Randian thought; and as you know, I categorize Paul's outlook as conservative. This is backed up by the fact that Paul—like most Neo-Randians—feels more comfortable in the nation's more conservative party, the Republican, rather than the nation's more liberal one, the Democratic. There is good reason for this. At its core Randian philosophy is based on extreme intellectualization and correspondingly a total rejection of any empathic initiatives in regards to public policy. It is no accident that its proponents call themselves objectivists. They revel in being objective, as in dispassionate. This is consistent with the Right's hard-line positions on fiscal priorities at the expense of human concerns such as injustice and inequality. Therefore, like their mainline conservative brethren, they reject societal attempts to mitigate even the worst of life's imbalances.

If the vast majority of the population does poorly, it's by definition their own fault and never the result of a flawed system. So issues like 5 percent of the population controlling 95 percent of the wealth (it's currently 72 percent)[16] are not seen as issues at all, since they are nothing to be concerned about. The same would be true if businesses and other institutions had policies of racial exclusion. Randians wouldn't necessarily see the victims of racism as responsible; but as already stated they aren't in favor of placing enforceable restrictions on abuser practices. However, on this question it must be noted that while this ideology has nonracist adherents, one shouldn't ignore the fact that Rand herself wasn't averse to engaging in racism. For example, when talking about particular ethnic classifications Rand often spoke with a broad brush, as when she asserted that Native Americans deserved to be stripped of their land because they had failed to create a heroically productive capitalist society.[17] Such sentiments are in tandem with William F. Buckley's ignoble contention that African Americans deserved their second-class citizenship because they had not achieved as much as whites (see Chapter VIII). Putting aside for the moment that some with this philosophy have no difficulty employing a broad brush against certain groups, Randians insist that they are virtually 100 percent about the individual and zero percent about any collective engagement. Racism notwithstanding, what remains is an intense individualism mixed with an aversion to any politics that is partial to sharing or caring, even one that attempts to address what may be the human toll of their own belief system.

Modern neuroscience questions this individualist philosophy by showing that a concern for the welfare of others is a genuine human emotion that benefits society and not, as Rand believed, a fraudulent hoax.[18] Her philosophy is contrary to not only the very soul of liberalism but also the best instincts of human nature. It's probably an understatement to say that, unlike those who participated in America's justice movements, Ayn Rand and her sympathizers wouldn't have been the best audience at the Sermon on the Mount.

Randian libertarianism is one of the most dangerous belief systems that we confront today. Her ideology embraces (without acknowledgment) the sociopathic ideal. Although most of its followers are not themselves sociopaths, it doesn't change the fact that their world outlook is a perfect fit for this personality type. For both, selfishness is the highest virtue and feeling obliged to assist your neighbors is an irrational anathema. In the previous chapter we saw the dangers inherent in any mindset that minimizes the importance of empathy. The Nazi era has shown us that although the vast majority of people—as in the millions who raised their arms and said "heil"—may not be individually sociopathic, the larger group when acting as an individual society can be. This is why the growth of Randian philosophy is of concern.

As with the proliferating Marxist ideologies in the late-nineteenth and early-twentieth century, twenty-first-century Randians can't imagine how the world they envision could lead to unspeakable tyranny. Yet the disturbing signs are all there. Like most ideologues, Rand displayed self-righteous absolutism in regards to matters of who was "entitled" and who was not. Her eagerness to ignore legally binding contracts and seize Native American lands, as well as her disdain for the statutory rights of working Americans whose earned income finances the social justice programs (like Social Security) that she (in theory) detested, are but two good examples. Reading Rand gives one an eerie feeling of how historic totalitarianism eyed the world. She saw no signs of grey in life. Rand had little tolerance for complexity or nuance. Her novels are very simplistic, with the "good" being really good and the "bad" being really bad. Invariably bad things happen to bad people; they are those who think they are owed something that has not been earned. They are the vast majority of human race; they are the losers. In contrast, the good people are a small minority of the population. It's mostly high achievers and life's winners that make this select list. The bottom line of this simplistic worldview is that Randian libertarianism has utter contempt for the losers, the preponderance of humanity. Included in this large group are history's heroic justice fighters. After all, why would life's winners be concerned about anybody but themselves? In her book *Atlas Shrugged* the star character, John Galt (who is really speaking for Rand), says:

> For centuries, the battle of morality was fought between those who claimed that life belongs to god and those who claimed that it belongs to your neighbors—between those who preached that the good is self-sacrifice for the sake of ghosts in heaven and those who preached that the good is self-sacrifice *for the sake of incompetents on earth.* And no one came to say that your life belongs to you and the good is to live it [my italics].[19]

In other words, why care about injustice to others who for the most part are undeserving "incompetents"; care first and foremost about you. As an aside it must be noted that although Randians claim that they oppose injustices like slavery, how are such evils ever disposed of if morality has nothing to do with caring about the plight of your fellow human beings and, if need be, making sacrifices to assist those who are in a less fortunate position than yourself? That's why when they or similar-minded libertarians attempt to deal with real events in history, injustices like slavery conveniently disappear by themselves, poof, without need of any human agency (see Chapter IX concerning the ideas of Thomas DiLorenzo). The bottom line is that unlike the abolitionists Rand did not believe that morality was directly related to how you treat others. Once again, John Galt (i.e., Ayn Rand):

> You who prattle that morality is social and that man would need no morality on a desert island-it is on a desert island that he would need it most ... reality will show him that life is a value to be bought and that thinking is the only coin noble enough to buy it.[20]

For Rand the morality of history's winners is grounded in the lone individual using his brain to survive (and achieve); it has little to do with his connectedness to any larger group. And of course there is good reason for this; for as stressed in her writings over and over again, the losers aren't worth it.

In *Pity the Billionaire,* Thomas Frank notes that after reading *Atlas Shrugged* libertarian economist Ludwig von Mises wrote Rand and said:

> "You have the courage to tell the masses what no politician told them: you are inferior and all the improvements in your conditions which you simply take for granted you owe to the efforts of men who are better than you."[21]

To which Frank aptly comments:

> It is hardly a democratic formula. Indeed, democracy is part of the problem for Rand ... [22]

For people with views like Rand and Mises, democracy is dangerous to the extent that it gives the loser majority decision-making power. They are out of place in this position. Although it may not be so visibly obvious to her fans, Rand's view of the proper fate of the masses is not much different from that of a serf's lot in life. As in feudal times, it's a winner-take-all world; no idea of the greater community need exist.

In lacking any meaningful concept of the common good, Randian ideology, like conservative philosophy in general, sees no need for a fair playing field. Wealth and social position are to be inherited without any societal limitations. Randians have a steadfast belief that "supermen" will always triumph no matter what side of the divide they are born on. For Rand, it's the supermen who really count.[23] For this reason the world must be constructed for their benefit alone. In the introduction to the twenty-fifth anniversary edition of her book *The Fountainhead* Rand writes:

> Since my purpose is the presentation of an ideal man, I had to define and present the conditions which make him possible and which his existence requires.[24]

After speaking about what kind of internal fortitude it takes to achieve the standing of her "ideal man," she hypotheses on the number of men who possess it:

> It's an emotion that a few—a very few—men experience consistently ... [25]

Two pages later she adds:

> It does not matter that only a few in each generation will grasp and achieve the full reality of man's proper stature—and that the rest will betray it.[26]

Once again she stresses that only a few people are worthy of her praise, with the vast majority of humanity being contemptible cowards. Therefore it's no surprise that most of us fail to qualify as being the ideal "man" she speaks of; and as a result, a fair start in life wouldn't do us any good. But for those who qualify any amount of unfairness wouldn't do them any harm. Yet most important is that in our betrayal of their (her) ideals, most of us are really anti-ideal men, i.e., the enemy. It then follows that a properly ordered society should care little about the gross number of people who would be adversely affected by being born into unfavorable circumstances. In fact, the good society must be purposely constructed to neutralize the negative influences of the larger portion of these people (i.e., the masses). Obviously, this perspective is well complemented by the typical right-wing belief that justice shouldn't be an automatic entitlement but must be earned by one's own individual efforts.

When Randian libertarianism doesn't live up to its farcical view of reality, it's then we will see the curtain open and the not-so-visibly obvious show its face. What happens when inequality becomes stifling? What happens when the real-life situation on the ground leads to an overflowing social unrest that endangers the entire political and economic order? What happens when the only governmental functions that Randians view as legitimate—courts, police, prisons, and the military—just happen to be coercive entities?[27] What happens when a response to a dangerously escalating disorder is necessary and these institutions are the only ones available? What happens when leaders blame the victims and have utter contempt for the mass of the population, the disgruntled "losers"? What happens when those on top see it appropriate to respond to social upheaval in the same violent and tyrannical manner as the men Ayn Rand "worshipped," the robber barons?[28] What happens when their model of industrial organization and hierarchical governance permeates everything? What happens when the only morality that leaders recognize is naked self-interest (an excuse for the absence of morality)? What happens when private tyrannies rule the world without any meaningful checks on their prerogatives? What happens in times of human crisis in a society whose very existence, its reason for being, is dependent on the rejection of altruism and compromise?

The untold truth is that Randian philosophy is a rigid, unbending, simplistic, and highly negative world outlook that has little room to grow or adjust to unforeseen and unwanted realities. And what doesn't bend will usually break. In caring nothing about the human toll, it has no real standards by which to judge itself. It is right by definition, no matter the body count. That eerie feeling of how totalitarian societies saw things surfaces once again. The potential for a real Randian dystopia is clearly evident in a piece by Stephen Cox of the University of California, San Diego, written for the *Journal of Libertarian Studies*. He notes that Rand amended her language in the 1959 edition of her book *We the Living*. She claimed that it was due to her mistakes using English (her native tongue was Russian). Cox writes:

> For instance in the original version, Andrei observes that "we can't sacrifice for the sake of the few" and Kira replies *"You can! You must. When those few are the best."* In the 1959 edition her declaration is replaced by a question: "Can you sacrifice the few?" A little later Kira's remark that she knows *"no worse injustice than justice for all"* is replaced by the more rational *"I know no worse injustice than the giving of the undeserved"* [my italics].[29]

Cox thinks that the change in Rand's last sentence is ideological, not linguistic. In this regard he says "she tries to reduce the violence of the novel's contempt for the "masses."[30]

Although he may think that this is satisfactory, in my estimation it's not much of a reduction. No matter how you phrase it, Rand saw most people as being undeserving—in a figurative sense, another species. What's more, linguistic change or not, she really didn't believe that those she labeled as undeserving (most of us) were even entitled to justice. If this isn't a prescription for a nightmare world, nothing is. The totality of Randian thought, like the Nazi ideology in Germany, sets the stage for the larger society to act like an individual sociopath.

Rand hasn't been the only prolific libertarian writer. In addition to her popular books there have been a number by well-known libertarian economists. One of them, Ludwig von Mises, was quoted above. As you saw, his view of the masses is very much in line with Rand's general outlook. While assessing the differences between various libertarian writers isn't the purpose of this book, we still need to dig a little deeper into the broader nature of this ideology.

Of the scholarly libertarians, economist Friedrich Hayek, previously mentioned in Chapter IX, is probably the most renowned. His famous book, *The Road to Serfdom,* has become a classic for the libertarian intelligentsia. This work was written in the early 1940s and was seen as a commentary on the rising tide of totalitarianism that was then engulfing large parts of the world. It is important to note that Hayek is far more complicated and nuanced than Rand. Unlike Rand, he does attempt, albeit somewhat disjointedly, to separate out at least some of the differences between a legitimate desire for social justice and an outright totalitarian ideology that tries to employ this yearning to justify tyranny. For example, he writes:

> Nor is there any reason why the state should not assist the individuals in providing for those common hazards of life against which, because of their uncertainty, few individuals can make adequate provision. Where, as in the case of sickness and accident, neither the desire to avoid such calamities nor the efforts to overcome their consequences are as a rule weakened by provision of assistance … *the case for the state's helping to organize a comprehensive system of social insurance is very strong* [my italics].[31]

Nevertheless, this collection of sentences does not fit very well into his overall perspective. He repeatedly stresses the necessity of having an unrestricted marketplace by asserting that its end result will never be based on a subjective and arbitrary decision by some institutional authority; that for him is the utter negation of freedom. Of course "in providing for those common hazards of life" some authority (legislative or otherwise) has to arbitrarily decide what exactly these hazards are and how much to provide for them. In other words, any existing society, especially a humane one, has to make human judgments that are outside the scope of the marketplace. Therein lays the rub in *The Road to Serfdom*, for Hayek doesn't really reconcile the necessity of arbitrary group actions with that of an unrestricted nonarbitrary (everyone is supposedly in the same boat and subject to the same unknown risks) marketplace. This may explain why Hayek's book chooses to portray social justice as most frequently being the enemy of freedom, for in doing so he avoids this rough edge. Hayek disagrees with those who claim that socioeconomic rights (i.e., positive freedom) are just a natural extension and the next evolutionary stage of previously established political rights (i.e., negative freedom). In speaking about these two different types of freedom, he says:

> And, although the word was used in a different sense by the two groups, few people noticed this and still fewer asked themselves *whether the two kinds of freedom promised could really be combined* [my italics].[32]

In his later works his opposition to social justice hardens even more and becomes exceedingly severe. It should be noted that when *The Road to Serfdom* was written the political-intellectual spectrum of thought was much further to the left than it would be in future years. In other words, as his audience moved to the right so did he. When there was less of a need to be conciliatory, he became less so. Therefore I see the reasonable concessions he once made to collectively provide "for those common hazards of life" to be taken with a grain of salt. By the end of his life social democracy (or New Deal liberalism in the U.S.), and not actually existing totalitarianism, was seen by Hayek as the primary enemy of freedom. He would subtly (or not-so-subtly, depending on your perspective) claim that states committed to alleviating social injustice were on a slippery slope to Stalinism.[33] While he was proved right about the future of Marxist-Leninist economics and style of governance, the exact opposite was true regarding the fate of nations with highly developed social safety nets. For this reason, in order to defend his legacy many of his present day followers are quick to (selectively) quote some of his conciliatory passages in the *The Road to Serfdom* like the one above (see footnote 31"). This is of course an admission of sorts that while history has swept away Soviet communism, the successes of the social justice movements are in another category altogether.

In a broader conceptual sense, it isn't the specifics of Hayek's philosophy that interest me the most but the ironic title he chose for his most famous work. Obviously it was meant to exemplify the worst that could happen. The reader was being warned that if the bad guys win, this is going to be your fate. And what was selected to represent the nightmare hanging over everyone's head? As we now know it was serfdom, the status of the vast majority of the medieval (European) population living under the social system known as feudalism.

I have always thought that this title was quite telling. After all, Hayek was implying that just about the worst state of affairs imaginable was life under feudalism. So what were this system's characteristics? Let's zero in on the four that most affected people's lives:

- The almost complete absence of any central authority, including the lack of virtually any enforceable universal standards—most power was local;
- The almost complete absence of any public commons, including civil governance—all assets, agriculture, and authority were in private hands;
- The almost complete absence of any semblance of equality—a small segment of the population laid claim to most of the world's land, water, and resources, all of which was earmarked to be passed on to their heirs alone;
- The almost complete absence of formal laws—traditional private arrangements (obligations) substituted for modern day legality, most people were restricted by perpetual debt (in-kind) owed to these family oligarchies, and the resulting system had essentially zero public debt and zero public bureaucracy.[34, 35, 36]

A society in which there is no powerful central authority to ensure enforcement of universal standards, no public commons, ownership, mandates, debt or bureaucracy, no concern about massive economic or power disparities, and where everything of value is privatized, is held to be the classic prototype of tyranny; go figure.

Of course, this is where I completely agree with Hayek's choice of a title. Yet I differ with his view of what system is most likely to move the world in such a direction. This nightmare seems to more closely resemble the end goals of libertarian capitalism than the ones at the liberal end of the spectrum. I know that some will say that despite some similarities to feudalism libertarianism is different, because unlike this past medieval arrangement it's democratic. Unfortunately, this is less a convincing argument than a lame excuse.

The great philosophers of libertarianism, like Rand and Mises, where not impressed by the concept of "one man, one vote" and far more amenable to the idea of "one dollar, one vote." As Thomas Frank implied, their primary concern with democracy wasn't that wealthy individuals or corporations would exercise their economic clout to rig the system, but rather that jealous voters would use their numerical majority to rob the rich. In even privatizing civil authority, feudalism put to rest their biggest worry and established a situation much closer to what leading libertarians have seen as the ideal relationship between political and economic influence.

As there cannot be any meaningful freedom in a patch of quicksand, you can't have a free society without universal standards and a robust public commons. If you could, feudalism would have been the freest society ever. Hayek's book would have been entitled *The Road away from Serfdom*. The fact that it's not speaks volumes.

Yet the story doesn't end here. In his famous 1977 work *The Alternative in Eastern Europe*, Rudolf Bahro discusses some interesting links between capitalism and feudalism. I think that his insights shed even more light on the nature of libertarian ideology. He writes:

Original capitalism, however, has only existed where this feudalism developed beforehand, with its immanent tendency of transformation. Feudalism–capitalism is essentially a single development, the dialectical unfolding and extension of one (or if Japan is included two) of the many human civilizations.[37]

Bahro is saying that it's no accident that modern capitalism first appeared in places that had a prior period of feudalism. The only non-European part of the world that went through a period akin to Western-style feudalism was Japan. And Japan is the one Eastern country where capitalist institutions emerged indigenously. In other words, the indigenous existence of capitalism is dependent on feudalism; they are interconnected systems.

When capitalism first began its rise, merchants supported a powerful king and the development of a strong central government.[38] This included universal standards and a civil bureaucracy to enforce them. In the process a public commons came into existence. It comprised water, lands, buildings, and institutions that weren't for the sole benefit of the few but at the disposal of the many. There had always been private book and art collections, but for the first time in a millennium, public libraries and museums sprang up.[39] Now everyone could have access to great creative works and consequently advanced knowledge. The development of capitalism and democracy went hand in hand with the growth of a public commons. As we now know, it would go as far as elected government, public services, infrastructure, parks, schools, and even social safety nets.

So what's the thinking behind the push to reverse course? The libertarian vision of a society where almost everything imaginable is once again back in private hands—with all that is public reduced, as Grover Norquist likes to say, to what can be drowned in a bathtub—is understood as simply capitalism just being itself, completely unadulterated. If feudalism is capitalism's other face and libertarianism is its purest form, the similarities between the two historical periods may become more obvious as capitalism becomes less diluted. This would explain why it is that no matter the designer, all libertarian models of society rearrange its parts into a mass network of private relationships with an overall structure reminiscent of the extreme social stratification and dispossession of feudal times. It may not be a fluke that, given the close and possibly circular relationship between the two supposedly different socioeconomic systems, the most extreme form of capitalism looks a lot like feudalism.

In the Princeton University journal *Philosophy and Public Affairs*, there is a paper by Samuel Freeman, "Illiberal Libertarians: Why Libertarianism is Not a Liberal View," that speaks to the ideology's inherent propensity to reestablish feudal arrangements (i.e., private tyrannies are once again at the pinnacle of society) and, more importantly, to our central question: Is any part of it liberal? He writes:

in the end, libertarians reject essential liberal institutions. Correctly understood, libertarianism resembles a view that liberalism historically defined itself against, *the doctrine of private political power that underlies feudalism.* Like feudalism, libertarianism conceives of justified political power as based in a network of private contracts. It rejects *the idea, essential to liberalism, that political power is a public power, to be impartially exercised for the common good* [my italics].[40]

He proceeds to say that the libertarian concept of liberty is none other than a property right and as such is in total opposition to the basic tenets of liberalism. He notes that liberals see liberty not as property but as an inalienable right. He elaborates further:

> More important for our purposes, *the idea of basic liberties also includes their inalienability: a person cannot contractually transfer basic liberties or give them up voluntarily.* No liberal government would enforce a contract or agreement in which one or more persons tried to *sell themselves into slavery or indentured servitude* [my italics].[41]

This paragraph explains why the existence of constitutionally established enforcement mechanisms to ensure the effectuation of agreed-upon universal standards is so important; without them there can be no inalienable rights. Americans witnessed this firsthand when, at the consternation of the majority of the local population, both the judicial and executive branches of the federal government enforced the Constitution and ended the South's traditional practice of state-sanctioned racial segregation. In a world of unbounded contracts between individuals and groups (common interest or regional) anything is possible, including slavery. At its core libertarianism, unlike liberalism, sees liberty as just another property to be brought and sought at the marketplace. It transforms an inalienable right into a property right, thereby making slavery not only possible but most likely.

If you don't believe me read Robert Nozick. His classic work *Anarchy, State, and Utopia* was so praised by the libertarian intelligentsia that it was held to be the definitive libertarian answer to the liberal concept of justice put forth by John Rauls. Interestingly, Rauls and Nozick were actually competing colleagues in the same academic department at Harvard. In *Anarchy, State, and Utopia,* Nozick takes the libertarian logic that everything constitutes a property relationship and therefore is marketable to its ultimate conclusion: a free society must allow slavery. He tells us that:

> The comparable question about an individual is whether a free system will allow him to sell himself into slavery. I believe that it would.[42]

This viewpoint enunciated by one of the twentieth century's most heralded libertarian scholars explains why fellow travelers like Ron Paul and Thomas DiLorenzo are able to hold that a slave society like the Confederacy— and not the United States—was the side that best represented the ideal of freedom during the Civil War. At the root of their ideology is the view that the existence of legal slavery is no big deal, or at least not one that's big enough to be a defining impediment to their understanding of liberty. Speaking of the casualness in which this institution is held, Nozick even takes the time to hypothesize about the monetary nuances of a free (!) slave market. Once again from *Anarchy, State, and Utopia*:

> even though in it (Utopia) they are abject slaves—their payoff will not be bid up in a competitive market.[43]

After some 350 pages of this esteemed Harvard professor's highly intellectualized analysis, including the use of abstract mathematical representations and innumerable referencing of the words liberty and freedom, we are right back to the antebellum South and the proslavery arguments of Thomas R. Dew. Remember, Dew held that a viable slave market was the hallmark of a genuinely free society. We see an offshoot of this perspective when libertarians argue for the right of living individuals to sell their own, as well as other people's, healthy body parts (i.e., kidneys) for profit in a free marketplace that trades in human organs as if they were just another commodity. I know that some may say that the libertarian idea of slavery is different, since as with selling one's organs it is based on a person's voluntary choice. These are the same people who believed that "separate but equal" (the legal rationale behind segregation) was really equal. Imagine an alternate libertarian universe where during the Great Depression millions of unemployed, homeless, and hungry unfortunates opted to sell not just their body parts but their entire selves into a legally binding contractually legitimized version of slavery. Instead of Social Security, unemployment insurance, child labor and worker safety protections, the legacy of that era would have been a large slave population. After all the clever rationalizations, the libertarian idea of freedom is no more than the freedom of the strong to exploit the weak, the freedom to take what you can get away with, the freedom of a jungle that would be, for most of humanity, indistinguishable from a patch of quicksand. Yes, this is the real (and quite ugly) face of freedom in a libertarian universe. We shouldn't ever forget that being on the correct side of a particular issue is not being right if it is for the wrong reason. This is even truer if that same reason, when fully played out, is horrifying. It is finally time to return to the overarching question: Is any part of this deceptive and dangerous ideology liberal? You tell me.

Chapter XII

Final Thoughts

The United States has always been a staunchly capitalist nation. The free-market ideas popularized by Adam Smith were embraced by many of our Founding Fathers. The country's astonishing economic growth has been in large part the result of a thriving market economy. Yet as we have seen, this fact in itself did not guarantee a decent life for everyone. Many Americans have still been plagued by terrible injustices—slavery, total disenfranchisement of women, socioeconomic restrictions on suffrage, racial segregation, exploitation of children and working people, to name but a few. What's more, this shameful list doesn't even include what amounted to genocide against the original native population. Fortunately for us the story didn't end—and won't end—with these or other atrocities. I have tried to show that throughout American history there have always been people who were outraged by injustice and dedicated their energies towards assisting its victims in redressing the wrongs imposed upon them. While some of these heroes were merchants, it wasn't marketplace concerns that energized them. It wasn't a striving for personal profit or self-gain; it was their strong sense of justice and their intuitive understanding that fundamental fairness was its main embodiment.

Yet the task before them was never easy; they had to battle the most powerful forces of their day. These included slaveholders who were primarily concerned about the financial catastrophe that would befall them if abolition succeeded, rich property owners who fought public education because they didn't want to pay higher taxes to educate other people's children, industrialists who opposed child labor and worker safety protections because they were worried about their profits being reduced, and on and on. The lesson to be learned from these very real historical struggles is that what we have become as a nation wasn't shaped by avoiding a financial catastrophe for slaveholders or higher taxes for wealthy landlords or increased labor costs for large corporations; it was a broader vision of humanity and our connection to it. Contrary to the perspective of Ayn Rand and her following, high-level civilization cannot be achieved by economic and technological accomplishments alone. If it could, Nazi Germany would have been the epitome of civilization. The fact that the exact opposite was true is evidence that quality existence rests on far more fundamental factors.

Only with this in mind can we understand America's true story. We see that a thriving capitalist economy in and of itself would not have produced the tale we now know. Those who were only concerned about "what's in it for me" could not have forged such an account. The history presented in this book has attempted to highlight the fact that it's our most distinctively human side—our capacity for empathy—that is primarily responsible for laying the groundwork for the real American narrative. Progressing from the Declaration of Independence[1] to the Gettysburg Address to Martin Luther King Jr.'s "I Have a Dream" speech, America's ongoing epic has been chronicled by its most empathic visionaries. It is no accident that this is the one quality that the Right makes fun of, mocking it to no end. They have negatively characterized fighters against injustice by their empathetic proclivities. Derogatory terminology such as "do-gooders," "bleeding hearts," "[n-word]-lovers," and "peaceniks" are but a few nasty names used to dehumanize those who identified with the distress of others. These verbal assaults epitomize the Right's disdain for empathy. Nevertheless, it has been as vital to our country's success as its economic system or its original Constitution. Take it away from the scene and you would see an unrecognizable America with anything but an awe-inspiring story.

Yet most essential, we mustn't forget that the final chapter doesn't end with the present. If we are going to continue this great saga for the benefit of future generations, we must never put aside the very human qualities that made it all possible. For this reason I have purposefully focused on how empathic concern and its blood relative—the pursuit of justice—is the primary agent for achieving meaningful social change. Never mistake these attributes for an artificial construction like the concept of "tough love." What I am referring to is the innate human propensity to identify with the plight of others. Everywhere we look in the world we see its positive potential, the fruits of which transcend any particular nation or people. This is the one quality that is able to bypass even the worst of ideologies. An excellent example would be the unlikely heroics of Oskar Schindler, the person heralded in Steven Spielberg's 1993 classic, *Schindler's List*. At the time he joined the Nazi Party, Schindler didn't question its goals or core beliefs. In fact, he was considered to be a loyal party member right up to the war's end. And it must be said that for someone with Schindler's intelligence it shouldn't have been that difficult for him to understand the nature of the Nazi movement. Unfortunately in this instance his intellect failed him. Yet when confronted with the kind of hard-core truth that couldn't honestly be denied he responded like a human being, not an ideologue. He chose to save Jews by preventing them from being taken to the gas chambers. It goes without saying that he took a very big chance. In all likelihood the potential consequences of his courageous action weren't something that he cared to think too much about. An abundance of in-depth thought wouldn't have aided such high-risk behavior. Doing the right thing wasn't an intellectual endeavor. What Schindler observed with his own eyes dictated his response, not any preconceived ideology and certainly not any clever, self-indulgent philosophizing.

I have attempted to demonstrate that it's this very same human quality that has expressed itself in all the great justice movements and as such has not only shaped the face of our current world but will be called on again to shape our future one. This is why people on the right not only detest this quality but also find it extremely threatening. This fear expresses itself in their efforts to rewrite history for the purpose of belittling the accomplishments of the great justice movements. They revel in dredging up justice fighters who possessed some hurtful and even barbaric attitudes to prove they were not what they claimed to be or were really conservatives. For example, Thomas DiLorenzo likes to focus in on selected nineteenth-century abolitionists who (like Schindler) didn't give many of the prejudices of their day too much thought. This is also true in regards to his handling of Lincoln. However, no matter how much they or Lincoln accepted the false but common belief in the significance of innate racial differences, they didn't try to use it to rationalize away the unfairness of slavery. When they were confronted with the institution's stark reality, their revulsion of injustice and instinctive capacity for identifying with the misery of other human beings got the upper hand.

This is the bigger picture that the Right chooses to ignore. It results in them never asking the most meaningful question: When a person is in the midst of a horrendous situation that runs counter to her acquired prejudices, does she respond like Schindler did or instead does she attempt to rationalize the brutality away? The choice between making a meaningful human connection that results in positive action and its opposite, self-serving intellectualization, has always been a crucial theme in human history. Fortunately, America has had good people who were outraged by the blatant evils that anyone with eyes could see. Their empathic concern for the victims would drive them to battle for a more just nation. The conservatives who opposed them all too frequently fell back on a comforting (free-market) ideology to justify everything from dangerous working conditions to the naked exploitation of children. In every case, seeing the world through ideological blinders is as sanctimonious as it is contrived. In contrast, seeing ourselves in others and seeking to redress injustice is as human as it is real. No matter the period, the truth lies beneath the arguments, with humanity's quest for justice representing the best in ourselves. This is why if we want America's true story to continue we mustn't ever allow this great nation's "bleeding heart" to stop beating.

Afterword

I think it necessary to speak to one last point. I know that many of the heroes I selected to showcase are both white and male. This doesn't mean that progressive accomplishments were primarily driven by this or any other group of people. The picture that I presented can be seen from many other legitimate angles. For example, a book could be written about the essential contributions that were made by those who came solely from persecuted groups, and its message could be just as (or even more) valid than what is contained in this book. Truth comes in degrees and from a multitude of perspectives. The perspective I chose reflects who I am.

I don't mean being white and male, although the shoe does fit. What I am referring to is my Jewish heritage. I was born of a Jewish mother and grew up in a neighborhood where there were many families of Jewish refugees, whose youngsters were among my closest friends. The parents in these families and correspondingly those of my childhood buddies were overwhelmingly Holocaust survivors. As a youth I would go into their living rooms, kitchens, and backyards with the same ease that I would my own home. Although unaware of it at the time, I was subtly picking up much of their values and world outlook.

I think this explains the fascination that I have always had with "righteous gentiles," the non-Jews who risked everything to protect Jews from the Nazis. Instead of being embittered against all gentiles, Holocaust survivors reserve a very special place in their hearts for these people, affording them the highest esteem imaginable. From the Garden of the Righteous among the Nations in Jerusalem to memorials in Holocaust museums throughout the world, righteous gentiles are honored time and time again. Yet the very best example of this is Steven Spielberg's elevation of Oskar Schindler. The first major motion picture about the Holocaust made by a child of Holocaust survivors memorialized a card-carrying member of the Nazi Party. This says it all when assessing how much respect Jews have for righteous gentiles.

Nevertheless, for whatever the reason the righteous gentiles have always intrigued me. I was driven to read books and do research on them. The more I got to know them, the more amazing they became. For the most part they were quite ordinary people, virtually nondescript, who did the most extraordinary things. They made the uttermost commitment to justice imaginable. To save strangers they not only put their own lives at risk but also those of their spouses, siblings, and even children! Yet they were very few in number and therefore no ordinary people. I came to understand full well why they are held in such high esteem. In fact, if anyone of us were put in the same position and faced the same terrifying risk, I doubt that we could honestly say for sure that we would be one of them. It isn't that difficult to imagine Jews putting everything on the line to oppose Nazism, but it is really another story altogether to imagine non-Jews taking the ultimate risk when the only certain fruits were fear and dread. The truth is that if there were ever a group that epitomized justice in human form it is the righteous gentiles.

I think this is why when I delve into American history I am so fascinated with people who remind me of them. Included are the Quakers, other white abolitionists, men who advocated for gender justice even before most women did, and so on. If I overrepresented these heroes it's because I can only come from where I come from; I can only write about what grabs me. As I have already said, it doesn't mean that there aren't other stories out there that are every bit as truthful and important. This book looks at history from one key angle among many. However, this fact doesn't in any way devalue the veracity and significance of the account you have just read.

Postscript

Just minutes after stepping into my local bookstore to have a look around, I noticed the August 26–September 2, 2013, issue of *Time* magazine. It was a double issue celebrating the fiftieth anniversary of Martin Luther King Jr.'s "I Have a Dream" speech. A large profile of Mr. King was on the magazine cover, with the words "Founding Father" in large capital letters. I quickly reached for the magazine and pored over the articles. There was one very interesting article by Jon Meacham entitled "One Man. A New Founding Father." Meacham introduces his piece by stating:

> One Man. With a single phrase, Martin Luther King Jr. joined Jefferson and Lincoln in the ranks of men who've shaped modern America.[1]

In the final paragraph he sums it all up by saying that:

> King brilliantly argued for *expansion* of the founders vision … In doing so, a preacher from the South *summoned* a nation *to justice* and won his place in the American pantheon [my italics].[2]

While Meacham's viewpoint is not exactly the message of this book, it's surprisingly close. King is as much of a legitimate Founding Father as any of those men who wore wigs. His accomplishments shaped our country as much as any of theirs did.

But what are the (subtle) differences between the focus of the article and this book? We can begin with the fact that King wasn't the first "Founding Father" without an eighteenth-century birth date or a White House address. What's important is that King represents a significant breakthrough. As stated in Chapter VIII, in celebrating King's birthday as a national holiday we finally got it right. One could add that it took long enough. There have been others like King who unfortunately didn't receive the credit they rightfully deserved—Garrison, (Frederick) Douglass, and Anthony, to name a few. All of them had a profound effect on what America is today. Like King, their contributions shaped our country to a degree that revivals the nation's original founders.

Second, I don't think King or any of the others wished to be so personally glorified that they ended up in stone like the make-believe "Founding Founders" of conservative lore. For King and the others, the real America was a work in progress, a masterpiece of infinite possibility and hope. The real heroes were its people; they were only the stand-ins. Their America could never be characterized by any exclusive club of invented deities. They understood that the list of our founders would only grow as we continued in the direction envisioned by Jefferson— namely, towards that less barbarous society.

NOTES

Chapter II

1. Sean Carroll, "Guest Post: Joe Polchinski on Black Holes, Complementarity, and Firewalls," *Cosmic Variance* (blog), *Discover*, September 27, 2012, accessed January 3, 2014, http://blogs.discovermagazine.com/cosmicvariance/2012/09/27/guest–post–joe–polchinski–on–black–holes–complementarity–and–firewalls/#.UsbcBLQlf5M.

2. John Rawls, *A Theory of Justice* (Cambridge, MA: The Belknap Press of Harvard University Press, 1971; rev. 1999), ch. III, sect. 25: "The Rationality of the Parties," 123.

3. John Rawls, *Justice as Fairness: A Restatement*, ed. Erin Kelly (The Belknap Press of Harvard University Press, 2001), pt. III, sect. 25:1: "Formal Constraints and the Veil of Ignorance," 86.

4. Ibid, pt. II, sect. 17.3: "Who Are the Least Advantaged?" 59–60.

5. Ibid, 60.

6. Thomas Pogge, *John Rawls: His Life and Theory of Justice*, trans. Michelle Kosch (New York: Oxford University Press, 2007), ch. 5: "The First Principle of Justice," 83.

7. John Rawls, *Justice as Fairness,* pt. I, sect. 6.2: "The Idea of the Original Position," 15.

8. Ibid, sect. 5.2: "Limits to our Inquiry," 14.

9. Ibid, pt. III, sect. 26.2: "The Idea of Public Reason," 89–90.

10. John Rawls, *A Theory of Justice*, pt. III, ch. VIII, sect, 72: "The Morality of Principles," 415.

11. Thomas Pogge, *John Rawls*, ch. 9, sect. 9.2, "Rawls and Communitarianism," 186.

12. Golnaz Tabibnia and Matthew Lieberman, "Fairness and Cooperation are Rewarding: Evidence from Social Cognitive Neuroscience," *Annals of the New York Academy of Sciences* 1118 (November 2007): 90–101, pub. online November 28, 2007, accessed December 13, 2013, http://www.cmu.edu/dietrich/sds/docs/tabibnia/fair–coop–rewarding.pdf.

13. Ibid, 94–95.

14. Paul Massari, "Just Rewards," *Harvard Gazette*, June 28, 2011, accessed December 14, 2013. http://news.harvard.edu/gazette/story/2011/06/just–rewards/.

15. Ibid.

16. Ibid.

17. Peter Reuell, "Figuring out Fairness," *Harvard Gazette*, September 13, 2012, accessed December 14, 2013, http://news.harvard.edu/gazette/story/2012/09/kids–merit/.

18. Ibid.

19. Sylvia A. Morelli, Lian T. Rameson, and Matthew D. Lieberman, "The Neural Components of Empathy: Predicting Daily Prosocial Behavior," *Social Cognitive and Affective Neuroscience* (advance access, September 29, 2012), 5, 8, accessed December 15, 2013, http://www.scn.ucla.edu/pdf/Morelli%28InPress%29SCAN.pdf.

Chapter III

1. Merrill D. Peterson, *The Jefferson Image in the American Mind* (Charlottesville, VA: Thomas Jefferson Memorial Foundation and the University Press of Virginia, 1998; originally published New York: Oxford University Press, 1960), 25–27.

2. Daniel Webster, *The Private Correspondence of Daniel Webster*, ed. Fletcher Webster, vol. 1 (Boston: Little, Brown and Company, 1857), 371.

3. "Thomas Jefferson and Slavery," Thomas Jefferson Foundation, Monticello, accessed October 17, 2013, http://www.monticello.org/site/plantation-and-slavery/thomas-jefferson-and-slavery.

4. "Missouri Compromise," Library of Congress: Digital Reference Section, modified July 30, 2010, accessed October 17, 2013, http://www.loc.gov/rr/program/bib/ourdocs/Missouri.html.

5. Thomas Jefferson to John Holmes, April 22, 1820, Thomas Jefferson Papers, Library of Congress, accessed November 12, 2013, http://www.loc.gov/exhibits/jefferson/159.html.

6. Ibid.

7. Ibid.

8. Thomas Jefferson to William Short, April 13, 1820, Thomas Jefferson Papers, Library of Congress, transcribed and ed. Gerard W. Gawalt, Manuscript Division, accessed October 17, 2013, http://memory.loc.gov/cgi-bin/query/r?ammem/mtj:@field%28DOCID+@lit%28ws03101%29%29.

9. Ibid.

10. Jefferson to Holmes, April 22, 1820.

11. Ibid.

12. Ibid.

13. James Madison to James Monroe, February 10, 1820, James Madison Papers, Library of Congress, from *The Writings of James Madison*, ed. Gaillard Hunt, accessed October 17, 2013, http://memory.loc.gov/cgi-bin/query/r?ammem/mjmtext:@field%28DOCID+@lit%28jm090013%29%29.

14. James Madison to Marquis de Lafayette, February 1, 1830, The Founding Era Collection, University of Virginia Press, early access document, accessed October 17, 2013, http://rotunda.upress.virginia.edu/founders/default.xqy?keys=FGEA-chron-1830-1830-02-01-1.

15. Ibid.

16. Ibid.

17. James Madison to Robert J. Evans, June 15, 1819, James Madison Papers, Library of Congress, from *The Writings of James Madison*, ed. Gaillard Hunt, accessed October 17, 2013, http://memory.loc.gov/cgi-bin/query/r?ammem/mjmtext:@field%28DOCID+@lit%28jm080168%29%29.

18. Ibid.

19. James Madison to Robert Walsh, November 27, 1819, James Madison Papers, Library of Congress, from *The Writings of James Madison*, ed. Gaillard Hunt, accessed October 17, 2013, http://memory.loc.gov/cgi-bin/query/r?ammem/mjmtext:@field%28DOCID+@lit%28jm090009%29%29.

Chapter IV

1. "American Anti-Slavery and Civil Rights Timeline," compiled by V. Chapman Smith, ushistory.org, Independence Hall Association, accessed October 8, 2013, http://www.ushistory.org/more/timeline.htm.

2. Richard S. Newman, *The Transformation of American Abolitionism: Fighting Slavery in the Early Republic* (Chapel Hill, NC: The University of North Carolina Press, 2002), "Abolitionist Transformations."

3. Ibid.

4. Bertram Wyatt-Brown, "American Abolitionism and Religion—The Two-Nation emergence of Antislavery Evangelicalism," Divining America, TeacherServe®, National Humanities Center, accessed October 8, 2013, http://nationalhumanitiescenter.org/tserve/nineteen/nkeyinfo/amabrel.htm.

5. James Brewer Stewart, "Abolitionist Movement," The Reader's Companion to American History, ed. Eric Froner and John A. Garraty (Houghton Mifflin Harcourt Publishing Company, 1991), accessed October 8, 2013, http://www.history.com/topics/abolitionist-movement.

6. Wyatt-Brown, "American Abolitionism and Religion."

7. Ibid.

8. Stewart, "Abolitionist Movement."

9. Ann Hagedorn, *Beyond the River: The Untold Story of the Heroes of the Underground Railroad* (New York: Simon & Schuster, 2002), 274.

10. Ibid, 58.

11. John Rankin, *Letters on American Slavery, Addressed to Mr. Thomas Rankin* (Boston: Isaac Knapp, 1838), 5th ed., 52.

12. Ibid, 20.

13. Ibid.

14. Ibid.

15. Lynn Pioneer, "Frederick Douglass," book review from *The Liberator*, May 30, 1845, Documenting the American South (University Library, The University of North Carolina at Chapel Hill, 2004), accessed October 8, 2013, http://docsouth.unc.edu/neh/douglass/support1.html.

16. Frederick Douglass, *Narrative of the Life of Frederick Douglass, an American Slave, Written by Himself* (Boston: The Anti-Slavery Office, 1845), 7.

17. Ibid, 10.

18. Frederick Douglass, speech given in Sheffield, England, on September 11, 1846, in John Blassingame et al., *The Frederick Douglass Papers, Series One—Speeches, Debates, and Interviews*, vol. 1 (New Haven: Yale University Press, 1979), 195.

19. Wendell Phillips, *Speeches, Lectures, and Letters: By Wendell Phillips* (Boston: Lee and Shepard, 1872), vol. 1, 98.

20. Ibid, 99.

21. Ibid, 101–102.

22. William Lloyd Garrison, *The Liberator*, January 1, 1831, from The Liberator Files, accessed October 8, 2013, http://www.theliberatorfiles.com/commitment-to-purpose.

23. Henry Mayer, *All on Fire: William Lloyd Garrison and Abolition* (New York: St. Martin's Press, 1998), *Book 5: And an Immortal Crown* [1859–1879], 618.

24. William Lloyd Garrison, "To the Public," *The Liberator*, January 4, 1834, from The Liberator Files, accessed October 8, 2013, http://www.theliberatorfiles.com/purpose-of-the-liberator.

25. William Lloyd Garrison, "Guilt of New England," *The Liberator*, January 7, 1832, from The Liberator Files, accessed October 8, 2013, http://www.theliberatorfiles.com/45.

26. *The Liberator*, July 28, 1832, from The Liberator Files, accessed October 8, 2013, http://www.theliberatorfiles.com/on-slavery.

27. Quote from the Milledgeville, GA *Federal Union*, *The Liberator*, March 12, 1836, from The Liberator Files, accessed October 8, 2013, http://www.theliberatorfiles.com/reward-for-capturing-an-abolitionist.

28. Copy of a resolution in Georgia ..., *The Liberator*, August 3, 1833, from The Liberator Files, accessed October 8, 2013, http://www.theliberatorfiles.com/georgia-resolution-against-garrison.

29. William Lloyd Garrison, *An Address Delivered in Marlboro Chapel, Boston, July 4, 1838* (Boston: Isaac Knapp, 1838), 12.

30. Ibid, 5.

31. Ibid, 8.

32. William Lloyd Garrison, *No Compromise with Slavery: An Address Delivered in the Broadway Tabernacle, New York, February 14, 1854* (New York: American Anti-Slavery Society, 1854), 9.

33. Henry Mayer, *All on Fire: William Lloyd Garrison and Abolition, Book 4: A Heavenly Race Demands Thy Zeal* [1844–1858], 390.

34. Wendell Phillips Garrison and Francis Jackson Garrison, *William Lloyd Garrison 1805–1879: The Story of his Life told by his Children* (Boston and New York: Houghton, Mifflin and Company, 1885 and 1889), vol. 3 [1841–1860], 390.

35. Letter from Thomas Ingersoll, *The Liberator*, March 26, 1847, from The Liberator Files, accessed October 8, 2013, http://www.theliberatorfiles.com/the-slavery-of-wages.

36. *The Liberator*, May 26, 1848, from The Liberator Files, accessed October 8, 2013, http://www.theliberatorfiles.com/working-mens-revolution-meeting.

37. "Capital and Labor," *The Liberator*, October 26, 1849, from The Liberator Files, accessed October 8, 2013, http://www.theliberatorfiles.com/capital-and-labor.

38. Horace Seldon, "A Life of Purpose," The Liberator Files, accessed October 8, 2013, http://www.theliberatorfiles.com/a-portrait-of-purpose.

39. Henry Mayer, *All on Fire: William Lloyd Garrison and Abolition, Book 3: And Press with Vigor On* [1836–1844], 293. According to Henry Mayer, as early as 1840 during his visit to England, Garrison expressed his support for the workingmen's protest taking place under the banner of Chartism.

40. Ibid, 322–323.

Chapter V

1. George Fitzhugh, "Black Republicanism in Ancient Athens," *DeBow's Review, Agricultural, Commercial, Industrial Progress and Resources*, ed. J.D.B. DeBow (New Orleans), 23:1 (1857), 20–26.

2. William Harper, "Memoir on Slavery," *The Pro-Slavery Argument: As Maintained by the Most Distinguished Writers of the Southern States, Containing the Several Essays, on the Subject, of Chancellor Harper, Governor Hammond, Dr. Simms, and Professor Dew* (Charleston: Walker, Richards & Co., 1852), 1.

3. Ibid, 18.

4. Ibid, 69.

5. John Patrick Daly, *When Slavery Was Called Freedom: Evangelicalism, Proslavery, and the Causes of the Civil War* (Lexington: University Press of Kentucky, 2002), 2–3.

6. Ibid, 3.

7. Ibid.

8. Ibid, 2.

9. Ibid, 3, 5.

10. Thomas R. Dew, "Professor Dew's Essays on Slavery," *The Pro-Slavery Argument*, 317.

11. Daly, *When Slavery Was Called Freedom*, 5.

12. George Fitzhugh, *Cannibals All! Or, Slaves Without Masters* (Richmond: A. Morris, 1857), excerpt titled "The Universal Law of Slavery" in Africans in America, PBS, accessed October 31, 2013, http://www.pbs.org/wgbh/aia/part4/4h3141t.html.

13. "Northern Free Negroes and Southern Slaves," *Staunton Spectator* (Staunton, Va.), January 17, 1860, retrieved from Valley of the Shadow: Two Communities in the American Civil War, Virginia Center for Digital History, University of Virginia, accessed October 31, 2013,
http://vshadow.vcdh.virginia.edu/saxon/servlet/SaxonServlet?source=/xml_docs/valle y_news/newspaper_catalog.xml&style=/xml_docs/valley_news/news_cat.xsl&level=b rowse_paper&paper=ss.

14. "The Southern Argument for Slavery," ushistory.org, Independence Hall Association, accessed October 31, 2013, http://www.ushistory.org/us/27f.asp.

15. *Staunton Spectator*, "A Southern Newspaper Concludes 'We are all therefore slaves'," *HERB: Resources for Teachers*, accessed October 31, 2013, http://herb.ashp.cuny.edu/items/show/935.

16. John C. Calhoun, "Slavery a Positive Good," speech before the U.S. Senate, February 6, 1837, from Teaching American History.org, accessed October 31, 2013, http://teachingamericanhistory.org/library/document/slavery-a-positive-good/http://teachingamericanhistory.org/library/document/slavery-a-positive-good/.

17. Ibid.

18. James Henry Hammond, speech before the U.S. Senate, March 4, 1858, in "The Mudsill Theory," Africans in America, PBS, accessed October 31, 2013; http://www.pbs.org/wgbh/aia/part4/4h3439t.html.

19. Ibid.

20. Ibid.

21. Daly, *When Slavery Was Called Freedom*, 10.

22. William Harper, "Memoir on Slavery," *The Pro-Slavery Argument*, 21.

23. Daly, *When Slavery Was Called Freedom*, 41.

24. Daly, 11.

25. Steven Crowder, "Detroit in Ruins (Crowder Goes Ghetto),"
LouderWithCrowder.com, YouTube video, 13:03, accessed October 31, 2013,
http://www.youtube.com/watch?v=1hhJ_49IeBw.

26. John C. Calhoun, *The Essential Calhoun: Selections from Writings,
Speeches, and Letters*, ed. Clyde N. Wilson (1992; paperback with new material
added, New Brunswick: Transaction Publishers, 2000), Forward by Russell Kirk: viii.

27. Richard Hofstadter, *The American Political Tradition and the Men Who
Made It* (New York: A. A. Knopf, 1948; Vintage Books Edition, 1989), 116–117.

28. Susan Gardner, "19 Things Conservatives Insist on Comparing to Slavery,"
Daily Kos, January 17, 2014, accessed January 19, 2014,
http://www.dailykos.com/story/2014/01/17/1270213/-19-things-conservatives-insist-
on-comparing-to-slavery?detail=hide.

29. Ibid.

30. Ibid.

Chapter VI

1. Lysander Spooner, *Unconstitutionality of Slavery* (Boston: Bela Marsh, 1845;
3rd edition, 1860), retrieved from Letters on Slavery, accessed December 3, 2013,
http://medicolegal.tripod.com/spooneruos.htm.

2. *Constitution of the Confederate States*, March 11, 1861, Article 1, Sec. 9 (4),
retrieved from the Avalon Project, Lillian Goldman Law Library, Yale Law School,
accessed December 3, 2013, http://avalon.law.yale.edu/19th_century/csa_csa.asp.

3. Ralph Raico, *Great Wars and Great Leaders: A Libertarian Rebuttal* (Auburn,
AL.: Ludwig von Mises Institute, 2010), viii–ix.

4. "John Brown," on History.com (A+E Networks, 2009), accessed December 3,
2013, http://www.history.com/topics/john-brown.

5. *The Lysander Spooner Reader*, George H. Smith, ed. (San Francisco: Fox &
Wilkes, 1992), vii–xix, retrieved from The Voluntaryist, accessed December 3, 2013,
http://voluntaryist.com/spooner/smithspoonerreader.html.

6. Lysander Spooner, *Address of the Free Constitutionalists to the People of the
United States* (Boston: Thayer & Eldridge, 1860), retrieved from Library of Liberty,
December 3, 2013, http://oll.libertyfund.org/titles/2230.

7. Frederick Douglass, speech in Washington D.C. on the 79th anniversary of
Lincoln's birth, February 12, 1888, retrieved from the Frederick Douglass Papers,
Library of Congress, December 2, 2013,
http://www.loc.gov/resource/mfd.25001/#seq-15, see 16–17.

8. Frederick Douglass, speech on the occasion of the unveiling of the
Freedmen's Monument in memory of Abraham Lincoln, April 4, 1876, retrieved from

the Frederick Douglass Papers, Library of Congress, December 2, 2013, http://memory.loc.gov/mss/mfd/23/23004/0011.jpg, 10.

9. Frederick Douglass, "The Fugitive Slave Law," speech to the National Free Soil Convention at Pittsburgh, August 1, 1852, retrieved from University of Rochester Frederick Douglass Project, December 2, 2013, http://www.lib.rochester.edu/index.cfm?PAGE=4385.

10. Lysander Spooner to Charles Sumner, Boston, October 12, 1864, retrieved from Library of Liberty, December 3, 2013, http://oll.libertyfund.org/titles/2233.

11. Lysander Spooner, *To the Non-Slaveholders of the South*, 1858, retrieved from the Library of Liberty, December 3, 2013, http://oll.libertyfund.org/titles/2229.

12. Ibid.

13. Ibid.

14. Ibid.

15. Ibid.

16. Ibid.

17. John Brown, *Provisional Constitution and Ordinances for the People of the United States*, in Douglas O. Linder, "The Trial of John Brown" (University of Missouri at Kansas City, 2005), Article XXXIX, accessed December 3, 2013, http://law2.umkc.edu/faculty/projects/ftrials/johnbrown/brownconstitution.html.

18. Ibid, Article XL.

19. Spooner, *To the Non Slave-holders of the South*.

20. Lysander Spooner, *No Treason. No. II. The Constitution* (Boston: Published by the Author, 1867) Part 1, retrieved from Library of Liberty, accessed December 3, 2013, http://oll.libertyfund.org/titles/2213.

21. Elsie Freeman, Wynell Burroughs Schamel, and Jean West. "The Fight for Equal Rights: A Recruiting Poster for Black Soldiers in the Civil War," *Social Education* 56: 2 (February 1992): 118–120; revised and updated by Budge Weidman, 1999, "The Fight for Equal Rights: Black Soldiers in the Civil War," National Archives: Teaching with Documents, accessed December 3, 2013, http://www.archives.gov/education/lessons/blacks-civil-war/.

22. Lysander Spooner, "No Treason, No. II. The Constitution," *DeBow's Review, Devoted to the Restoration of the Southern States*, ed. R. G. Barnwell and Edwin Q. Bell (Nashville and New York), 4:5 5 (1867), 393.

23. Lysander Spooner, *No Treason. No. I.* (Boston: Published by the Author, 1867), retrieved from LysanderSpooner.org, December 3, 2013, http://lysanderspooner.org/node/44.

24. Lysander Spooner, *A Plan for the Abolition of Slavery*, 1858, point no. 11, retrieved from the Library of Liberty, December 3, 2013, http://oll.libertyfund.org/titles/2229.

Chapter VII

1. "Signers of the Declaration of Sentiments," First Women's Rights Convention, Seneca Falls, N.Y., July 20, 1848, online at Women's Rights, National Park Service, accessed November 12, 2013, http://www.nps.gov/wori/historyculture/signers-of-the-declaration-of-sentiments.htm. Every signer from the list of male signers whose biography I could locate online was active in some manner in the antislavery movement.

2. Ida Husted Harper, *The Life and Work of Susan B. Anthony: Including Public Addresses, Her Own Letters, and Many from Her Contemporaries during Fifty Years* (Indianapolis and Kansas City: Bowen-Merrill, 1899), vol. 1, 13–14.

3. Shane Mountjoy and Tim McNeese, *The Women's Rights Movement: Moving Toward Equality* (New York: Chelsea House, Infobase Publishing, 2008), 70.

4. "Biography of Susan B. Anthony … Suffragist," National Susan B. Anthony Museum and House, accessed November 12, 2013, http://susanbanthonyhouse.org/her-story/biography.php.

5. "The Revolution," compiled by the editors, Encyclopedia Britannica, accessed November 12, 2013, http://www.britannica.com/EBchecked/topic/500612/The-Revolution.

6. Elisabeth Griffin, *In Her Own Right: The Life of Elizabeth Cady Stanton* (New York: Oxford University Press, 1984), 137–138.

7. Sue Davis, *The Political Thought of Elizabeth Cady Stanton: Women's Rights and the American Political Traditions* (New York and London: New York University Press, 2008), 163.

8. "Biography of Susan B. Anthony … Labor Activist," National Susan B. Anthony Museum and House, accessed November 12, 2013, http://susanbanthonyhouse.org/her-story/biography.php.

9. Susan B. Anthony, "Suffrage and the Working Woman," speech given in 1871, originally collected in Ellen DuBois, *Elizabeth Cady Stanton, Susan B. Anthony, Correspondence, Writings, Speeches* (New York: Schocken Books, 1987), 139–145, accessed November 12, 2013 at Archives of Women's Political Communications, Iowa State University, http://www.womenspeecharchive.org/women/profile/speech/index.cfm?ProfileID=90&SpeechID=513.

10. Ibid.

11. Ibid.

12. Ibid.

13. Grover Cleveland, excerpt of speech given in 1905, cited in "Women's Suffrage and Other Visions of Right-Wing Apocalypse," *The New Republic*, December 21, 2009, accessed November 12, 2013, http://www.newrepublic.com/article/womens-suffrage-and-other-visions-right-wing-apocalypse#.

14. Griffin, *In Her Own Right*, 132.

15. Ibid, 130.

16. Davis, *The Political Thought of Elizabeth Cady Stanton*, 142–144.

17. Ibid, 141.

18. Louise Michele Newman, *White Women's Rights: The Racial Origins of Feminism in the United States* (New York: Oxford University Press, 1999), 4.

19. Griffin, *In Her Own Right*, 140.

20. Ann D. Gordon, "Stanton, Elizabeth Cady," American National Biography Online, February 2000, accessed November 12, 2013; http://www.anb.org/articles/15/15-00640.html

21. Elizabeth Cady Stanton, May 1869, quoted in Griffin, *In Her Own Right*, 140.

22. Elizabeth Cady Stanton, letter to a friend, c. 1865–1870, in Griffin, *In Her Own Right*, 139.

23. Gordon, "Stanton, Elizabeth Cady."

24. Eugene V. Debs, " Liberty," speech given on November 22, 1895, Eugene V. Debs Internet Archive, accessed November 12, 2013, http://www.marxists.org/archive/debs/works/1895/liberty.htm.

25. Eugene V. Debs, "A Call to the People," originally published in the *Social Democrat*, Chicago, Ill. (August 26, 1897), retrieved from Eugene V. Debs Internet Archive, November 12, 2013, http://www.marxists.org/history/usa/parties/spusa/1897/0823-debs-calltothepeople.pdf.

26. Eugene V. Debs, "The Martyred Apostles of Labor," originally published in *The New Time* February, 1898, from "Collected Speeches and Writings of Eugene Victor Debs," Library of Congress, retrieved from Eugene V. Debs Internet Archive, November 12, 2013, http://www.marxists.org/archive/debs/works/1898/martyred.htm.

27. Eugene V. Debs, "The Socialist Party and the Working Class," speech given on September 1, 1904, in Indianapolis, Ind., from the Socialist Party Convention Minutes, retrieved from Eugene V. Debs Internet Archive, November 11, 2013, https://www.marxists.org/archive/debs/works/1904/sp_wkingclss.htm.

28. David Pietrusza, *1920: The Year of Six Presidents* (New York: Carroll & Graf Publishers, 2007; New York: Basic Books, 2008), 269–270.

29. Nicholas Lemann, "Progress's Pilgrims: Doris Goodwin on T.R and Taft," Books, *The New Yorker*, November 18, 2013, 81.

30. "Agitation and Agitators," unsigned article attributed to Eugene V. Debs, published in Locomotive Firemen's Magazine, Terre Haute, Ind., August, 1890, retrieved from Eugene V. Debs Internet Archive, November 12, 2013, http://www.marxists.org/history/usa/unions/blf/1890/0800-debs-agitation.pdf.

31. Caleb Crain, "It Happened One Decade: What the Great Depression Did to Culture," Books, *The New Yorker*, September 21, 2009, accessed November 12, 2013,

http://www.newyorker.com/arts/critics/books/2009/09/21/090921crbo_books_crain?cu
rrentPage=all.

32. Carolyn Kott Washburne, *America in the 20th Century: 1930–1939* (New
York: Marshall Cavendish Corporation, 1995; 2nd ed. 2003), 505.

33. John L. Lewis, "Labor and the Nation," speech given on September 3, 1937
in Washington, D.C., John L. Lewis papers, 1879–1969 (Sanford, N.C.: Microfilming
Corporation of America, 1979), retrieved from American Rhetoric: Top 100 Speeches
on November 12, 2013,
http://www.americanrhetoric.com/speeches/johnlewisrightsoflabor.htm.

34. Ibid.

35. John L. Lewis, *Testimony of John L. Lewis before Congressional Committees
on Centralia Mine Explosion* (Washington, D.C.: Labor's Non-Partisan League,
1947), 24.

36. Ibid, 19.

37. John L. Lewis, undated quote, in "UMWA History," United Mine Workers
of America/AFL-CIO, CLC , accessed November 12, 2013,
http://www.umwa.org/?q=content/john-l-lewis.

38. Jill Quadagno, *One Nation, Uninsured: Why the U.S. Has No National
Health Insurance* (New York: Oxford University Press, 2005) 110–112.

39. Victor G. Reuther, *The Brothers Reuther and the Story of the UAW: A
Memoir* (Boston: Houghton Mifflin, 1976), 249.

40. "Nobody Leaking a Word: Auto Makers Quiet on Reuther's Offer," *Toledo
Blade*, August 22, 1957, 3, retrieved from Google.com News on November 8, 2013,
http://news.google.com/newspapers?nid=1350&dat=19570822&id=iPxOAAAAIBAJ
&sjid=0gAEAAAAIBAJ&pg=7212,1899908.

41. Nelson Lichtenstein, *Walter Reuther: The Most dangerous Man in Detroit*,
(New York: Basic Books, 1995, by arrangement with Harper Collins Publishers), 347.

42. Walter Reuther, undated quote, retrieved from Stubby's Labor Quotes
("Brotherhood") on November 8, 2013,
http://laborquotes.weebly.com/brotherhood.html.

43. Walter Reuther, Labor Day Address, September 1, 1958, retrieved from "No
Greater Calling: The Life of Walter Reuther," Walter P. Reuther Library, November 8,
2013, http://reuther100.wayne.edu/pdf/Labor_Day_Address.pdf.

44. Ibid, 4.

45. Ibid, 3.

46. Ibid.

47. Sarah Anderson, "People Power Pushed the New Deal: Roosevelt Didn't
Come Up with All Those Progressive Programs on His Own, *Yes! Magazine*, June 5,
2009, accessed November 13, 2013, http://www.yesmagazine.org/issues/the-new-
economy/people-power-pushed-the-new-deal.

48. Robert McHenry, "A Man and His Plan," *The American*, online magazine of the American Enterprise Institute, December 30, 2009, accessed November 13, 2013, http://www.american.com/archive/2009/december-2009/a-man-and-his-plan.

49. Ibid.

50. Dr. Francis E. Townshend, *New Horizons: An Autobiography*, ed. Jesse George Murray (Chicago: J.L. Stewart Publishing Co., 1943), excerpt on Social Security History, Social Security Website , accessed November 10, 2013, http://www.ssa.gov/history/towns8.html.

51. Edwin Amenta, *When Movements Matter: The Townsend Plan and the Rise of Social Security* (Princeton, NJ: Princeton University Press, 2006), 242.

52. Townshend, *New Horizons*, dedication: "Poverty Breeds War," accessed November 10, 2013, http://www.ssa.gov/history/towns8.html.

53. Ibid, 160–165.

Chapter VIII

1. Lincoln's birthday is a legal celebration in a number of states, including Ariz., Conn., Ill., Mo., N.J., N.Y., and Ind.; *Wikipedia*, accessed December 6, 2013, http://en.wikipedia.org/wiki/Lincoln%27s_Birthday.

2. Ann S. Manheimer, *Martin Luther King Jr.: Dreaming of Equality* (Minneapolis: Carolrhoda Books Inc., Lerner Publication Group, 2005), 103.

3. "Montgomery Bus Boycott (1955–1956)," Online Encyclopedia, Martin Luther King Jr. Research and Education Institute, accessed December 6, 2013, http://mlk-kpp01.stanford.edu/index.php/encyclopedia/encyclopedia/enc_montgomery_bus_boyc ott_1955_1956/.

4. Ibid.

5. Martin Luther King Jr., Letter from Birmingham Jail (containing quotes from the Sermon on Mount), April 16, 1963, African Studies Center, University of Pennsylvania, accessed December 6, 2013, http://www.africa.upenn.edu/Articles_Gen/Letter_Birmingham.html.

6. Martin Luther King Jr., "My Pilgrimage to Nonviolence," September 1, 1958, Martin Luther King Jr. Papers Project, Stanford University, 473, accessed December 6, 2013, http://mlk-kpp01.stanford.edu/primarydocuments/Vol4/1-Sept-1958_MyPilgrimageToNonviolence.pdf.

7. Ibid, 477.

8. Ibid, 478–479.

9. Paul Wood, "The Unbroken Chain," *LAS News*, Spring 2009, College of Arts and Sciences, University of Illinois, accessed December 6, 2013, http://www.las.illinois.edu/alumni/magazine/articles/2009/tolstoy/.

10. Brice Tennant, "Tillich and Civil Rights: The Tillich–King Correspondence," Paul Tillich Resources: Tillich and Popular Culture, Boston University, accessed December 6, 2013, http://people.bu.edu/wwildman/tillich/resources/popculture_civilrights01_tennant.htm.

11. Ellen M. Ross, "Quakers, Culture, and the Transforming Power of Love," *Friends Journal*, December 26, 2012, accessed December 6, 2013, http://www.friendsjournal.org/quakers-culture-and-the-transforming-power-of-love/.

12., Michael P. McDonald and Samuel L. Popkin, "The Myth of the Vanishing Voter," *American Political Science Review* 95 (December 2001): 967, accessed December 9, 2013, http://polisci2.ucsd.edu/ps100da/McDonald%20%26%20Popkin%20%20APSR%20Myth%20vanishing%20Voter.pdf.

13. "The Road to Civil Rights: Getting to the March on Washington, August 28, 1963," Highway History, Federal Highway Administration, U.S. Dept. of Transportation, accessed December 6, 2013, http://www.fhwa.dot.gov/highwayhistory/road/s33.cfm.

14. "The Goals of the Poor People's Campaign, 1968," Eyes on the Prize: America's Civil Rights Movement 1954–1985, PBS: "American Experience," August 23, 2006, accessed December 6, 2013, http://www.pbs.org/wgbh/amex/eyesontheprize/sources/ps_poor.html.

15. "Memphis Sanitation Workers Strike (1968)," Online Encyclopedia, Martin Luther King Jr. Research and Education Institute, accessed December 6, 2013, http://mlk-kpp01.stanford.edu/index.php/encyclopedia/encyclopedia/enc_memphis_sanitation_workers_strike_1968.

16. Ibid.

17. Martin Luther King Jr., "I Have a Dream" address, March on Washington, August 28, 1963, Martin Luther King Jr. Papers Project Speeches, accessed December 6, 2013, http://mlk-kpp01.stanford.edu/kingweb/publications/speeches/address_at_march_on_washington.pdf.

18. King, Letter from Birmingham Jail.

19. Title VII of the Civil Rights Act of 1964, U.S. Equal Employment Opportunity Commission, accessed December 6, 2013, http://www.eeoc.gov/laws/statutes/titlevii.cfm.

20. Title IX Enforcement Highlights, Office for Civil Rights: U.S. Department of Education, June 2012, accessed December 6, 2013, http://www2.ed.gov/documents/press-releases/title-ix-enforcement.pdf.

21. William F. Buckley Jr., "Can We Desegregate, Hesto Presto?" *National Review*, November 11, 1961, 122, digital excerpt at Buckley Online, Hillsdale College, accessed December 7, 2013, https://cumulus.hillsdale.edu/Buckley/.

22. Ibid, 125.

23. Ibid, 126.

24. Ibid, 127.

25. Ibid, 124–125.

26. William F. Buckley Jr., "The Issue at Selma," syndicated column "On the Right," February 18, 1965, digital excerpt at Buckley Online, Hillsdale College, accessed December 7, 2013, https://cumulus.hillsdale.edu/Buckley/.

27. William F. Buckley Jr., "Why the South Must Prevail," *National Review*, August 24, 1957, 338, digital excerpt at Buckley Online, Hillsdale College, accessed December 7, 2013, https://cumulus.hillsdale.edu/Buckley/.

28. William F. Buckley Jr., "Let Us Try at Least to Understand," *National Review*, June 3, 1961, digital excerpt at Buckley Online, Hillsdale College, accessed December 7, 2013, https://cumulus.hillsdale.edu/Buckley/.

29. Ibid.

30. William F. Buckley Jr., *Up from Liberalism* (New York: McDowell, Obolensky, 1959), 37.

31. Ibid, 125.

32. William F. Buckley Jr., "Why the South Must Prevail."

33. Ibid.

34. William F. Buckley Jr., *Up from Liberalism*, 118.

35. Ibid, 119.

36. Richard Weaver, "Integration is Communization," *National Review*, July 13, 1957, 67–68.

37. Will Herberg, "Civil Rights and Violence: Who Are the Guilty Ones?" *National Review*, September 7, 1965, 769–770.

38. James P. Lubinskas, "The Decline of *National Review*," *American Renaissance*, April 9, 2012, quoting a July 2, 1963, *National Review* editorial, accessed December 8, 2013, http://www.amren.com/news/2012/04/the-decline-of-national-review/.

39. Ibid, quoting a June 2, 1964, *National Review* editorial.

40. Ibid, quoting a March 9, 1965, *National Review* article by Russell Kirk.

41. "Before the Purge," AlternativeRight.com (August 19, 2012), quoting a September 28, 1957, *National Review* article by James J. Kilpatrick, accessed December 8, 2013, http://www.radixjournal.com/altright-archive/altright-archive/main/blogs/district-of-corruption/before-the-purge.

42. Ibid, quoting a September 24, 1963, *National Review* article by James J. Kilpatrick.

43. Ibid, quoting an April 20, 1965, *National Review* article by James J. Kilpatrick.

44. Ibid.

45. Description of the *Claremont Review of Books, Wikipedia*, accessed December 7, 2013, http://en.wikipedia.org/wiki/Claremont_Review_of_Books.

46. William Voegeli, "Civil Rights and the Conservative Movement," *Claremont Review of Books*, Summer 2008, accessed December 7, 2013, http://claremont.org/index.php?act=crbArticle&id=624.

47. "Jim Crow Laws," Martin Luther King Jr. National Historic Site: Georgia, National Park Service, accessed December 7, 2013, http://www.nps.gov/malu/forteachers/jim_crow_laws.htm

48. Voegeli, "Civil Rights and the Conservative Movement."

49. James Sanders, *South Africa and the International Media, 1972–1979: A Struggle for Representation* (London and Portland, Oregon: Frank Cass Publishers, 2000), 37.

50. Jacob Heilbrunn, "Apologists without Remorse," *The American Prospect*, December 12, 2001, accessed December 7, 2013, http://prospect.org/article/apologists-without-remorse.

51. Douglas Martin, "William F. Buckley Jr. Is Dead at 82," *New York Times*, February 27, 2008, accessed December 7, 2013, http://www.nytimes.com/2008/02/27/business/media/27cnd-buckley.html?pagewanted=all.

52. Lee Edwards, "William F. Buckley Jr.: Conservative Icon," The Heritage Foundation, December 18, 2012, accessed December 7, 2013, http://www.heritage.org/research/reports/2012/12/william-f-buckley-jr-conservative-icon.

53. Heidi Przbyla and Judy Woodruff, "Buckley Says Bush Will Be Judged on Iraq War, Now a 'Failure'," Bloomberg.com, accessed December 7, 2013, http://www.bloomberg.com/apps/news?pid=newsarchive&sid=anN._IfoJo1M.

54. James Joyner, "Bill Buckley and the Gays," Outside the Beltway, February 28, 2008, accessed December 7, 2013, http://www.outsidethebeltway.com/buckley_and_the_gays/.

Chapter IX

1. Ron Paul, interview, *Morning Joe*, MSNBC, December 27, 2007, retrieved December 13, 2013, from Heritage Not Hate Productions ("Ron Paul Speaks out about Lincoln and the War for Southern Independence"), http://www.youtube.com/watch?v=sRx-trdMGtY.

2. Ibid.

3. Ibid.

4. Ron Paul, interview with Bill Maher, *Real Time with Bill Maher*, HBO, November 8, 2007, retrieved December 13, 2013, from Me Hugger /Green News and Eco Friendly, http://www.mehugger.com/green-articles/ron-paul-interview-with-bill-maher/.

5. Thomas J. DiLorenzo, *The Real Lincoln: A New Look at Abraham Lincoln, His Agenda, and an Unnecessary War* (Roseville, California: Prima Publishers, 2002; reprint edition New York: Three Rivers Press, 2003), 48.

6. Ibid, 261.

7. Ron Paul, speech given at the Southern Historical Conference in Schertz, TX, 2003, retrieved December 12, 2013, from a YouTube post by Charles Johnson ("Ron Paul Promotes Revisionist Civil War History in Front of Giant Dixie Flag"), http://www.youtube.com/watch?v=B85TJJyKyKw.

8. Ibid.

9. Ron Paul, interview by Tim Russert, *Meet the Press*, NBC, December 23, 2007, transcript accessed December 12, 2013, at http://www.nbcnews.com/id/22342301/#.Uqsc37Qlf5M.

10. DiLorenzo, *The Real Lincoln*, 258–259, 279.

11. Paul, speech given at the Southern Historical Conference, 2003.

12. Ibid.

13. Thomas J. DiLorenzo, *Lincoln Unmasked: What You're Not Supposed to Know about Honest Abe* (New York: Three Rivers Press, 2006), 40.

14. Ibid, 41.

15. DiLorenzo, *The Real Lincoln*, 61.

16. Ibid, 273–274.

17. Ibid, 218.

18. "Mississippi Ratifies 13th Amendment 148 Years after Slavery Abolished," CBS News, February 21, 2013, retrieved December 13, 2013 from WFMY CBS News 2, http://www.digtriad.com/news/article/270499/1/Mississippi-Ratifies-13th-Amendment-148-Years-After-Slavery-Abolished.

19. Teresa Santoski, "Mississippi Ratifies the 13th Amendment (which abolishes slavery) today in 1995," *Telegraph*, Hudson, N.H., March 16, 1995, accessed December 13, 2013, http://www.nashuatelegraph.com/news/674558-196/daily-twip--mississippi-ratifies-the-13th.html.

20. Constitution of the Confederate States, March 11, 1861, art. I, § 9(4), retrieved December 13, 2013 from the Avalon Project, Lillian Goldman Law Library, Yale Law School, http://avalon.law.yale.edu/19th_century/csa_csa.asp.

21. DiLorenzo, *The Real Lincoln*, 49–50.

22. DiLorenzo, *Lincoln Unmasked*, 27–28, 48.

23. Paul, interview, *Morning Joe*, MSNBC, December 27, 2007.

24. Ibid.

25. DiLorenzo, *Lincoln Unmasked*, 25.

26. DiLorenzo, *The Real Lincoln*, 29, 283.

27. Harold Holzer, "Pre Civil War Peace Conference," *America's Civil War*, November 8, 2010, retrieved December 13, 2013 from Weider History Network, http://www.historynet.com/pre-civil-war-peace-conference.htm.

28. Amendments Proposed by the Peace Conference, February 8–27, 1861, art. XIII, §§ 3 and 6, retrieved December 13, 2013, from the Avalon Project, Lillian Goldman Law Library, Yale Law School, http://avalon.law.yale.edu/19th_century/peace.asp.

29. Harold Holzer, "Why did the Peace Conference in Washington Fail in its Mission?" *A House Divided* (blog), *Washington Post*, January 31, 2011, accessed December 13, 2013, http://voices.washingtonpost.com/house-divided/2011/01/harold_holzer_why_did_the_peac.html.

30. Articles of Confederation, March 1, 1781, art. XIII, retrieved December 13, 2013, from the Avalon Project, Lillian Goldman Law Library, Yale Law School, http://avalon.law.yale.edu/18th_century/artconf.asp.

31. Stephen Douglas, Fourth Lincoln–Douglas Debate, Mark E. Neely Jr., *Abraham Lincoln Encyclopedia* (New York: Da Capo Press, 1982), retrieved December 13, 2013, from Lincoln Home National Historic Site, National Park Service, http://www.nps.gov/liho/historyculture/debate4.htm.

32. Ibid.

33. Ibid, Abraham Lincoln.

34. Abraham Lincoln, Seventh Lincoln–Douglas Debate, from Neely, *Abraham Lincoln Encyclopedia*, accessed December 13, 2013, at http://www.nps.gov/liho/historyculture/debate7.htm.

35. Stephen Douglas, Fifth Lincoln–Douglas Debate, from Neely, *Abraham Lincoln Encyclopedia*, accessed December 13, 2013, http://www.nps.gov/liho/historyculture/debate5.htm.

36. Ibid, Abraham Lincoln.

37. J.D.B. (James Dunwoody Brownson) DeBow, Director Biographies, U.S. Census Bureau, U.S. Department of Commerce, accessed December 13, 2013, http://www.census.gov/history/www/census_then_now/director_biographies/directors_1840_-_1865.html.

38. "The Northern Press—'The Day-Book'," *DeBow's Review, Agricultural, Commercial, Industrial Progress and Resources*, ed. J.D.B. DeBow (New Orleans), 29: 6 (1860), 793.

39. "Drapetomania," David Pilgrim response to a 2005 Question of the Month, Jim Crow Museum of Racist Memorabilia, Ferris State University, accessed December 13, 2013, http://www.ferris.edu/jimcrow/question/nov05.htm.

40. Ibid.

41. Ibid.

42. Reginald Horsman, "Josiah C. Nott," Encyclopedia of Alabama, Alabama Humanities Foundation, accessed December 13, 2013, http://www.encyclopediaofalabama.org/face/Article.jsp?id=h-1484.

43. Josiah C. Nott, *Two Lectures on the Natural History of the Caucasian and Negro Races* (Mobile, Alabama: Dade and Thompson, 1844), Lecture II, 24.

44. Stephen Douglas, Fourth Lincoln–Douglas Debate, from Neely, *Abraham Lincoln Encyclopedia*, accessed December 13, 2013, http://www.nps.gov/liho/historyculture/debate4.htm.

45. "Alexander Hamilton Stephens, 1812–1883," retrieved December 13, 2013, from Civil War Biographies, Shotgun's Home of the American Civil War, http://www.civilwarhome.com/stephens.htm.

46. Alexander H. Stephens, speech in Savannah, Georgia, March 21, 1861, in Henry Cleveland, *Alexander H. Stephens, in Public and Private: With Letters and Speeches, Before, During, and Since the War* (Philadelphia: National Publishing Company, 1886), 717–729, retrieved December 13, 2013, from Teaching American History.org, Ashland University, http://teachingamericanhistory.org/library/document/cornerstone-speech/.

47. Ibid.

48. Ibid.

49. Ibid.

50. Bruce Caldwell, "Hayek on Socialism and on the Welfare State: A Comment on Farrant and McPhail's 'Does F.A. Hayek's *Road to Serfdom* Deserve to Make a Comeback?'" (working paper, September 2010), 12, accessed December 13, 2013 at Duke University Center for the History of Political Economy, http://hope.econ.duke.edu/sites/default/files/Road%20to%20Serfdom%20comment.pdf.

51. Ralph Raico, *Great Wars and Great Leaders: A Libertarian Rebuttal* (Auburn, AL: Ludwig von Mises Institute, 2010), iv: "Foreword" by Robert Higgs.

52. DiLorenzo, *The Real Lincoln*, 282–285.

53. Gordon Rhea, "Why Non-Slaveholding Southerners Fought," address to Charleston Library Society, January 25, 2011, retrieved December 13, 2013 from Civil War Trust: Saving America's Civil War Battlefields, http://www.civilwar.org/education/history/civil-war-overview/why-non-slaveholding.html.

54. DiLorenzo, *Lincoln Unmasked*, 26.

55. Ibid, 156–159.

Chapter X

1. Noam Chomsky, conversation with Jonathan Freedland, "The Role of the State," March 19, 2013, prelude to Propaganda: Power and Persuasion, British Library exhibition, accessed December 14, 2013, http://www.youtube.com/watch?v=O0D0E42AA4landfeature=player_embedded.

2. Ibid.

3. Noam Chomsky, interview with Bill Moyers, *Bill Moyers' World of Ideas*, PAT, November 4, 1988, accessed August 9, 2014, http://billmoyers.com/content/noam-chomsky-part-2/.

4. George Lakoff, *Moral Politics: How Liberals and Conservatives Think* (Chicago: University of Chicago Press, 1996; second edition, 2002), 4.

5. Ibid, 5–7.

6. Ibid.

7. Ibid, 12.

8. Ibid, 14–17.

9. Ibid, 33–35.

10. Ibid, 108–119.

11. *The Liberator*, August 20, 1831, from "Call to Women," The Liberator Files, accessed December 14, 2013, http://www.theliberatorfiles.com/call-to-women/.

12. George Lakoff, *Don't Think of an Elephant!* (White River Junction, VT.: Chelsea Green Publishing Company, 2004), 113.

13. George Lakoff, *Moral Politics*, 65–71.

14. Daniel Goleman, "New View of Mind Gives Unconscious an Expanded Role," *New York Times*, February 7, 1984, accessed December 14, 2013, http://www.nytimes.com/1984/02/07/science/new-view-of-mind-gives-unconscious-an-expanded-role.html.

15. "How Big is the Unconscious Mind?" *Horizon: Out of Control?* BBC Two, March 6, 2012, accessed December 14, 2013, http://www.youtube.com/watch?v=w3mrZ0b8LHc.

16. George Lakoff, "The Brain and its Politics," Humanities Center, University of Oregon, July 14, 2010, accessed December 14, 2013, http://www.youtube.com/watch?v=mEb__-szK4k .

17. Ibid.

18. John A. Bargh and Ezequiel Morsella, "The Unconscious Mind," *Perspectives on Psychological Science* (Yale University), 3:1 (2008): 77–78, online at http://www.yale.edu/acmelab/articles/Bargh_Morsella_Unconscious_Mind.pdf.

19. Lakoff, "The Brain and its Politics."

20. Mario F. Mendez, "Neurobiology of Moral Behavior: Review and Neuropsychiatric Implications," *CNS Spectrums* 14:11 (November 2009): 608–620, retrieved December 14, 2013, from National Institute of Health Public Access, U.S. National Library of Medicine, http://www.ncbi.nlm.nih.gov/pmc/articles/PMC3163302/.

21. Katrin Riedl, Keith Jensen, Josep Call, Michael Tomasello, "No Third-Party Punishment in Chimpanzees," *PNAS* 109: 37 (2012): 14824–14829, accessed December 14, 2013, http://www.pnas.org/content/109/37/14824.long.

22. Monte Morin, "Crime, Punishment, and Chimpanzees," *Los Angeles Times*, August 29, 2012, accessed December 14, 2013, http://articles.latimes.com/2012/aug/29/science/la-sci-sn-chimp-punishment-20120828.

23. William Harms, "Psychopaths Are Not Neurally Equipped to Have Concern for Others," *University of Chicago News*, April 24, 2013, accessed December 16, 2013, http://news.uchicago.edu/article/2013/04/24/psychopaths-are-not-neurally-equipped-have-concern-others.

24. Mendez, "Neurobiology of Moral Behavior."

25. Ibid.

26. Ibid.

27. Ibid.

28. Stanley C. Loewen, "Characteristics of a Sociopath," Health Guidance, accessed December 15, 2013, http://www.healthguidance.org/entry/15850/1/Characteristics-of-a-Sociopath.html.

29. "Empathy Represses Analytic Thought, and Vice Versa: Brain Physiology Limits Simultaneous Use of Both Networks," *Science Daily*, Case Western Reserve University, October 30, 2012, retrieved December 14, 2013, http://www.sciencedaily.com/releases/2012/10/121030161416.htm.

30. Martha Stout, *The Sociopath Next Door: The Ruthless Versus the Rest of Us* (New York: Broadway Books, 2006), 125.

31. Chris Mooney, *The Republican Brain: The Science of Why They Deny Science—and Reality* (Hoboken, NJ: John Wiley and Sons, 2012), 112–116.

32. St. Augustine, *Enchiridion*, trans. Albert C. Outler, stanzas 12–15, accessed December 14, 2013, at the Tertullian Project, http://www.tertullian.org/fathers/augustine_enchiridion_02_trans.htm#C4.

33. John B. Arden, *Rewire Your Brain* (Hoboken, NJ: John Wiley and Sons, 2010), 8–10.

34. Sharon Begley, *The Plastic Mind* (New York: Ballantine Books, 2007; London: Constable and Robinson, 2009), 303–317.

35. Sharon Begley, "The Brain: How the Brain Rewires Itself," *Time*, February 19, 2007, 1–5, accessed December 14, 2013, http://www.time.com/time/magazine/article/0,9171,1580438,00.html.

36. Lakoff, *Moral Politics*, 147.

37. Susan T. Fiske, "Look Twice," June 1, 2008, Greater Good: The Science of a Meaningful Life, Greater Good Science Center, UC Berkeley, accessed December 14, 2013, http://greatergood.berkeley.edu/article/item/look_twice.

38. Rand Paul, interview with Rachel Maddow, *The Rachel Maddow Show*, MSNBC, May 20, 2010, retrieved December 14, 2013, from "Rachel Maddow Corners Rand Paul on His Extremist View of Civil Rights," webcast at http://crooksandliars.com/nicole-belle/rachel-maddow-corners-rand-paul-his-e.

Chapter XI

1. Thomas Jefferson to H. Tompkinson, July 12, 1816, Quotations on the Jefferson Memorial: Panel Four, Monticello.org, accessed December 21, 2013, http://www.monticello.org/site/jefferson/quotations-jefferson-memorial.

2. Tom Jewett, "Jefferson and Religion," *Early America Review* (Summer/Fall 2009), Archiving Early America, accessed December 21, 2013, http://www.earlyamerica.com/review/2009_summer_fall/jefferson-and-religion.html

3. Ibid.

4. Thomas Jefferson to Peter Carr, August 10, 1787, in *Jefferson: Writings*, Merrill D. Peterson, ed., (Ann Arbor: University of Michigan, 1984; New York: Library of America, 2011), 902.

5. Thomas Jefferson to John Adams, June 15, 1813, in *The Works of Thomas Jefferson*, Paul Leicester, ed., 1905, vol. 1: *Correspondence 1808–1816*, accessed December 21, 2013, at Library of Liberty, http://oll.libertyfund.org/titles/807/88109.

6. Thomas Jefferson to Joseph Priestley, January 27, 1800, Thomas Jefferson Papers, Library of Congress, accessed December 21, 2013, at Thomas Jefferson and the Roots of Lewis and Clark, Envisaging the West, http://jeffersonswest.unl.edu/archive/view_doc.php?id=jef.00042

7. Ayn Rand, "Introducing Objectivism," *Times-Mirror Co.*, 1962, retrieved December 29, 2013, from Ayn Rand Institute Center for Advancement of Objectivism, http://campus.aynrand.org/more/ayn-rand-importance-philosophy/

8. Ibid.

9. Ayn Rand, *Atlas Shrugged* (New York: Random House, 1957; New York: Dutton, New American Library, Penguin Books, 1992), 1018.

10. "Ayn Rand," *Conservapedia*, last modified December 28, 2013, accessed December 29, 2013, http://www.conservapedia.com/Ayn_Rand

11. Jonathan Chait, "Wealthcare," review of *Goddess of the Market: Ayn Rand and the American Right*, by Jennifer Burns, and *Ayn Rand and the World She Made*, by Ann C. Heller, *New Republic*, September 14, 2009, accessed December 29, 2013, http://www.newrepublic.com/article/books-and-arts/wealthcare-0.

12. Sam Anderson, "Mrs. Logic," review of *Ayn Rand and the World She Made*, by Ann C. Heller, *New York Magazine*, October 18, 2009, accessed December 29, 2013, http://nymag.com/arts/books/features/60120/

13. Ibid.

14. Paul Varnell, "Ayn Rand and Homosexuality," *Chicago Free Press*, December 3, 2003, retrieved December 29, 2012 from Independent Gay Forum/Culture Watch, http://igfculturewatch.com/2003/12/03/ayn-rand-and-homosexuality/.

15. Joshua Holland, "Ayn Rand Railed against Government Benefits, But Grabbed Social Security and Medicare When She Needed Them," AlterNet, January 28, 2011, accessed December 29, 2013, http://www.alternet.org/story/149721/ayn_rand_railed_against_government_benefits,_but_grabbed_social_security_and_medicare_when_she_needed_them

16. Alan Dunn, "Average America vs. the One Percent," *Forbes*, March 21, 2012, accessed December 29, 2013, http://www.forbes.com/sites/moneywisewomen/2012/03/21/average-america-vs-the-one-percent/

17. Anderson, "Mrs. Logic."

18. "Introduction to Objectivism," Ayn Rand Institute Center for Advancement of Objectivism, accessed December 29, 2013, http://www.aynrand.org/ideas/philosophy.

19. Rand, *Atlas Shrugged*, 1011–1012.

20. Ibid, 1018.

21. Thomas Frank, *Pity the Billionaire: The Hard-Times Swindle and the Unlikely Comeback of the Right* (New York: Metropolitan Books, Henry Holt and Company, 2012), 150.

22. Ibid.

23. I offer an added note on the possible origins of Rand's vision of the ideal man (i.e., a superior man). When reading Rand I was immediately struck by what I felt to be the underlying presence of nineteenth-century German philosopher Friedrich Nietzsche. In fact a Nietzschean contempt for the ordinary person combined with his concept of the "ubermensch" (German for overman and somewhat analogous to the modern-day reference to a superman) jumped right out of the pages and hit me in the face. The difference was in presentation, as Rand cast her ideal man's (i.e., superior man's or ubermensch's, if you will) unrestricted prerogatives as none other than the essence of freedom. Yet at the time I was unaware of any documented connection between the two. However, I would later discover that my gut inclination concerning the origin of some of Rand's ideas may not have been that far astray. According to Barbara Branden, a longtime friend and biographer of Ayn Rand, in her youth Rand

was quite enamored with Nietzsche and his philosophy. See: Barbara Branden, *The Passion of Ayn Rand*, (Garden City, NY: Doubleday, 1986), 45.

24. Ayn Rand, *The Fountainhead* (New York: Bobbs-Merrill, 1943; Signet edition, 1993), Introduction to the Twenty-Fifth Anniversary Edition by Ayn Rand, May 1968, vii.

25. Ibid, ix.

26. Ibid, unnumbered last page of Introduction.

27. As an aside it should be noted that there are libertarian philosophers (including some neo-Randians) who try to (falsely) equate modern-day libertarianism with nineteenth-century anarchism. In this regard one must understand that with the possible exception of Germany (beginning in the 1880s) publically sponsored social insurance (justice) programs were virtually nonexistent in the nineteenth century. For the anarchists of the period, their rejection of government was in large part based on their distaste for the very same coercive institutions (i.e., courts, police, prisons, and the military) that the preponderance of twentieth- and twenty-first century libertarians (Rand included) hold to be either the only—or (at minimum) the most—legitimate agencies of government.

28. Ayn Rand, "The 'Robber Barons'," audiotape, Ayn Rand Institute Center for Advancement of Objectivism, retrieved December 29, 2013, http://aynrandlexicon.com/ayn-rand-works/robber-barons.html.

29. Stephen Cox, "Ayn Rand: Theory versus Creative Life," *Journal of Libertarian Studies* 8:1 (Winter 1986): 25–26, accessed December 29, 2013, http://mises.org/journals/jls/8_1/8_1_2.pdf.

30. Ibid.

31. Friedrich Hayek, *The Road to Serfdom* (Chicago: University of Chicago Press, 1944), 120–121.

32. Ibid, 26.

33. Paul Krugman, "The Conscience of a Liberal: Jack-Booted Insurance-Bringing Thugs," *New York Times*, April 2, 2013, accessed December 29, 2013, http://krugman.blogs.nytimes.com/2013/04/02/jack-booted-insurance-bringing-thugs/?_r=0.

34. Lynn Harry Nelson, "The Rise of Feudalism: 850–1000 AD" (Lectures in Medieval History, University of Kansas, Lawrence, 2001), accessed December 30, 2013, http://www.vlib.us/medieval/lectures/feudalism.html.

35. Richard Abels, "Feudalism" (web article for teaching, Dept. of History, United States Naval Academy, April, 2009), accessed December 30, 2013, http://usna.edu/Users/history/abels/hh315/Feudalism%20entry2.htm.

36. Jeffrey L. Singman, *Daily Life in Medieval Europe* (Westport, Ct.: Greenwood Press, 1999), 1–11, 70–73, 224–225.

37. Rudolf Bahro, *The Alternative in Eastern Europe* (London: NLB, 1977, Verso edition, 1981), 66.

38. Lynn Harry Nelson, "The National Monarchies: 1400–1500," (Lectures in Medieval History, University of Kansas, Lawrence , 2001), accessed December 29, 2013, http://www.vlib.us/medieval/lectures/national_monarchies.html.

39. Geoff Eley, "Nations, Publics, and Political Cultures: Placing Habermas in the Nineteenth Century," in Craig J. Calhoun, ed., *Habermas and the Public Sphere* (Cambridge, Mass.: MIT Press, 1992), 289–303.

40. Samuel Freeman, "Illiberal Libertarians: Why Libertarianism is Not a Liberal View," *Philosophy and Public Affairs* 30: 2 (2001): 107.

41. Ibid, 110.

42. Robert Nozick, *Anarchy, State, and Utopia* (New York: Basic Books, 1974), 331.

43. Ibid, 302.

Chapter XII

1. The Declaration of Independence is the one founding document where the reader can almost feel the author's righteous outrage over terrible injustices. The original draft of that author, a young and idealistic Thomas Jefferson, included a harsh denunciation of slavery's "assemblage of horrors," one of which was what Jefferson described as a "miserable death." Unfortunately, due to the influence of slaveholders, this section was removed from the final version. Nevertheless these highly emotive antislavery passages were fully in keeping with what were, at the time, the author's quite intense sentiments and more important with the proclamation's overall spirit, including the larger breadth of its intended appeal. This is why their absence is so noticeable and consequently has been seen as a gaping hole in the actual document itself. Just as unfortunately, the antislavery zeal of this very same author would lessen as the years passed. The following is an excerpt from the original draft, which begins with the particular grievances that are being levied against Great Britain (with the King George III being the official stand-in for that nation): " … he has waged cruel war against human nature itself, violating it's most sacred rights of life and liberty in the persons of a distant people who never offended him, captivating and carrying them into slavery in another hemispere, or to incure miserable death in their transportation hither. this piratical warfare, the opprobium of infidel powers, is the warfare of the Christian king of Great Britain. [determined to keep open a market where MEN should be bought and sold,] he has prostituted his negative for suppressing every legislative attempt to prohibit or to restrain this execrable commerce [determining to keep open a market where MEN should be bought and sold]: and that this assemblage of horrors might want no fact of distinguished die, he is now exciting those very people to rise in arms among us, and to purchase that liberty of which he had deprived them, by murdering the people upon whom he also obtruded them: thus paying off former crimes committed against the liberties of one people, with crimes which he urges them to commit against the lives of another" (spelling as in the original). Source: Rough Draft of the Declaration of Independence, 1776, "Africans in America," Part II (1750–1805), WGBH/PBS online, accessed January 9, 2014, http://www.pbs.org/wgbh/aia/part2/2h33.html.

Postscript

1. Jon Meacham, "One Man. A New Founding Father," _Time_, August 26–September 2, 2013, 36.

2. Ibid, 43.

CPSIA information can be obtained
at www.ICGtesting.com
Printed in the USA
FFOW02n1000021215
19033FF